TOMMY MACK

An Appalachian Childhood

A Memoir
&
Family History

THOMAS M. DIXON

TOMMY MACK: An Appalachian Childhood

The events and times included herein are all true, although some names have been changed.

Please visit Thomas' website at www.tommymackbooks.com for news of upcoming books and other communications.

This book is dedicated to:

Virginia and West Virginia coal miners; small farmers; and all other workers living by the sweat of their brow, through callused hands, and with a nagging hitch in their back—and especially to the children of alcoholic parents and those from broken and dysfunctional homes.

And in memory of:

Myrtle Virginia Dixon and

Odus and May Jones.

The Jones Family: Myrtle, Odus, Pauline, May, Catherine, and little Pansy c. 1932.

ACKNOWLEDGMENTS

I would like to thank all my family for their support and contributions to this endeavor. A heap of appreciations are in line for: Daisy, Wesley, Ronnie, Ginny, and Paul for the many hours of rehashing and fine tuning of family events. Even though more than forty-six years have elapsed since the end of this story, many of the events are still crystal clear in our minds. Other events were not as memorable to some, so it took several months of pestering on my part to nail down and secure all the important pieces of the puzzle. Thanks again for "putting-up" with me.

Even though they were too young, or just don't remember certain events, I also want to give thanks to my sisters, Donna and Debbie, and younger brothers, Gary and David, for their support—just being there as family and as part of our lives holds special meaning. They will, no doubt, play a more active role in my future writing endeavors.

Also, special thanks to my editor, Al Desetta, for his assistance with this project.

Finally, I can't express enough my gratitude and admiration for Mildred, my loving and wonderful wife. If not for her unwavering support and encouragement, this story may not have gone to print.

CONTENTS

INTRODUCTION

Everyone has a history and a story to tell, and many factors influence a person's decision to set that life to print. Since our memories have so much to do with who we are, I'm pretty sure my family and friends will be glad I shared mine. I'm hoping you will, too.

My father and mother revealed little to us about their childhoods. That fact has bewildered me, my nine siblings, and other family members for decades. Maybe their childhood memories were too unpleasant to remember, let alone relate to others. I'm sure my mother had wonderful dreams of raising a large family, providing for our health and comfort, and encouraging us to get an education. Like most mothers all over the world, she always maintained the hope that her children would live better and have more than she had. As my story will show, fate, circumstances, and bad choices can often deal good people very bad hands.

The first time I considered writing about my childhood was in the mid-1970s. After graduation from junior college, I was working for a large, well-known corporation. I was also married and thinking of starting a family. By this time I had shared many family stories with my new wife. Surprised that I had retained so many childhood memories, she gave me a notebook and encouraged me to jot down my thoughts. Now the year is 2011. I have evolved, and so has my book.

My birthplace, Boissevain, Virginia, is located northwest of the city of Bluefield, Virginia, in the southwest part of the state, across the border from West Virginia and in the shadow of the Blue Ridge Mountains. What started as a thriving coal mining town in the early 1880s has been reduced today to several dozen homes and trailers, a new post office (the ruins of the old post office and Company Store are still standing), and an old church (which may have been called the Old Donation Church) that was used mostly by the "colored folk" of earlier days. The family would leave and return to the place of my birth several times throughout my childhood. Although small and insignificant to most, Boissevain was an important part of my childhood and subsequently, this book.

Back then my father sometimes worked in the mines; that is, when he wasn't downtown on-a-drunk, or up in the woods making moonshine. He was often in trouble with the local law for selling his hooch. We never knew whether making or drinking the whiskey was Dad's greater passion. Either way, the grueling, dirty, and dangerous job of mining coal drove many men to various levels of alcoholism, crime, and abuse, and my father was no exception.

In fact, the word "abusive" could be a mild description of the way my father treated my mother. In one of her earliest attempts at self-defense, she smashed a cast iron frying skillet, still encrusted with the greasy remains of the morning's breakfast, against the side of his head. As someone in the family recalled, "he went out like a light." Yet even that wouldn't deter Dad from his regular abusive fits.

Many will probably wonder why my mother allowed such a man so many chances at redemption. Today, those who study abuse would most likely have classified my mother as codependent and my father as an alcoholic suffering from a hefty dose of narcissism. I certainly don't have all the answers, and those I do have may be somewhat biased.

First, my mother's love for her husband had to be strong, as it took many years for that love to diminish, let alone die.

Another answer would be the historical context of their times. Abuse has no national, geographic, or income boundaries, yet its severity and frequency in and about the southern Appalachian coal mining areas in the 1940s and 1950s were only surpassed by the degree to which it was ignored, if not condoned, by the average citizen and law enforcement. Not surprisingly, that social attitude cast a long and dark shadow upon our family.

Finally, Mom and some of my older siblings felt trapped and paralyzed by fear. Many things my mother did (such as maintaining the status quo) or refrained from doing (killing my father) were calculated to minimize the chances of losing custody of her children. To Mom, we were the primary reason for her existence. That both my parents had so little education only added more fuel to the fire.

Their silence about their growing up years profoundly influenced my desire to write this family history and memoir. My primary mission is to document a good part of my life, so that my family will get to know me as I know myself, with few questions. By exploring and sharing my early years, I hope to provide a fairly accurate glimpse into my siblings' lives and, hopefully, an understanding of my mother's life and the difficult choices she had to make. It is my wish that this book (and others to follow) will be an inspiration for my children, my children's children, and for many other readers. I've come to realize that we don't have to fear our feelings, memories, and dreams.

Furthermore, I offer this story to honor my mother: a simple, unselfish, and honest woman, who wanted so little in life, yet gave so much.

Thomas Dixon
July 12, 2011

Though he slay me, yet will I trust Him.

Job 13:15

I

THE
HERALDING

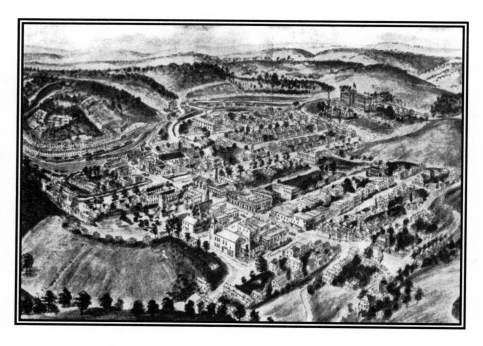

<u>Aerial Sketch of Pocahontas, Virginia c. 1880's.</u>

It was early May, 1964. Birds were singing and not a cloud shielded the brilliance of the Saturday afternoon sun. Mom's prized daffodils and tulips were still in full bloom. After several days of balmy weather and little rain, the steep and rocky land about our home was dry enough for spring planting and other outdoor tasks. The morning's work was done, and the afternoon's was waiting.

I was in the front yard with my brothers Paul, 16, and Gary, 10, taking a break from our chores. We'd finished our lunch and were roughhousing and playing fetch with our dog Prince, a black Lab with a silky coat that glistened in the sunlight. Mom was standing on the front porch enjoying the show.

Gary held on tight to Paul's worn-out baseball mitt as the dog snarled and growled, yanking at the leather in a vigorous tug of war. Prince weighed nearly 70 pounds, and every time Gary eased up the dog buried his canines deeper into the glove's stuffing and an inch closer to his hand.

"Gary, you better let go," Mom warned, "he's gonna take your hand with it."

My little brother let go, startled by the blaring of a car horn. Our brother Ronnie and his friend Ricky were dropping off our father. As Dad climbed out of the car, I could tell in an instant he'd been drinking too much.

"He's all yours Mom!" Ronnie shouted from the car window. "The sheriff down in Pocahontas told me I should take him home before he got himself locked up."

Mom just smiled as Prince rushed to greet Dad.

"Get out of the way, you mangy mutt!"

Dad followed this with a fierce kick to the dog's chest. I could hear Prince whimper in pain.

Mission accomplished, Ronnie and Ricky wasted little time leaving Dad and the developing ugly scene, far behind.

"Did you kids get that trash pile cleaned up? Or have you been goofin' off all day?"

"We have most of it done," Paul said.

My father walked to the edge of our yard and gazed down at our progress.

"You were told I wanted to start plantin' here this weekend. You should have finished the job by now."

Again, Paul came to our defense. "We were tired and just takin' a break, Dad."

"Dammit," Dad shouted, "I want all of you to get in the house, now!"

Paul and I hesitated, staring at each other. When our father told us to go inside the house, it was usually because he was about to say or do something pretty darn mean and ugly, and he didn't want the neighbors to overhear and call the sheriff.

"I said *now!*"

We rushed to the porch and into the house.

I cowered with my brothers on the sofa. Dad stood over me, a wide, black leather belt in his hand. It seems that I had sassed my father by telling him I didn't want to work on the trash pile anymore that day. With each strike of the belt, I could feel its searing heat through my pants. I raised my knees to my chest and released a flurry of hard kicks, hoping to repel him and the burning belt. This only infuriated him more. Grabbing my arm, he jerked me off the sofa.

"I think you're way overdue for a beat'n, boy!"

Around the corner, out of sight, our mother was busy preparing lunch. She had learned which battles to pick with her husband, and this wasn't going to be one of them.

After giving me the worst beating of my twelve years, Dad finished me off with a vicious kick to my behind. While he turned his attention to his next victim, I stumbled my way up the stairs and dove onto my bed.

As I cried, I questioned how my young life had progressed to the point where I despised my father. He had been in jail so often that I hardly recognized him when he arrived home from prison eight months before.

A few months into his last incarceration, I visited him at White Gates Jail in Bland, Virginia. It was late 1959, just before he was moved to Richmond State Penitentiary. Dad had been rotting at White Gates for a while when Mom decided to bring some of her kids to visit him.

I stood on a cold stone floor with some of my siblings, gazing up at a heavy steel door and the iron bars of the visitors' conversation window. As a seven-year-old, I was too short to see anything more than the top of Dad's head, so Mom picked me up and held me in front of the window.

I saw a familiar face from the past: pale yellow from years of heavy cigarette smoking and minimum exposure to sunlight, wrinkled beyond its years. The voice was far from soothing and calm. Instead, he seemed to squawk and cackle like a witch on steroids, salivating over the chance to toss an unsuspecting child into the oven.

Dad told me I was becoming a big boy, and I should visit him more often. His smile and tone of voice chilled me, and I began to squirm. Mom, sensing my discomfort, lowered me to the floor.

There were plenty tales and rumors about the bad times my older brothers and sisters had endured when Dad was at home, and especially when he was drinking. I had now received a very small dose of my old man's medicine.

Two years earlier, my brother Gary and I were baptized. We'd committed ourselves to behaving in God's way and accepting Him as our savior.

Now, as I lay in bed sobbing from the beating, I prayed that God would look over the family and keep us safe from Dad's harmful ways. I also had another request.

"Please God, if you can make my dad go away forever, I'll never ask you for anything again."

With those words, my eyelids grew tired and closed ever so slowly. Sleep took me, and I was at rest.

II

ROLL CALL
c. 1937-1955

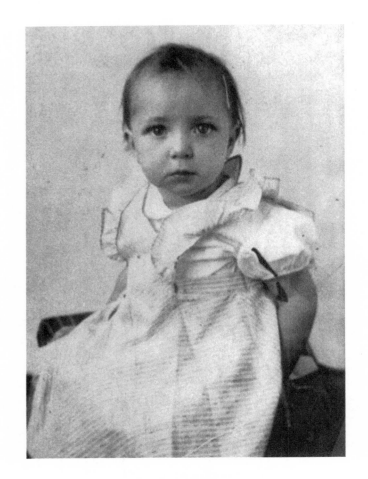

Little Daisy (2) c. 1940

The Early Years, c. 1937- 1945

My mother, Myrtle Virginia Jones, was born in Jenkinjones, West Virginia. She seldom spoke of her parents, Odus and May Jones, but when she did she gave us the impression they respected one another. Nevertheless, in 1937, family tension may have forced her to drop out of school at the age of fifteen and marry my father, Harold Lucas Dixon. Meanwhile, Japan invades China (July 7th), starting World War II in the Pacific.

My father was born in Boissevain, Virginia, a mountain away from Jenkinjones. His mother, Minnie (Mama) Dixon, lived in a sturdy two-room house high on a hill in the town. From here on, it will be known as Boissevain Mountain.

Dad was 19, with less than a third grade education when he married my mother. He still hadn't learned to print, let alone sign his name. They were married by the local justice of the peace in a small and informal ceremony where only a handful of relatives and friends were present. Mom wore her very best—a plain, light colored, cotton dress. She wore no makeup, as was her habit. Nevertheless, my Aunt Gertie (Dad's sister) said my mother was a beautiful bride.

On September 29, 1938, Germany, Italy, Great Britain, and France sign the Munich agreement which forces the Czechoslovak Republic to cede the Sudetenland, including the key Czechoslovak military defense positions, to Nazi Germany. It was one of Hitler's "sleight of hand" maneuvers that brought Europe closer to war.

Two months later (November) while Mom and Dad were living with her parents in Jenkinjones, my sister **Daisy** was born. She was a healthy baby with strong bones and fair skin. Daisy was destined to become nursemaid, caregiver, and teacher for her younger siblings.

Around the spring of 1940, Dad moved the new family to Boissevain Mountain and the homestead they called "under the hill." It was a small shack less than a stone's throw from his mother's house. On May 24, 1940, Mama helped deliver my parents' first son, **Billy Joe**. Although prone to illness, as the first-born male he was expected to carry a heavy load.

Sometime between the U.S. Selective Service Act (draft) in September, 1940, and the Japanese attack on Pearl Harbor on December 7, 1941, Dad was called up to defend his country. Fortunately for him and his family, he couldn't pass the physical. It was probably flat feet and the lack of an education that saved him. Two weeks after Pearl Harbor, and just before Christmas, Mom gave birth to another boy, **Wesley Harold**. He would grow tall and strong, with a fair complexion and thick, dark curly hair.

While the world was at war, family life continued unabated in the quiet corners of Appalachia.

Although the country had revved up its war machinery and coal production and factory outputs were smashing records, the winter of 1941-1942 proved bitter and harsh towards our budding family. Spring had barely arrived when Billy Joe succumbed to pneumonia just a few weeks shy of his second birthday. The loss of a child at any age would be painful enough, but losing one so young and so soon must have been disheartening. Our tiny big brother was buried in a family plot high upon Jenkinjones Mountain, but the long walk up steep and rough terrain prevented many family and friends from attending the services.

Mom and Dad added another son, **Ronnie Milburn**, near the middle of October 1943. Ronnie, the fourth child born with the world at war, was a scrawny kid with blond hair and a fair complexion. He would grow to be somewhat ornery, picking on and irritating his younger siblings. Now, with Billy gone, Ronnie and Wesley were in line for some major chores. But let's get them walking first.

In the summer of 1945, Dad got into trouble with the law, thereafter serving a brief period of time in jail. It could have been for selling illegal whiskey, public drunkenness, or one of several bar-fights. Or maybe it was because he mistreated my mother. Most likely there was more than one charge, and he was out of the family picture for a few weeks.

At the time Mom was pregnant and, with three children under the age of seven, living under the hill was too much to endure without a husband and provider. She packed up the kids and moved back with her parents on Jenkinjones Mountain.

Dad returned just in time to witness his wife walking circles around the in-law's house, trying to ease her labor pains. Her breathing was labored and heavy. Every lap or two she paused and leaned against the wall.

"Shortie," Dad said, "you better get inside and let your mother take care of you." As was customary for the times, he rarely, if ever, witnessed his wife giving birth.

In October 1945, six weeks after Japan's formal surrender, Grandma Jones helped deliver our second sister, **Virginia** (Ginny). Along with a full head of curly brown hair, she also was graced with a fair complexion and destined to take Daisy's place as assistant caregiver and performer of household tasks. She may have been Dad's favorite.

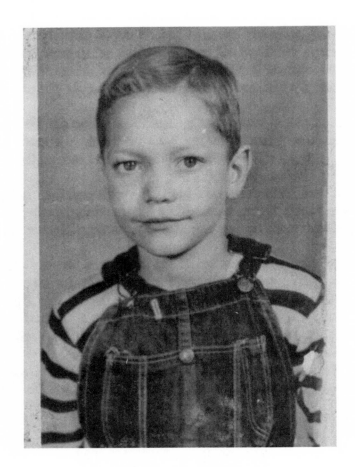

Wesley (8), c.1949.

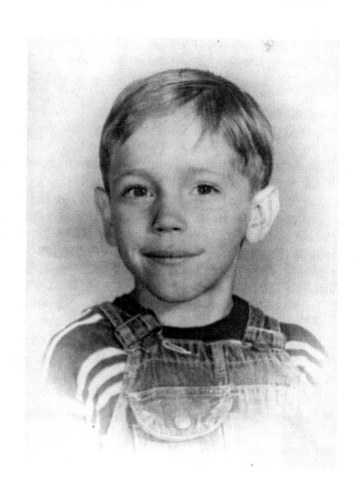

Ronnie (7), c.1950.

Tipple Hollow, c. 1946 – 1950

Little Ginny had barely messed her first diaper when Dad got drunk again, punched Mom in the face, and chased her upstairs. She locked herself in one of the bedrooms while Dad banged away on the door.

"Shortie, if you don't open this damn door, I'm gonna break it down!"

Mom, as usual, remained quiet.

Dad kept banging away at the door until Grandma walked onto the scene.

"Harold!" she shouted. "You'd better leave her alone. If you hit my girl again, I'll … I'll put a hole in ya!"

Dad couldn't believe what he was hearing. Did she say "put a hole in me"? He poked his head around the corner, looked down the stairway, and laughed when he saw his mother-in-law standing at the bottom, gripping a .38 revolver.

"You wouldn't dare shoot your son-in-law!" he shouted, and returned to banging on the door.

"Harold … if you don't leave this house in ten seconds, I'm gonna shoot ya!"

Grandma began her count. When she got to five, Dad grabbed the iron from the ironing board nearby and tossed it at grandma as she began climbing the stairs. It missed by inches and struck the sewing machine, breaking one of its cast iron foot pedals. Grandma was infuriated. The argument had just become extra, extra personal; that sewing machine had been in the family for over thirty years—five years longer than her daughter.

Just as Dad ducked behind the wall, she pulled the trigger. The blast, cloud of plaster dust, and bullet hole just above his head apparently got his attention. Shocked into sobriety, he ran into an empty bedroom, jumped out the window, and fled down the mountain. As far as we know, Dad never set foot in the Jones's house again.

In addition to a part-time job at the mines, Dad was working part-time at a saw mill in early 1946. Now gainfully employed, he convinced our mother to pack up the kids and move with him to a new family dwelling in Boissevain. It was just as well because my mother's parents were getting older and their health was failing.

Tipple Hollow was a dirty place. The access road, Tipple Hollow Road, originated smack-dab in the middle of railroad and coal mining operations and snaked through this hollow of mud holes in a northwesterly direction. Paved with dirt, gravel, and coal slag, it dead-ended about three quarters of a mile up the hollow, where thirty to forty identical two-room houses—most with tin roofs and tin-covered porches—were situated on both sides of the road. A small stream ran parallel with the road on its western side. All of the dwellings on the western side were provided with a small footbridge for crossing the stream. Only a few of the houses enjoyed close proximity to a handful of auto bridges.

The homes (shanties really) were owned by the Pocahontas Fuel Company, a joint railroad and landholding company. During World War I, the United States Navy and the Royal (British) Navy insisted on the (soft) bituminous Pocahontas Coal to fuel their ships. The nearby town of Pocahontas derived its name from The Pocahontas Fuel Company, and the town and company soon became major employers for many of the surrounding Virginia and West Virginia counties. These "coal operators" needed to invest minimal capital to open a mine. The mines' major requirements were a tipple, a coal processing facility, houses for 30 workers, and a store.

The Company houses were wired with electricity but had no plumbing or running water. A spring at the bottom of the steep hill behind our house provided drinking and cooking water. Rain provided water for most everything else. For health reasons, a company official made sure the outhouses were situated downhill from the drinking water supply.

Our shanty was divided into two sections: a bedroom with two beds to the left of the front entrance; a multi-use room with a bed, sofa, sofa-chair, heat stove, and cook-stove against the back wall, along with a kitchen cabinet, table, and chairs. There was no space or need for more than the bare essentials.

Two of my siblings would be born in this hollow. Also, my mother's parents died during the family's stay in Tipple Hollow. They were buried in the family plot on Jenkinjones Mountain.

Our father did not dote upon his children, but there were times when peace and quiet prevailed—when he was sober, the little ones were up from their naps, diapers were fresh, and little tummies were full. Dad would burp his children, bouncing them on his knee while making all kinds of silly and strange faces. And as long as one of us didn't spit up on him, he could be amusing for the better part of an evening.

Just when family matters would start to improve, Dad always seemed to get himself into trouble. One evening after sundown in August 1947, Dad and my brother Wesley, 5, were walking near the entrance to the hollow. The rumor was Dad was trying to make a deal with two men when tempers flared. Because his son was with him, Dad walked away. But he wasn't known to avoid trouble for too long. After he and Wesley had walked about a hundred yards into the hollow, Dad stopped, turned to his son, and said, "Wait here, Wesley."

My brother waited anxiously in the faint moonlight. Minutes rolled by as Wesley became more and more terrified. Then he heard men shouting. Seconds later: *Pop! Pop!* Wesley flinched at the sound of gunshots, followed by rapid footsteps getting louder and closer. He remembered a rush of air as he was swooped-up by Dad and carried away, faster and more scared than he had ever been.

Dad had cut a man that night; a man he knew from working at the mines, and the man was looking for revenge.

The argument continued at work the following day in the miners' changing room when Dad was dressing for work. Armed with an iron poker from the coal stove, the man charged Dad intent on doing him serious harm. Dad managed to deflect the poker strike away from his head using his forearm, duck under his assailant, and gain control from behind him with a strong bear-hug. Unfortunately for the man, Dad had been expecting trouble and was ready with a weapon of his own. The blade of Dad's razor sharp, hawk-bill knife (the same knife he had cut the man with the night before) was already open and pressed against the side of the man's stomach. Dad gave a loud growl, and with firm pressure on the blade, swiped the knife from one side of the man's stomach to the other, exposing and laying open some of his intestines. It was more than enough to put a stop to the fight.

While everyone present rushed to attend the victim, Dad hurried to get dressed.

"You all saw it!" he shouted. "You all saw it! It was self-defense!"

That afternoon, Dad ran out the back door into the wooded hollow when he saw the sheriff and two deputies approaching the house. Wesley stood on the back porch watching the law chase his father up the steep terrain of Tipple Hollow at Boissevain Mountain, firing angry shots from their hand guns and a rifle. The familiar trees saved him that day, deflecting serious harm, until the law caught up with him on Boissevain Mountain.

"Don't shoot," Dad shouted from behind a tree, "can't you see I'm unarmed?"

Dad had screwed up again. He spent several weeks locked up until he and a few witnesses were able to prove it was self-defense. Meanwhile, he was unable to work and provide for the family.

The man's injuries were serious, but he recovered well and lived for decades recalling, "Sleepy hurt me real bad that day."

Continuing to bear children at two-year intervals, my mother delivered **Paul Kenneth** in September 1947. The third surviving son, Paul grew straight and strong. He had dark hair and a matching complexion (from his father's side of the family), and a calm, quiet disposition (from his mother's side, no doubt).

Wesley, Ronnie, and Daisy attended the Boissevain Grade School near Tipple Hollow. A few times each week the school cook, a colored woman named Miss Janie, would give Ronnie cafeteria soup. About the tastiest soup the family had ever eaten; it was stored and transported to the family in clean, one-gallon paint cans. While Miss Janie knew we needed help, she may not have realized just how important this simple act of kindness was to our family.

For Wesley and Daisy, getting good grades was especially difficult since they were absent a large percent of the time. That's because they often had to share a single pair of shoes. One day Wesley wore the shoes and Daisy stayed home. The next day Daisy wore the shoes and Wesley stayed home. That was in the winter. In warmer weather, someone—and it wasn't Daisy—would be stuck going to school barefooted. But this didn't have as big of an emotional or psychological impact as one would imagine, since ours wasn't the only family going through hard times. However, my brothers were known to go barefoot well into the winter, even after a snowfall or two. How they managed this, I can't begin to imagine.

Sometimes, when Dad was away mostly, Ronnie would cast aside his pride and go begging when the miners changed shifts. A scrawny, sickly looking kid, he stood with his palm out as the workers came and went. A few took pity and dropped hollowed-out coins (called script) into his hand. The script could be used to buy anything, but only at Company stores. The not-so-subtle control by the mining companies was pervasive and often contributed to worker frustration and feelings of hopelessness. The 1955 song "Sixteen Tons", made popular by Tennessee Ernie Ford, rings true with the line, "I owe my soul to the company store."

Since The Company owned a large portion of the real estate in the area, many families struggled to pay off their debts. You had to play and bide by Company rules or quit the game (so to speak). Most played because they felt they had no other option.

Ronnie usually kept five or ten cents worth of the script for himself and gave the rest to Mom, which she would trade for family necessities.

Bordering on malnourishment, the family scraped through the seasons at Tipple Hollow.

Not only did my siblings have food, clothing, and their father's drinking and temper to worry about, they also had to worry about their physical safety when Dad carried out some of his crazier notions. In

1949, Dad had acquired himself a beat-up old pickup, and no doubt wanting to impress his sons with his courage and new-found knowledge, he dragged his young sons into the dangerous business of dynamiting coal seams and hauling coal.

The Pocahontas Fuel Company didn't "cotton to" poor people mining their coal. It didn't matter that the company was no longer interested in mining certain seams; they just wanted everyone to buy their coal at the going price. The Company tried to deter scavengers by periodically caving in abandoned mines. They said they did it for the "safety" of the families and kids living in the area, but most of the people involved knew *economics* was their major concern.

Somehow our father and a handful of others managed to uncover and revive some of the caved-in mines around Boissevain Mountain. The process began with drilling holes into the seams of an abandoned mine. Sticks of dynamite with blasting caps and detonator wires were inserted, and dummy charges were carefully packed into the remaining space. After that, the tail-ends of the detonator wires were strung out to a safe distance. When the last wire was connected to a battery terminal, the charge exploded.

Although it was a lot more dangerous, dynamiting beat the hell out of digging coal with a pick. To drill, setup, and blast open a seam took all morning, but blasting supplied a heck of a lot more loose coal than could be dug in four hours. At age eight, Wesley's job was to attach the two (positive and negative) detonator wires to the battery terminal posts. This set off an enormous Boom! The earth shook under his feet, his ears rang, and his hands trembled as if he were a feeble old man. Wesley's nerves were unraveling, and he dreaded hearing his father's command, "Go ahead, Wesley!"

Digging or blasting—it was hard, dirty, sweaty, and dangerous work.

Dad and Wesley were driving home with a truck-load of coal one night, when they found themselves blinded by the brightness of the new street light near the entrance to Tipple Hollow.

"Dammit!" Dad shouted. "I can't even see the road on account-a that damn light! If I had a gun, I'd shoot it out."

Wesley said, "Hey Dad, the .22 rifle's behind the seat there. Why don't you use it?"

"Yeah, you're right boy. I forgot about that."

Dad stopped the truck, loaded a round into the rifle and shattered the light with the first shot. They drove away not realizing that a neighbor had recognized Dad's truck and reported the deed to the sheriff the following day.

Meanwhile, on their way up the newly-darkened hollow, the truck splashed two young girls with mud from a mud puddle as they walked by. The girls squealed. Dad and Wesley laughed all the way home.

Back at the house, Mom said, "Harold, I'm gonna have the baby any time now."

"You are?"

"Yeah, I just sent Daisy and her friend to fetch Doctor Porter. Did you happen to see them?"

"See em," Dad laughed, "I think I just splashed mud all over em!"

Dad had to work several days for the county to pay his fine, court costs, and the price of a new street light.

Donna Marie was born mid-January 1950, the last to be born in Tipple Hollow. Donna enjoyed being close to her mother and helping out around the house, and would become known as the family tattle-teller.

Donna's birth also marked her as the family's "Great Contributor," since she arrived just before the entire family (Dad, Mom, and the other five kids) came down with the mumps. Ronnie and Ginny still have vivid memories of tying Birdseye diapers around their faces to support swollen and sagging jaws.

Mining Tipple at Jenkinjones, WV.

<u>Mining Tipple at Boissevain, Virginia.</u>

Under the Hill, c. 1950 – 1954

During the spring of 1951, the family left Tipple Hollow and moved back under the hill where the family had started. This was a section of property owned by Mama.

Just a stone's throw northeast of Tipple Hollow, Tank Hill Road was the only road to the top of Boissevain Mountain. The road got its name from the large water storage tank located on the side of the mountain looking down upon the mining tipple. When the mine at Tipple Hollow was operating, the tank supplied water for various equipment and mining tasks. The road was mostly dirt, with a thin layer of slate (or red dog) to help prevent vehicles from getting stuck in the mud.

On the right, about halfway up the road, Mama lived in a modest four-room house. My dad's sister, Aunt Christine (Tini), lived in a trailer on the lot next to Mama's house. A tertiary dirt road with a treacherous, steep grade slid over the hill from this property to our house under the hill.

Including the kitchen, our home here consisted of three rooms. One bedroom with two beds served five children. A large multipurpose room contained Mom and Dad's bed, the baby's bed, a sofa, sofa chair, and a pot-bellied stove. The family had electricity for lighting, the radio, and occasionally the washing machine.

It was during our stay here that Ginny, now seven, caught her hand between the rollers of the wringer washing machine. Her arm was drawn all the way to the bicep while the rollers kept spinning, until Mom rescued her by hitting the release mechanism. It took several days for the severe bruises and abrasions to heal. The accident was a good lesson, and we all stayed clear of the rollers after that.

Many times the washer was broken and Mom had to use the scrub board to do our laundry. My older siblings still remember our mother's dry, cracked, and bleeding hands. At times they were so chafed she couldn't even lick cake batter from her finger. That's when my older brothers and sisters took over the job of "stomping clothes" and washing the dishes. While standing in a tub of water, detergent, and laundry, they stomped until either the stompers were exhausted or the clothes were clean.

Just as in Tipple Hollow, our outhouse stood at attention forty feet from the back porch, bath water collected in tubs and barrels when it rained, and drinking water was gathered from a spring dug into the side of the mountain at the far edge of the garden. I have often referred to this spring as the Spring of Cognition; for it was here I recall my earliest memories: Mom taking me by the hand and guiding my first clumsy, stumbling steps to the spring, and Daisy allowing me the honor of using the dipper to fill the family water bucket. Tired from the trip, I was usually carried back to the house.

A large vegetable garden bordered the house on two sides. It supplied plenty of food during the summer and early fall and a bounty of canned goods that helped us get through the winters. Everyone worked in the garden, even young Ronnie. And we can't forget the hard work supplied by Dad's brother Jessie and his horses, which broke ground in the spring just before planting.

Wesley recalls that one of the horses collapsed and died while plowing our garden under the hill. It was dark by the time Dad and Jessie finished digging a shallow grave at the lower edge of the garden. They were tired, and it was late. So, they left the burial for daylight and the cooler hours of the morning.

By sunrise, rigormortis had set in; the animal was too stiff to fit into the hole.

Uncle Jessie cursed and drove his shovel into the ground. "Well, we best start diggin' a bigger hole."

"To hell with that," Dad replied. "I did all the diggin' I'm gonna do last night."

Dad walked to the house and returned with a small bow saw. After sawing off the horse's legs, he tossed them into the grave along with the carcass.

"I did my part," Dad said, stepping away from the hole. "Now it's your turn. Cover it up, Jessie."

It probably would have been just as easy to dig a bigger hole, but Dad had a funny way of looking at things. Why dig when you can butcher?

Tommy Mack (yours truly) was born in the shack under the hill by the side of the hollow between Tank Hill Road and Phipps Road. It was late January 1952. I was a healthy baby with fair skin and wavy brown hair. A natural explorer, I was prone to having accidents and getting hurt.

Much later in my life, my dear friend John referred to my birth as being "spit-out," signifying my very first accident and a good way of describing the family's reproductive rate in those days.

My sister Daisy has painful recollections about the day of my birth. My mother's labor pains were coming on real strong, and she knew I was about to make a grand entrance.

With an agonizing voice, Mom said, "Daisy … run up the hill and fetch your Aunt Tini … the baby's about to come."

Sis didn't hesitate for an instant. After all, this would be the eighth time for Mom, and she figured her mother knew pretty well what was going to happen—and when.

After fetching my aunt, Daisy was overly anxious to return to her mother's side, so she ran ahead at full steam down the steep hill. Spurred by an apparent influx of adrenaline she attempted to leap onto the porch, but her momentum didn't match her ambition. She scraped her thigh from knee to groin on the edge of the porch floor. Through years passing, the scar has been a vivid reminder of the day her little brother, Tommy Mack, entered the world. I guess you could say I made a certain impression upon her.

In February 1953, a little more than a year after my birth, Mom was expecting again. Daisy, 14, Wesley, 11, and Ronnie, 9, were bearing down under their parents' directions, doing whatever it took to make living bearable on the tiny farm. At the same time, sibling rivalry was common and arguments were frequent—especially between Wesley and Ronnie:

One of their arguments reached a peak one day as they stood outside the house. Ronnie pushed Wesley, and Wesley's elbow smashed through the kitchen window, resulting in a deep five-inch gash. It wasn't the first time they were injured while fighting, and it wouldn't be their last. Even though they carried the physical scars for life, forgiveness came quickly; for hard work and responsibility requires a good team working together, and true brotherhood does not harbor resentment. My siblings and I remember our scars fondly and enjoy recalling the stories behind each and every one.

My brother Paul loved to play with plastic toy soldiers and Indians on the banks of the dirt road leading to our house. It was a common pastime for children of that era, and Paul could do so for hours at a time.

Late in the day, Mom called Paul into the house for dinner, which probably consisted of the usual pinto beans, corn bread, and any combination of mixed vegetables and fruit we could get our hands on. At the time, Dad was serving another short stint in jail. We all lived hungry in those days, especially since we played hard and worked hard, so there were few or no complaints about the menu.

After dinner, there weren't many things to do between sundown and bedtime. One was waiting to take your turn at bath, which most of the time consisted of a pan of water and a washcloth (or, as some call it, a sponge bath). When anyone (especially the boys) started to smell a little ripe, Mom would insist we take a real bath in large galvanized metal tubs.

The following morning, Mom fed us cornmeal fritters (pancakes) with Karo syrup. Paul was really enjoying the meal that morning. Actually, he seemed to be making a pig out of himself, which caused him to begin choking and gasping for air. Those at the breakfast table thought he was fooling around until he began vomiting. The vomit looked like strings of spaghetti, something we rarely ate and no one had seen at the breakfast table. The situation drew gasps from everyone present, especially Mom.

The next thing that happened would astound the most stoic of onlookers—spaghetti started to extrude from Paul's nose. Unable to breath freely, his tearful eyes were filled with fear and panic. He began clawing and pulling at the strings to clear his nose and mouth. All of a sudden, the family realized that what Paul was clearing from his sinuses was alive, since spaghetti doesn't squirm and move on its own. My brother was vomiting worms, eight to twelve inches long.

Realizing this, Paul jerked his shoulders back in an effort to get away from his attackers. His sudden panic caused the chair to tumble backwards, and before anyone could catch him, Paul's head struck the floor leaving him unconscious for a few seconds, just long enough for Mom to clear out the worms and for Paul to regain his breath.

There were squirming worms all over the table and floor. No one in the family had ever seen such a sight. Mom was hysterical.

As soon as Paul was able to stand, Daisy hoisted him on her back, carried him briskly out of the house, and all the way down to the bottom of the hill where our neighbors, the Phipps, lived. One of the Phipps boys transported Paul and Daisy to Doctor Porter's office in Pocahontas.

The doctor examined Paul and asked him and Daisy several questions. From the evidence gathered, the doctor surmised that the worms resulted from Paul's playing in the dirt with the toy soldiers. Over a period of days or weeks, Paul had ingested the parasitic worms by placing his dirty fingers and/or toys in his mouth. The parasites grew and multiplied, seeking an exit. The sweet syrup and fritters could have been the primer that hastened their flight from an unwilling host.

The next day Paul was running around and playing just like a normal, healthy five-and-a-half-year-old boy.

Paul's close call was an unusually stressful event, but we learned a valuable lesson about proper washing and hygiene, along with keeping objects and fingers out of our mouths. The worm incident was never repeated again—by any of us.

The Fourth of July was less than a week away and Mom thought the family should relax by having a picnic. We celebrated that year at Laurel Creek. Everyone enjoyed the rare occasion—baloney and cheese sandwiches, watermelon, and other fruits were abundant.

Dad had returned from jail. He was standing in the living room with a tricycle in one hand and the other hand behind his back.

"Who's been a good boy while I was away?" Dad asked.

Ronnie, Paul, and Ginny all jumped in, shouting, "I was! I was!"

Dad didn't hesitate to put Ginny in her place.

"This is for the good boys," he said, handing the tricycle to Paul. Ginny looked hurt and disappointed, but Dad was quick to suppress any serious pouting. "I have something else here for good girls."

Dad took his hand from behind his back to offer Ginny a package wrapped in a brown paper bag. She opened it to find a small doll with a cotton dress—her very first.

During the next several days, Paul and Ginny took turns sharing the tricycle. While waiting his turn, Paul began the habit of walking in circles around the wood stove, dragging and sliding his bare feet along the wooden floorboards while pretending to be a railroad locomotive.

"Choo-choo-choo-choo!" he'd bellow. "Choo-choo train coming down the track!"

It would have been an innocent and harmless way for him to amuse himself if not for the rough wooden floorboards behind the stove. (Some of the floors in the house were covered with linoleum and other parts were polished smooth from the high volume of human traffic, but that wasn't the case where Paul was walking.)

Paul let out a piercing howl. A splinter, about a half-inch wide and nearly one and a half inches long, had penetrated an inch or more into the bottom of his foot. Paul fell to the floor, screaming in agony. Dad was called into the room to attend to his son, and using a pair of pliers, he was able to pull out the entire splinter in one piece. Lucky Paul. It took a lot longer to restrain him than it did to remove the splinter.

Oh, by the way: the tricycle that Dad gave the boys wasn't around very long. Ginny and Paul argued so much over who was next to ride it that Dad hauled it away, never to be seen again.

In November 1953, Mom had to stay in the Bluefield hospital because of pregnancy complications. Daisy was worried about her mother being there alone, so Dad promised her the two of them would take the train from Boissevain to Bluefield to visit her.

A day later, in anticipation of her own birthday and the visit to see her mother, Daisy cut her hair. Maybe a little too short, she thought. She also scrounged up a new dress to wear.

The following morning she was ready and waiting for Dad to take her to the train station. When Dad walked into the kitchen, Daisy proudly displayed her new hair and dress.

"What do you think, Dad?" she said, smiling ear to ear.

Dad stared at Daisy with a painful expression.

"What the hell did you do to your hair girl? You look like shit."

Daisy felt like she had been punched. She stood silently, in shock. Dad turned his back on Daisy and raised a dipper-full of water to his mouth, saying, "You're not going anywhere with me looking like that."

Daisy ran crying from the room, devastated that her father would treat her in such a manner. Two days later, she was allowed to visit her mother, but only after Dad forced her to wear a kerchief to hide her "botched" hairdo.

While our mother was resting in the hospital, I was placed in the hands of my Aunt Tini for temporary safekeeping. The family thought this was most likely Dad's idea. Tini already had three daughters of her own, each of them as cute as a kitten on a ball of yarn. Darlene was around my age (two), Barbara was a little older, and Garnell was seven. My aunt loved her children and wanted the best for them.

Like my father, his sister Tini was an alcoholic, and asking her to take good care of me was a reluctant leap of faith for my mother. Tini's stunning looks should have attracted pick-of-the-litter male suitors; but, due to her drinking and age, her choices were all-too-frequently limited to other alcoholics and shady male admirers. Along the way she adapted, learning how to maximize the returns from her investments.

Her children were curious of the many male admirers who came to visit. One day Garnell asked, "Mommy, are any of those men my daddy?"

"Listen sweetie," Tini replied, "when you're thrown into a briar patch, you don't know which thorn stuck you."

Were it not for Aunt Tini's addictive relations with alcohol and men, Mom would have considered her the perfect caregiver for a toddler like me. Since she had no boys (and I was Mom's fourth son) Tini pressured Mom relentlessly to allow her to adopt me. Mom said, "No way!"

Still, my cousins were tickled to death to have me as their temporary little brother. For years Aunt Tini and my cousins fussed over me like I was a prince. I can fondly remember them chasing me around their property, tickling and hugging me as I giggled up a storm.

Mom gave birth to **Gary Lee** near the middle of November 1953, at the Bluefield Sanitarium hospital. As far as we know, Gary was the first to be born in a hospital. He was a healthy baby with fair skin, straight, light-brown hair, and an inquisitive, mischievous disposition.

Unfortunately for Daisy, our new brother was born the day before her 15th birthday. Her teacher and classmates had scheduled a little birthday party for her, but Daisy missed it because she had to stay home and take care of Mom and the young ones.

At the time, Dad and Wesley were working at the sawmill. Daisy, Ronnie, Ginny, Paul, and Donna were all present to fuss over the newest baby's arrival. I wasn't even two—too young for that kind of fussing. Some might think that after six or more babies, the novelty would have ceased to exist. Well, for most of the family, it hadn't.

It was around noon and Daisy had prepared a big lunch to take to Dad and Wesley at the mill. It was not unusual for her to prepare and deliver lunch to our father, but this time she was also delivering news of the new family addition. Needless to say, the best Dad could respond was, "Christ, another mouth to feed."

After missing two days of school, Daisy returned the following Monday, where her teacher gave her the late birthday present. It was a small blue bottle of "Evening in Paris" perfume, a very popular fragrance at that time. Daisy loved it.

When it came to chores, it didn't matter whether Dad was in jail, working in the mines at Tipple, or working at the sawmill; Wesley and Ronnie always worked the hardest. In addition to attending school, they (and sometimes Daisy) were responsible for collecting coal and wood for heating and cooking. Occasionally a coal company foreman, in one of his better moods, showed pity and gave them permission to gather loose chunks of coal that had fallen from the rail cars. "Quick," the foreman would say, "pick it up and get out of here before someone else sees you."

Some days they walked a mile or so to the slate dump and collected coal slate. On Sundays when the mines had shut down, Dad, Wesley, and Ronnie sometimes sneaked to the top of the coal chutes at Tipple and, being quiet and careful that no one saw them, picked the chutes clean of leftover coal.

One Sunday, while they were working the chutes, Dad and Ronnie saw an old colored man approaching.

"Quiet!" Dad shouted. "Someone's coming."

As they hid behind some metal beams, they watched the man pass beneath them, walking with a cane. The old man stopped and, thinking he had heard something, looked about.

"Who dat?" he shouted, somewhat startled.

Dad said, "Who-dat?"

The old man said, "Who-dat!"

Ronnie said, "Who-dat?"

Again, the old man said, "Who-dat!"

"Who-dat keep say'n 'who-dat' to my who-dat?" Dad demanded.

The old man wrinkled up his face in frustration.

"Dat us!" Ronnie shouted, breaking into an uncontrollable bout of laughter. Dad and Ronnie kept laughing as the old man hurried on, limping his way into Tipple Hollow.

It was usually when Dad was locked up that my brothers had to work the hardest. Mom was afraid of automobiles, and she wasn't about to let her twelve and ten year old sons drive their father's truck—no matter how eager. So, whether it was coal or slate, Ronnie and Wesley always loaded it into burlap sacks until it weighed as much as 30 pounds. Worried that their stash might be taken by thieves, they each carried two full bags about a hundred yards up the mountain. While keeping the bags in sight, they returned for two more filled bags to carry back up the mountain again. Wesley and Ronnie continued this method all the way home.

The same procedure was often used to carry home government supplied commodities, which often consisted of cheese, lard, powdered milk and eggs, peanut butter, and canned meat handed out at the church for Colored folk (Old Donation Church) at the bottom of Tank Hill Road. Each bag of commodities also weighed twenty to thirty pounds, and my brothers carried two bags at a time to evenly distribute the load.

Wesley loved dogs and dogs loved Wesley. Stray dogs were always trying to follow him. Dad, on the other hand, had very little patience for small animals. Dogs and cats were a waste of time and resources; unless, of course, the dog was good at hunting. If the animal couldn't provide milk, meat, or wool, you had better be able to ride it or plow by it. Otherwise, Dad said he wouldn't be held responsible for what happened to the animal. He was serious and often proved it.

One day Wesley and Ronnie were returning home from collecting several bags of coal from the Tipple area. Along the way they picked up a stray dog that wouldn't stop following them. He was so cute they couldn't force themselves to get rid of it. So, against their better judgment, they allowed the dog to trail them home. When they arrived, Dad was disappointed with the amount of coal Wesley and Ronnie had gathered.

"I think you boys were wastin' time playing with that stray mutt there, instead of doing your work."

"I think we did a good job today, don't you Ronnie?"

Before Ronnie could reply, Dad grabbed Wesley.

"Don't you use that tone with me boy!"

Then, using a nearby stick, he began to beat Wesley.

The stray dog didn't hesitate; first growling and biting at Dad's legs, he then attacked the hand that had struck my brother. Dad redirected his attention to the dog, and the poor stray didn't have a chance. After a few blows with the stick and several hard kicks to the ribs, the stray bounded away, yelping.

Later that week, my brothers came upon the same dog. When it began to follow them again, they had to throw rocks at it to keep it away. Ronnie and Wesley were beginning to realize the futility of having a pet while Dad was living at home.

It was Easter Sunday, April 18, 1954. My Aunt Tini was planning on getting married. She packed up her three girls along with a cooked ham dinner and most of the trimmings, and dropped them off at our house. In exchange for the dinner, Mom and Daisy would have to watch her three young children for six days while she was away getting married and enjoying her honeymoon.

Daisy had developed a strong predisposition to say whatever was on her mind, which sometimes got her into trouble. So, before my aunt and her fiancé left our house to be married, Daisy spoke up.

Having known him for some time, she said, "Leo, don't marry her. My aunt's no good for you." My sister suspected that neither one of them were the marrying kind.

But Leo was a grown man and in no mood to explain to a 15-year-old the complexities of his relationship with our aunt. Nevertheless, he tried his best to let Daisy know that they were both aware of what they were getting into. Apparently Daisy wasn't convincing enough, and Tini and Leo were married that Sunday as planned.

Late in the summer of 1954, Dad had scrounged up enough cash from his illegal whiskey sales and work at the mill to purchase a 1930 Ford Model "A" Sedan at a real cheap price. His old pickup was junked, and Dad needed another one so he could continue hauling coal and other things. He was frustrated at not being able to find another pickup at a reasonable price. A few friends and acquaintances suggested that he take the sedan and chop it up, and they knew some men in that type of racket who could do a good job, and at the right price. So Dad paid two men to chop away the back half of the sedan's cab, close in the new cab, and install a six-foot bed. A week after he bought the Ford, he brought the truck version home and proudly showed off its features to Mom and the older kids.

The next day he put Mom in the cab and piled some of us kids into the back of the pickup for a trip to Pocahontas. On the way he became agitated by the way the vehicle was handling. He cursed the men who did the work and swore he'd get even with the "son-of-a-bitches" for "screwing him over." Meanwhile, he was driving recklessly with kids aboard.

"Harold, slow down. You're gonna drive us in a ditch."

Well, weren't no woman gonna tell him how to drive! Dad began driving even faster.

"Dammit Harold, there's kids back there! Slow down!"

Dad got pissed off at Mom for yelling at him and started punching her about the face as he was driving. Daisy and some of the other kids started crying, screaming, and yelling from the back of the truck.

"Stop it, Dad! Please, stop hitting her! Stop it, stop Dad! Please!"

As soon as the truck slowed to a roll in Pocahontas, Daisy jumped out, ran into the sheriff's office, and told the deputy what our dad had done. Mom refused to press charges. But—charges or not—the sight of Mom's bloody nose and battered face was too much for the deputy. Dad was detained for 24 hours and released. It was the only legal thing the law could do under the circumstances.

Along with Dad's abuse, his severe and often unfair punishment didn't promote any warm-and-fuzzy feelings from his kids in those days. Most of the time he elicited so much fear and loathing that Ronnie and Wesley just tried their best to stay out of his way.

There were many opportunities for revenge, the best being when he was severely pickled (drunk) or sleeping. But Dad always slept with his eyes half open, and the cold black stare of those eyes would always send a chill to the bones of anyone with an ill will in mind. Whether he was laid out in bed at home or on a sidewalk somewhere downtown, it was difficult to discern if our father was awake or asleep. That's why the law and many others called him Sleepy Dixon. So loathing was all anyone could muster.

Dad got drunk the night he got home from jail. He continued to rant and rave about the Ford and the men who "screwed" him. He passed out about midnight. The next day he drove the Ford to the garage and accosted the men in Sleepy Dixon fashion. The men knew Dad well and were able to calm him down enough to point out the problem.

Apparently, Dad needed to install a stabilizer and suspension kit so the vehicle would handle more like a truck when hauling a load. Dad said, "Oh, and how much will that cost?" When they told him the price, Dad had a cussing fit.

"You gotta be … kiddin' me! I'll … do it my own self!"

Dad bought the kits and within a few days had figured out how to install them. But having the materials and knowing how to do the job was the easy part. With his two oldest sons reading the instructions and lending a hand, Dad managed to install the kits without anyone getting seriously hurt. As Wesley recalls, "It was a whole lot harder than Dad thought it would be." They busted a few knuckles doing that job.

After Mom's last beating, the sheriff and deputy must have decided to keep a close watch on our father. It didn't take long for them to spot something. Dad grew overly confident while driving his new toy. On November 21, he was caught and charged with operating a motor vehicle under the influence. He stayed locked-up in the county jail until February of the following year (1955), when he was arraigned and pled guilty. The crime was a misdemeanor; but when the court considered Dad's history, he was sentenced to six months, minus time already served in the Tazewell County Jail. He was also fined $234.69. Unable to pay such a large sum of money, Dad had to work on public roads for nearly three months until the fine was paid in full.

Also in February, around the time of Dad's arraignment, Daisy quit school. Due to the family's ups-and-downs she couldn't concentrate, the lessons weren't sinking in, and she just couldn't take it anymore. Something had to give and, unfortunately, it was her education. She was hoping to be more helpful to her mother around the house.

III

ABB'S VALLEY
c. 1955-1956

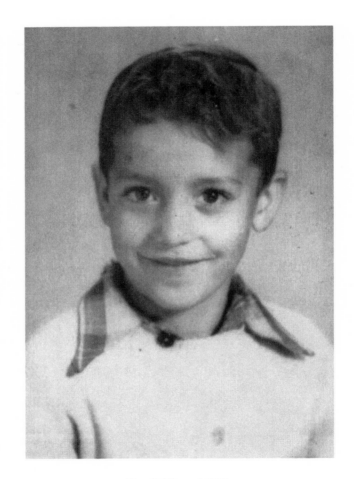

Paul (6) c. 1953.

A Converted Schoolhouse

Abb's Valley! What a beautiful place. To this day I love visiting its scenic meadows and farmland, dotted with barns and quaint, well-kept ranch houses.

Two pioneers, James Moore and Robert Poage, were the first to settle in Abb's Valley, Virginia, in about 1770. Sixteen years later, Shawnee Indians raided the valley, killing and capturing some of the Moore family. Early settlers of Southwest Virginia and West Virginia were plagued by Indian attacks until around the year 1800 when the various tribes were defeated. A tall yet somewhat inconspicuous stone historical marker on the right side of Abb's Valley Road, about one and a half miles west of Tank Hill Road, gives a brief explanation of those events.

The roads around Abb's Valley were paved and well maintained by the state. Of course it would not be country if there weren't a few sheds, shacks, and barns scattered along Abb's Valley Road, some suffering from advanced stages of decomposition. Close proximity to the occasional country store and gas station meant the locals saved time and money when they didn't have to drive into the city.

By late spring of 1955, Dad was home and he had moved the family again. Somehow he managed to secure rental on what used to be a little one-room schoolhouse in Abb's Valley. The defunct county-owned

43

schoolhouse was located off the main road and several hundred feet uphill into a hollow. It had been converted from a one-room building into a family dwelling by partitioning half of the space into two bedrooms, and the other half into a living room where Mom and Dad slept, and a kitchen. The front door opened into the large living room and kitchen area, with the boys' room to the right and the girls' room to the left. Just about everyone had to share a bed, and often with more than one sibling. When faced with two pair of feet at the foot of the bed and one or two pair at the head, it was not unusual for someone to complain about the smell of dirty feet. Instead of plumbing and running water, we made do with yet another outhouse and spring out back.

A few weeks after we moved there, Donna, Gary, and I came down with the mumps. Again, just as in Tipple Hollow, we donned Birdseye diapers to provide comfort and support for our swollen and sagging jaws.

Dad liked the location here because it was another ready-to-go hollow. In addition to a small chicken coop within smelling distance of the house, the place had a great set-up for raising hogs. That we did pretty well. But Dad liked the place best because we were somewhat isolated from the road and neighbors. With privacy, Dad could do the things he wanted to do without being seen or heard.

First, he could make and sell his moonshine. Dad frequently assigned Paul, Wesley, and Ronnie the task of hiding it. Sealed tightly in mason jars, the brew was usually hidden under tree stumps. My brothers didn't mind the assignment—they considered it a challenge and competed with each other to see who was best at hiding the jars. Whenever Dad was in a drinking mood or had a buyer waiting, he sent one of his sons to fetch the stashed jars.

Secondly, the seclusion allowed Dad and his drinking and brewing cohort, John Wyseloiff Jr., to get drunk without being locked up. John was rarely called by his real name. We suspect he was known as "June Guinea" because of the many loud and irritating Guinea Hens that ran wild around his property. The fact that few people could pronounce his last name provided further justification for the nickname, and other than the usual courthouse clerk, there were few attempts at spelling either name.

Dad and June took turns whipping up a batch of the stuff in our kitchen, and more frequently, in June's kitchen and other places on Boissevain Mountain. If Dad or June passed out at their respective homes, they couldn't be arrested for public drunkenness.

There was a third reason Dad liked our secluded location. It allowed him to beat his wife and kids away from prying ears and eyes.

Early one afternoon, Mom and Daisy were in the kitchen area preparing laundry for the rinse cycle in our recently repaired electric washing machine. A few minutes earlier, Mom and Daisy had lifted a large galvanized metal tub half full of steaming hot water from the stove and placed it on the floor beside the kitchen cupboard. It was to be used to temper the wash water for rinsing.

The house was a little quieter than usual. Donna, little Gary, and I were traipsing about the house in our bare feet, while Wesley, Ronnie, Ginny, and Paul were in school, finishing up the last few days of the school year. Mom was probably thinking that pretty soon they'd all be home and the peace and quiet would be gone. Awake from a short nap, I strolled into the kitchen and immediately noticed that Donna and Gary were sharing a peanut butter and jelly sandwich.

"Where's my sandwich?" I complained.

Donna was in an antagonistic mood. "You're too late, Tommy. You don't get one."

"Mommy, where's my sandwich? Don't I get one too?"

Nobody seemed to hear me. I kept insisting on having a sandwich. Why was everyone ignoring me? Angry and impatient, I looked about the kitchen and spotted the evidence: two jars, one containing peanut butter and another containing some of Mom's canned blackberry preserves left over from the previous summer. They sat high atop the cupboard counter, right next to a partially consumed loaf of Sunbeam bread.

Using a nearby chair, I began my climb in pursuit of the forbidden fruit. A lick and a promise later, I was standing tall atop the chair between the kitchen table and cabinet.

I'll make a sandwich myself, I boasted silently.

As I leaned across the cabinet to reach the jar of preserves, Mom saw me in her peripheral vision. But it was too late. Before she could react, I slipped from the chair, headed for the tub of hot water.

"Tommy!" Mom screamed, and I matched her scream with my own.

If it wasn't for the shock and terror, Mom would not have responded so fast. In an instant, she pulled me from the painful grip of firewater.

It could have been worse. Thank goodness only a small section of my upper left side and arm had dipped into the tub. My head and the rest of me were spared. In less than a minute the flesh on my left triceps, forearm, and side began to peel away. Mom and Daisy poured cold water over my scalded skin, wrapped me in a clean sheet, and rushed me to the hospital. I was screaming so loud the neighbors could hear.

Someone notified the school to tell my older brothers and sisters what happened. Wesley rushed home with Ronnie, Ginny, and Paul.

No one recalls how they were able to get me to the hospital in Bluefield, West Virginia, or as fast as they did. Daisy and Mom stayed with me as I suffered that first night in the hospital. Daisy sat with me for another day or two until my cries for my mother's presence prevailed. I was too young to suffer so mature a pain. Daisy recalls that Mom wept uncontrollably at the sight of my discomfort. She blamed herself over and over for leaving the hot water uncovered and not watching me closer.

I don't recall the pain, only the hospital food. It was delicious. I had applesauce, pudding, Jell-O, and cold milk in wax-coated cardboard cartons that had to be opened for me. I especially remember the grape and orange juice, which I had rarely, if ever, experienced before. The sheets and pillow cases were bright and clean, and all the nurses fussed over me.

Days later, when there was little risk of my burns becoming infected, I was allowed to go home. It was only after my wounds healed and my usual spirits returned that Mom seemed to forgive herself. Aside from losing a child, it was the most wretched mishap to befall any of her young children. I still bear some minor physical scarring from my attempt to acquire the forbidden fruit.

Near the middle of that summer, Daisy, now 15, ran away from home. Chores, pressure from babysitting her siblings, and Dad's ceaseless nagging and occasional whippings had taken their toll.

Ginny was nine years old when Daisy left. She, more than any of us, began to miss her big sister. She recalls the times when Dad sent her a mile down the road to Creasy's store to fetch his weekly supply of cigarettes and chewing tobacco. It was usually after dark, and strangers often stopped and asked if she wanted a ride. Frightened, she always declined the offers. Dad would be waiting on the porch for her return.

About three weeks after running away, Daisy stopped by the house to visit us. Few people wanted to help her. Those who did, told her to go home and tough it out. Still, someone was helpful enough to provide the name of a nice lady willing to offer her a live-in job, and Daisy was foolish enough to ask for her father's permission.

"No, you can't!" Dad shouted. "Three weeks is enough. Now you get your ass back up there, pick up your belongings, and come on home. I know where you was staying. If you hadn't come home when you did, I was about to have the sheriff's deputy come get you and drag your sorry ass home."

Still fearful of Dad's retribution, Daisy gathered her belongings and returned home. Meanwhile, she began making phone calls and plans for a more permanent getaway.

Early in August, Dad and June redoubled their drinking and whiskey-making. Dad, as he often did, came home drunk one night. This time he accused Mom of fooling around with another man. He didn't have anyone particular in mind, but suspected one of the many men who came to the house to buy some of his nasty moonshine.

Daisy, true to her style, stood up to her father, insisting Mom was innocent. Dad thought she was sassing him and lying for her mother, which only made things worse. He grabbed Daisy by her long dark hair and swung her to the floor. Pinning her hair under one foot, he kicked away at her with the other.

47

When he was finished, Daisy was spitting and dripping blood. The next day she had multiple cuts, bumps, and bruises. It was an unbearable sight for her mother, an awful thing for her siblings to behold, and an unforgivable experience for Daisy.

Having taken her last abuse from her father, Daisy packed her clothes again and left home for good. She felt extremely sad. She felt guilty and was consumed by the nagging premonition that she was deserting her mother when she was most in need. No one knew Mom was three months pregnant; fertile as she was, Mom had to have known this. Nevertheless, Daisy had no choice. Her own survival was at risk, and she wouldn't be of any use to her mother if she was dead.

On the 16th of August, 1955, Dad and June were arraigned in court on felony indictments for the illegal manufacture of alcoholic beverages. Dad pled innocent and June pled guilty. Dad was sure someone had reported the two of them to the authorities and wondered for days who it could have been.

Less than a week later, June was fined an unknown amount plus court costs and sent on his way, having promised the judge that he would behave, abstain from violating any penal laws, and cease consuming alcohol. Initially they were both facing 18 months in the state penitentiary, but somehow June was able to slither away from the sentence.

Dad went to trial by jury and was found innocent of all charges. It didn't hurt having the sheriff testify in his defense. Whether he was leaning against his patrol car under a full moon or lounging in his favorite chair in the privacy of his own house, the sheriff and his wife often enjoyed putting-down a bottle or two of Dad's best hooch. They wanted to protect the county folk by making sure it was good for human consumption. Since most of the evidence for conviction was found at June's place, it was no surprise Dad was found innocent. My father's greatest skill was hiding his whisky-making habit.

The Welfare and Social Service Agencies often exasperated my mother in those days. She and many teachers were puzzled by the way families were treated at the local, state, and federal levels. The laws at the time stipulated that if the father was at home and able to work, the family could not collect welfare. It didn't matter if he was an alcoholic and constantly getting locked up, or if he didn't have a job simply because he couldn't find one. It also didn't matter that he wasn't earning a livable wage, or if the money he was earning was wasted on alcohol.

I guess one could say state agencies were just as exasperated with dysfunctional families like ours. But no matter how you look at it, the children are always caught in the middle.

Dad came home one day and told Mom his foreman had just fired him from his job of loading coal. In desperation, Mom walked to the mine and pleaded with the foreman to give our father another chance. She told him she had seven children at home to feed and clothe. Mom's pleading worked and Dad was given another chance. But within a few short weeks he screwed up again and was fired a second time. Mom was paralyzed with shame. She would never be able to look her husband's employer in the face again—let alone plead for our father's job.

Because of the laws at the time, it was always better for us when Dad was locked up long enough for the family to collect a welfare check. My older siblings sometimes wondered if Dad planned it that way. Perhaps he was thinking: I'll get locked up so that I can rest, and my wife and kids will be provided for.

Well, such thinking would smack of responsibility, and Dad wasn't responsible.

Cold Feet

Wesley, Ronnie, and Paul sometimes went to school barefooted. Sometimes their feet would bleed.

The teachers often overlooked bare feet in September because the weather was nice. To them, it was just a case of "country boys being tough country boys." But when frost coats the pumpkins, it became a different story.

In the fall of 1955, Ronnie, 12, and Paul, 8, were standing barefooted at the school bus stop. Their feet had stayed relatively warm while they were moving, but once they were standing still the ground seemed a lot colder. In fact, their feet were getting so cold that their bones were beginning to ache—all the way to their knees. To prevent frostbite, they stood back to back, keeping only one foot on the ground at a time. The resting foot was placed against the seat of the other's pants, to be warmed by body heat. Ronnie and Paul would alternate, warming one foot at a time until the bus arrived.

A few days later, Ronnie's teacher approached him at dismissal time.

"Ronnie, could you please stay in class for a few minutes? I want to have a talk with you."

She waited until all the other students were gone.

"Ronnie, I would be blind to not have noticed, but you haven't been wearing any shoes to school lately. Don't you have any?"

"No ma'am."

"Well, there are some shoes in the box under my desk. Maybe you can find a pair that will fit you."

Ronnie hunted through the box and found a fitting pair that he liked well enough.

The next day he returned to school with renewed confidence, knowing his feet were warm and protected like the rest of his classmates.

"Hey Ronnie," shouted a young Eddie Barrett, "why are you wear'n girl shoes?"

Ronnie was taken aback.

"They aren't girl shoes."

"Yeah they are," Eddie insisted, "my sister had a pair just like em'."

Sure enough, Ronnie had picked out a pair of girl's brown and white Oxfords that sported bright, multicolored laces.

"Well, it don't matter to me," Ronnie said. "I like 'em. So you kin kiss my ass, Eddie!"

My brother continued to wear the shoes until they wore out. These were indeed hard times. He might have been a little embarrassed, but Ronnie was tough!

Soon after that—thanks to the school and its teachers—Paul, Ronnie, and Wesley grew accustomed to wearing shoes to school regularly. They even gave Mom a warning: they would never go to school again without them.

Although difficult, Mom managed to squirrel-away a few dollars from the monthly welfare checks to buy us new clothes and shoes once or twice each year. That was usually when the hand-me-downs were too raggedy to be handed down any more. The new stuff usually came at the beginning of school or as presents at Christmas time.

Many of the teachers at Abb's Valley School were good seamstresses. My sisters usually had better clothes and shoes because they weren't as hard on them as the boys. Nevertheless, some teachers thought Ginny could use a couple of new skirts. In a combined effort to help our family, they pooled their skills and made several beautiful skirts for her. Like Ronnie in his new shoes, Ginny felt so proud when she wore her new skirts to school.

Around this time, one of Ginny's teachers came to doubt my sister's ethics. It all started one day when Ginny and her fourth-grade classmates were introduced to the Crayola Company's box of 48 crayons. Although produced in 1949, it had taken more than five years for a box set with that many crayons to make its way to her teacher's desk. Ginny had never seen so many pretty colors, and they came with several beautiful coloring books.

Although nervous about going through with it, Ginny developed a plan. Most of my brothers and sisters were given free lunches, and some were required to earn the meal. For Ginny it was cleaning the blackboard after school. She asked and received permission from her teacher to clean it during recess instead. She quickly erased but did not clean the blackboard. Then, using the rest of her chore time, she used the set of crayons to do some coloring in one of the books. When recess was over and Ginny heard the rest of the class returning, she shoved some of the crayons and the coloring book into her desk and closed the lid. What's out of sight is out of mind, she thought.

The teacher announced that the class was going to do some coloring. But now some of the crayons were missing. When the teacher asked the class for the crayons' whereabouts, Ginny panicked and said nothing. Within minutes the teacher found the crayons and coloring book in Ginny's desk.

Because she didn't admit to having used the crayons, Ginny was disciplined in front of the class. She cannot recall exactly how, but she knows the penalty for such an infraction was harsh.

By winter my scalding wounds were completely healed. Tired and weary from the endless cycle of chores, Mom was feeling a bit cooped-up. So when a neighbor offered to drive her to Bluefield, she jumped at the chance to get away. Mom put on a clean dress, grabbed Donna and me, and paid a visit to my father's other sister, our Aunt Gertrude (Gertie) near Bluefield, Virginia. My aunt's neighbor and long-term friend, Mrs. Thaye Matheny, stopped in to see Gertie while we were visiting. Thaye was (for unknown reasons) thinking of adopting a child of her own, and as she watched me play with my cousins, she became more and more enamored of the idea.

"Myrtle, how many children do you have?"

"I have seven living with me and one has left home."

"Well, that sure is a houseful. What's the name of your little boy there?"

"That's Tommy," Mom said.

"Myrtle, would you mind letting me keep Tommy for a while? I promise to give him back whenever you want, and I'd be willing to take him now if it's okay with you."

Mom was caught off guard by Thaye's frankness, but she wasn't about to give up her child—especially to a stranger.

"No ... I don't think so."

Aunt Gertie spoke up, thinking of Mom's welfare.

"Myrtle, you might want to consider Thaye's offer. Those kids must be a real handful, and it would help a lot if you had one less to feed, bath, clothe, and look after. You expecting again isn't going to help any."

There was a ring of truth to Aunt Gertie's words, and Mom was feeling pressured.

"I'll have to think on it."

During the next few days Mom thought about how fortunate she was to be so fertile, and how difficult it must be for a woman to hunger for a child and yet, for whatever reason, be unable to bear one. Aunt Gertie was working hard at putting Mom at ease about the offer. She was being proactive in convincing her that Thaye was a kind and honest person who would take good care of me. To Mom, it was beginning to make sense. She knew that she was getting older and her current pregnancy was going to be a rough one.

I suspect that Mom had not totally forgiven herself for the scalding. She may have started to believe that Thaye could offer me so much more than I could get at home, and especially since I, unlike most of my siblings, was so receptive to living with this nice lady from the city.

About a week later, Aunt Gertie and Thaye drove to Abb's Valley. They loaded me and an armful of my clothes into the car and whisked me away to Thaye's home, a very nice house high up on a hill in the city of Bluefield, West Virginia.

During my first Christmas there, she and her husband treated me to my one and only toy tractor—with wheels and pedals that work. The streets around Thaye's home were very narrow and steep—a bit too dangerous for my new tractor and me. The only safe places were the porch and a short sidewalk. It was nearly impossible to peddle the tractor more than several feet before I would have to pick it up, turn it around, and start pedaling again. That didn't seem like much fun for a four-year-old country boy.

Looking back, I'm surprised I didn't attempt a trip down their steep and dangerous driveway. Who knows, considering my tendency for accidents, maybe I did try it and survived. Or maybe, Thaye or someone was carefully watching over me.

I don't recall being traumatized or emotionally scarred from being shoveled out to the nicest bidder. I was a happy and well-adjusted child, and Thaye was doing a superb job as my substitute mother.

Those were good times with good memories. There was plenty of good food and delicious desserts to eat at Thaye's house —like my first chocolate snowball cake, filled with cream and covered with coconut and marshmallow. I was given nice clothes to wear and a hot bath just about every night. Television, a novel and most enchanting invention, sat in the corner of our living room most of the day. At night, the TV came alive with the introduction of successful Broadway musical fantasies like Peter Pan (July 2, 1955) and The Wizard of Oz (Nov. 3, 1956). Music and dancing with the big bands of The Lawrence Welk Show was a must-watch for Thaye and her husband on Saturday nights. I especially enjoyed the giant bubble display. Greatest of all, I got to flush the toilet instead of using a chamber pot, coffee can, or outhouse.

The first winter in Abb's Valley brought the usual snowy days and cold nights. In spite of the bad weather and our father's overbearing drunken fits, my older siblings managed to find opportunities to enjoy their youth and nature, especially with me tucked safely out of the way.

Back then, snow sledding was a frequent and popular family pastime, and we were lucky enough to be able to own or borrow a sled or two. On one particular weekend, some of my older siblings were out enjoying a bountiful snowfall. Wesley and Ronnie would often dare one another to do risky things. Ginny felt the winter outings would be more fun if her older brothers would stop making the activity so competitive. But being a perfect tomboy at heart, Ginny frequently allowed herself to get caught up in her brother's dangerous games.

Paul and Ronnie had just successfully performed a tricky maneuver where the two of them: 1) sledded down the steep hill at the entrance to our hollow, 2) shot across the road, and 3) threaded their way under the barbed wire fence on the other side.

It was Ginny's turn to prove that she was just as skilled with a snow sled as her big brothers. More importantly, she wanted to prove she was just as brave too. With her adrenaline pumping, Ginny stood at the precipice planning her route to victory.

"Ginny, keep your head down when you go through the fence," Ronnie warned.

"Yeah," Paul said, "watch out for the barbed wire."

"Okay."

Ginny hadn't taken into consideration the fact that her siblings had packed the snow tighter since her last trip down the hill. Her speed would be faster now. So, almost from the moment Ginny and the sled started moving, my brothers could hear her screaming. She tried to slow down by dragging her feet, but that didn't help. When she and the sled shot through the fence, the lower strand of barbed wire caught her across her left eyelid, producing a bloody gash.

Later that night, Mom had a good look at Ginny's damaged eye.

"What were you doing to get that?" she asked.

"I was sledding. Mom, I think my brothers are trying to get me killed."

"I don't think so, Ginny. You're gonna half-ta stay away from the boys and stop being such a tomboy before you do get yourself killed."

Ginny was lucky there was no damage other than a nasty scar.

After clawing their way for more than half a mile through briars and brambles, Wesley and Ronnie stood resting against a tree stump near the top of the mountain above our house. Looking about, they saw exactly what they were looking for. It was a tall, dead chestnut tree that offered more than a three-month supply of kindling for our heaters, and it provided just the right challenge for the two boys and their two-man bow saw.

With Ronnie helping, Wesley felled the tree in seconds, only to watch it jam itself between two standing trees. Wesley clambered aboard the partially downed tree and began to jump up and down in an effort to dislodge it. Tired and frustrated, he said, "Ronnie, get up here and help me!"

"I'm not climbing up there," Ronnie said. "It's gonna fall any second, and I don't want to be anywhere near it when it does."

"Don't be such a sissy. Now, get up here!"

Ronnie turned his back on Wesley and began to walk down the mountain, headed for home. When he saw his brother deserting him, Wesley was furious and close to an emotional breakdown. The pressures of being the oldest, the strongest, and the son with the most responsibility had been building inside him for months—maybe even years. He jumped to the ground, shouting, "Ronnie, if you don't get back here, I'm gonna hit you with a rock!"

Ronnie ignored Wesley and continued walking. Wesley found the perfect rock and threw a perfect strike, hitting Ronnie square in the back of his head. The force knocked him to the ground, where he almost lost consciousness.

Wesley didn't really plan to hit his brother, only to scare him. But now wasn't the time for regrets or apologies. He had to stop the heavy flow of blood from Ronnie's head and get him home. Wesley wrapped Ronnie's shirt around his hand and pressed the cloth against the back of his brother's head. Then he helped Ronnie back down the mountain. On the way he showered his younger brother with apologies, hoping Ronnie would tell Mom it was an accident.

At home, it took an unusually long time to stem the flow of blood from Ronnie's head. In fact, Ronnie lost enough blood to feel dizzy and lightheaded—so much so, that he wasn't able to enjoy the severe beating that Mom gave Wesley.

He learned a good lesson that day and never threw a rock again. Well, at least he didn't throw them at family.

In January 1956, the family moved one mile northeast of Tank Hill Road to another hollow called Hanges Branch, little more than a dirt road leading to another shack. A decade or two later, the state and its bulldozers erased the main road leading there along with all official references to Hanges Branch. Over time, the name ceased to exist—except in the minds of a few.

About the same time the family was settling in at Hanges Branch, I was at Thaye's celebrating my 4th birthday. Almost ready to deliver, Mom brought Ginny along for an evening birthday visit.

I had just taken a hot bath and was strolling about the house barefoot and squeaky-clean. Comfortably dressed in white pajamas with wine-colored vertical stripes, I was enjoying the companionship of Max, Thaye's bulldog. Ginny recalls that my normally chubby cheeks were gone and I looked thinner. This was possibly due to a healthier diet, riding my tractor, and perhaps a small growth spurt.

Thaye insisted that I take Ginny to my bedroom and put on some socks and my new house slippers so that Mom and Ginny could see them. I think it was an excuse for Mom and Thaye to be alone to discuss the topic of adoption. I took Ginny's hand and led her proudly through the master bedroom and into my bedroom. While in my clean and well-organized bedroom, I put on my slippers and showed her my new toy tractor. Ginny saw a few dollars and some change lying on the master bedroom dresser, and recalls thinking: That's more money than I've ever seen at one time.

Near the end of the visit, Thaye took a Polaroid picture of me feeding Max a biscuit while sitting in my rocking chair, smiling as if tickled about the whole thing. She gave the picture to Mom to keep. Ginny marveled at how soon I had recovered from my scalding and how well I was adapting to my new home and surroundings. On the way home, she shared her thoughts with Mom, saying, "Tommy seems so happy."

Just a few days later, Mom's labor complications were so severe that she had to be taken to the Bluefield Sanitarium Hospital. Marital stress and the move to a new place had contributed to a dangerous pregnancy.

Thanks to proper medical care, Mom successfully delivered **Deborah Sue** (Debbie) near the middle of February 1956. The second child to be born in a hospital, Debbie was a healthy child with a medium complexion and curly dark brown hair.

Tommy (4) feeding Max at Thaye's, Jan. 1956.

IV

ELGOOD
c. 1956-1957

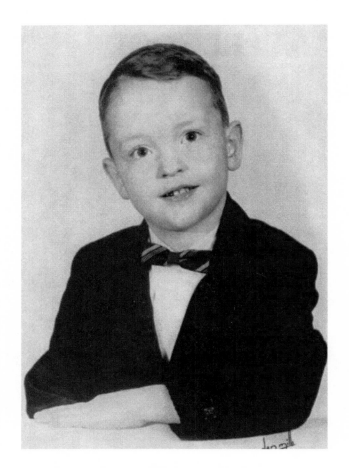

Tommy (5), Olan Mills special, Feb. 1957.

Sharecropping

Anyone who has ever traveled through Virginia and West Virginia will admit that both have some of the most beautiful real estate in the country.

Located just a few miles southeast of the town of Athens, the small unincorporated community of Elgood, W.V., proudly displays rolling hills and farmland that has—undoubtedly—been formed by a higher power. Indeed, God has bragging rights here. To this day the area is also a testament to the deep pride shared by the local farmers and landowners.

In the spring of 1956, our family was lucky enough to plant our feet on a piece of this heaven. Unfortunately, serious family frictions would taint our good times at Elgood.

The road to our farming property was one of many branching from Little Island Creek Road in the Island Creek section of Elgood. Lazy Lane was a rutty dirt road that wound 200 yards from the main road to a large barn, packed to the brim with hay, tools, and assorted farm equipment. Continuing another 30 yards or so, one would encounter a small stream of fresh water. A foot deep at best, the stream had a solid foundation of rock and pebbles that automobiles and rolling farm equipment could easily cross. Two long, wooden planks supported by large, flat rocks served as a pedestrian walkway when you didn't want to get your feet wet. Yep, used by the women mostly. The men and boys usually didn't care if their feet got wet or their shoes got muddy, except in the cold of winter or when you wanted to look your best in church. Of course sitting in church was a rare event for our family.

On the other side of the creek, the road began a slight and steady incline, curving here and there before disappearing 50 yards further, replaced by weeds and grass at our front yard.

A white picket fence surrounded the yard on three sides. Once through the gate, a visitor would be drawn to the big white farmhouse crowding the sky above it. A sturdy front porch sporting a couple of rocking chairs beckoned the weary to sit and admire the view. Sometimes Dad would sit there sipping his moonshine, chewin' and spittin' tobacco, and watching for the Revenuers. It was the nicest place our family had ever called home.

Dad and his brother, Uncle Bob, somehow worked out a deal with the property owner, Mr. Nash, that allowed our family to live on and farm the property, and in return we had to give back all the crops except what we needed to survive. We would be sharecroppers, working more than thirty acres—mostly corn and potatoes. As part of this arrangement, we were allowed to sell small amounts of fruits and vegetables for necessary cash income.

Ronnie earned 25-cents and Wesley earned 50-cents per hour (half the minimum wage) cutting brush and putting in fence posts. Dad forced his sons to sign their paychecks and hand them over. Then he cashed them and disappeared for days, spending their hard earned money on gambling, drinking, and who knows what else. It was a despicable act and loathing was the just reward.

Farming the property required tending a horse, several cows, sheep, pigs, and chickens. Bob, our big plough horse, could be mean and often unpredictable. Dad and Wesley were the only ones able to control him, and Dad said he didn't want anyone riding him, especially Wesley and Ronnie. Bob and his wooden sled, or harrow, were often the only means of transportation for the family. Since we didn't have a horse that could be ridden, my older siblings satisfied their equestrian desires by settling for an occasional ride on the back of an obliging cow or two. These "victims" always complained, saying, "Mooo-waa!" Or sometimes, when they were really annoyed, they'd say, "Umm-mooo-waa!"

In early June 1956, Mom informed the family that she was pregnant again. Considering little Debbie had been born just three months earlier, Mama and several of my aunts were concerned about her ability to bring a new pregnancy to a healthy full term. Mom was thirty-four years old—no spring chicken for birthing children. To add even more danger, there was Dad's behavior and the fact that the family would be living on and working a small farm. Just as important, Elgood was way out in the country and a considerable distance from supporting family and medical institutions.

The family had barely settled into the farming routine that summer when Dad started behaving in a bad way again. To avoid another beating from him and protect her unborn child, Mom ran away and didn't tell anyone where she was going.

Two or three days later and fifty miles from home, she was picked up by the sheriff while wandering the streets of Christiansburg, Virginia. Dirty and appearing homeless, she was charged with vagrancy and locked in a cell. Mom pleaded with the sheriff and his deputy. She showed them a picture of Daisy and told them she was trying to find her daughter. It was fortunate the sheriff's deputy recognized Daisy's picture. It was the familiar face of the pleasant young woman working at one of the local drive-in restaurants.

"Good morning deputy," Daisy said, with her usual tone of voice and polite smile, "what can I get for you today?"

The deputy said, "Daisy, I think we have your mom down at the station."

"Oh no," she said, "it can't be."

"Daisy ... I'm afraid she is. If you'll get in, I'll take you to her."

At the sheriff's office, Daisy was shocked to see Mom's uncombed dirty hair and her wrinkled, dirty, and torn clothes. She looked so haggard and worn out that Daisy barely recognized her and wept uncontrollably when Mom told her what had happened. She used her last fifteen dollars to pay Mom's fine and release her from jail.

Daisy helped Mom clean up and saw to it that she was delivered to a friend's place in Princeton, W.Va. Although it was painful to see her mother in such a state, Daisy was sure she could do nothing more. She had argued enough with her mother over the dangers of staying with Dad. She didn't expect another round of arguments to do any good. Mom stayed with her friend for a while before returning to the family in Elgood.

Each time she returned, Mom hoped her husband had missed her and would be glad she was back. Dad had missed her, but his memory could be as fleeting as the high from a pint of moonshine.

The daily pressures of running a farm can be overwhelming for even the toughest of families. There is little doubt that Mom; Wesley, now 14; and Ronnie, 12, were often worn out by suppertime. Dad, on the other hand, was good at making and avoiding work by getting drunk, passing out, and sleeping it off.

So, right after dinner a few days before Christmas, Dad started drinking and smacking Mom about her face. Her survival mode kicked in again, and she ran from the house again, disappearing into the dark. Around dawn someone went looking for her. Everyone hoped she would be at one of the neighbor's houses, but she was found hiding in the smokehouse. Not wanting to bother the neighbors, she had spent most of the night curled up in the fetal position, trying to keep herself and her unborn child warm.

Shivering violently from the cold, Mom was brought into the house, fed, and warmed by the pot belly stove in the living room.

"Shortie, you didn't have to stay out in the cold like that," Dad said. "I wasn't gonna hurt ya."

Mom said, "You're full of shit, Harold."

"Yeah, Dad," Wesley said, "Mom can't read your mind."

Later in the day, she developed fever with abdominal pains. Mom was escorted to a neighbor's house and driven to the Princeton hospital, where she went into labor.

On December 23, 1956, Mom delivered Julie Ann, her fifth daughter. About three months premature and weighing less than two pounds, she was stillborn.

I don't think our father ever realized how much he may have contributed to the loss of his daughter and our little sister. His life, and his way of living it, seemed to remain the same. No, actually it did change—it got worse.

On February 4, 1957, the Bishop #34 mine near Tazewell, VA, had an explosion that killed 37 miners. It was one mishap among many, not only in McDowell and the surrounding counties, but in the U.S. coal industry in general. Poor mining safety regulations and relaxed enforcement were par for the course.

While my mother made a speedy recovery, I was settled and quite happy at Ms. Thaye's home in Bluefield. After her recovery, however, Mom decided I should be at home sharing the joys of farming with the rest of the family. So, shortly after my fifth birthday in 1957, Thaye dressed me up to have my picture taken at a local Olan Mills studio. I was wearing a white collared shirt, black blazer, and black bow tie. She wanted to make sure, no doubt, that everyone had a good picture of me as keepsake.

It must have been a difficult drive when she and Aunt Gertie delivered me back to my mother. Thaye wanted so much to adopt me, but Mom wouldn't think of it anymore.

"I'm sorry, I just can't give him up," she said. "He's been away from home and family long enough." Mom didn't want to impose upon Thaye any longer, nor continue to build up her hopes of adopting me.

I was not torn between two mothers. I knew who my real mother was and didn't complain. Although I'm sure I was happier returning home to my real mother and the familiar faces of my siblings.

I was home less than two months when many of us witnessed Dad chasing our mother around the kitchen table. He was staggering drunk. This was not an affectionate or playful chase; although some of us little ones may have thought so. Mom knew if Dad caught her she was going to get another beating. The little ones were giggling-up a storm until Mom, in self-defense, grabbed an iron poker from a bucket of coal and struck Dad so hard across his chest that he fell backwards hitting his head on the floor. Everyone grew quiet. Gazing at our father lying flat-out on the floor, we expected him to rise up and continue the chase just the way he had done so many times before, but he didn't. The family left him lying there unconscious until morning. When Dad awoke he was furious. He looked for Mom inside the house and couldn't find her.

"Where's your mother?" he shouted. Honestly, at the time, no one knew where she was.

As Dad walked onto the front porch, he told us, "When I find her, I'm gonna beat the shit out of her and some of you kids too. Somebody better tell me where she is."

Fearing Dad's twisted sense of retribution, Wesley and Ronnie immediately locked the front and back doors. Dad walked completely around the house looking for Mom and when he returned to find the front door locked—he was pissed.

"Open the door or I'm gonna break it down!"

"I have the shotgun, Dad," Wesley shouted through the door, "so you better not come in!"

Dad didn't hear or just didn't care. Using our wood axe, he started chopping away at the heavy wooden door. The sound of the axe chewing away the front door was so loud and terrifying that Wesley dropped the shotgun and shouted for everyone to run to the back yard. Before Dad could chop his way through, all of us kids ran out the back door and across the yard and creek in a westward direction, before heading for the hills and woods.

Later that evening, under the cover of darkness, Wesley led our little group of seven as we snuck into the barn and entered the hayloft. It was barely springtime and the night air was cold. But that didn't bother us; we were all snuggled together inside the bales of hay, getting toastier and toastier by the minute. In fact, we were so comfortable that

Wesley thought some of us little ones were beginning to make too much noise.

"If we aren't quiet and Dad hears us," Wesley said, "he'll be up here with the loaded shotgun." Well, that did the trick. We all grew quiet and enjoyed a peaceful sleep that night.

Early in the morning we awoke hungry and dirty. Since we were afraid to return home, we marched over to our neighbor's house, where Mr. and Mrs. Butler fed us breakfast. They must have pitied us.

Most of us had finished eating by the time Dad drove his pickup into the Butler's driveway. He just sat there beeping his horn until Mrs. Butler went outside with a loaded shotgun to see what his problem was.

My siblings and I sat petrified at the kitchen table. Ronnie and Wesley recalled what took place then.

"What do you want, Sleepy?" Mrs. Butler shouted, as my brothers peeked through the curtains of the open front porch window.

"Have you seen any of those damn kids of mine?"

"No, I haven't!"

"You wouldn't be hide'n my old lady in there, would-ja?"

"Sleepy, you better get your ass on out of here. You're beginning to upset my nerves. Don't you see what I'm holding in my hands here?"

Dad would usually avoid upsetting his neighbors too much. His thinking was, "You never kin tell when ya might need a favor from one of em." But he wasn't thinking that way now. Dad started to harass and argue with Mrs. Butler, a woman not about to put up with any more of Dad's crap. When she lifted her shotgun and pointed it directly at him, he started turning the truck around and pretended to head home. Mrs. Butler had barely returned to the porch when Dad stopped and began beeping his horn again. Mrs. Butler swung her shotgun around and put a blast of shot through the truck's cab. Dad just sat there. He looked shocked and seemed frozen in place. He continued to stare at her, until he saw her eject the empty shotgun shell and prepare another. That's when he skedaddled out of there, disappearing across the mountain.

Whether he was drinking or sober, my father lived for excitement. He bragged for days after that how Mrs. Butler shot holes in his truck—but missed hitting him.

You know, that Mrs. Butler was tough!

We returned home that afternoon. Wesley and Ronnie were repairing the front door when, out by the barn, they saw Mom walking toward the house carrying little Debbie in her arms. Before she could cross the planks over the stream, Ronnie and Wesley were beside her. Ronnie took Debbie, as Wesley helped Mom across to the front yard and into the house.

Dad returned the following day, but before he could step onto the front porch he found himself staring at the barrel of another shotgun— his own. Dad pleaded and begged Mom to forgive him. After promising to behave himself, he was allowed to rejoin the family. Again.

Horsing Around

Some of my earliest memories go back to our second year of breaking ground on the farm. It was late in the morning when Wesley, Ronnie, and Dad were working in the fields near the barn. Bob was harnessed to and pulling the harrow, with Dad standing on top in control of the reins. They had been breaking up sod and combing out rocks most of the morning. Carrying a bucket of water with a dipper in it, Ginny, 11, headed for the fields to give the men a drink. Gary, 3, and I followed close behind her as we maneuvered our way around several piles of cow manure. We stopped in the shade of a tree at the edge of the field.

"Tommy," Ginny said, "you and Gary stay here while I give Daddy and your brothers a drink." Navigating and maneuvering barefooted about the freshly tilled furrows would have been a challenge for our tiny feet and legs.

As Ginny walked across the lumpy field toward my brothers, I plopped myself down on a grassy bank under one of the few trees in the area. To my right, I could see and hear Dad working and talking to Bob as he muscled his way, head and back straining, across the field toward us. "Gee! Haw! Gee-up!" he'd sometimes command.

Later in life, I would learn that the words meant right, left, and faster respectively. I was fascinated by those sounds, as I also was by the snapping of the reins, the crackling of new harness leather growing louder and more distinct, and the sight of Dad and our plough horse working in harmony on a warm spring day.

"Gary, don't put that in your mouth!"

Ginny's voice startled me to attention. But it was too late; Gary had wandered into the sun and plopped himself down beside a shiny new cow pie.

"For crying out loud, Gary. I can't leave you for one darn minute."

About that time, Dad arrived with Bob and the sled.

"Jesus Christ, Ginny! You're supposed to be watchin' those kids. Now take him over to the stream and clean em up."

Ginny gave Dad his drink and led Gary and me to the stream by the barn. While she cleaned the mess from Gary, I spotted Paul, 9, and Donna, 7, playing in the hayloft of the barn. I ran into the barn, and—all by my self—climbed the ladder to join them. A rowdy game of hide-n-seek ensued as we climbed, jumped, and tunneled among the randomly stacked hay bales. Fifteen minutes later, the three of us paused to catch our breath.

It didn't take long for Donna to catch hers. She was on top of me in a flash.

"Come on, Tommy. Let's wrestle."

Donna had me pinned tight, and I grunted, groaned, and struggled to push her off. Now that I was forced to lie on my back, my eyes and attention were drawn upwards into the barn's rafters. That's when I saw it.

"Hey, what's that hanging up there?"

"Tommy, you're just trying to trick me so I'll let you up."

"Wait a minute," Paul said. "There is something up there."

Finally Donna rolled off me and looked into the rafters. "I see it, too," she said. "It looks like one of Dad's black belts."

As we stared at the object, it seemed to stare back, moving and swaying in the breeze. Donna was getting excited. "Look, Paul, the wind is blowing it."

Paul jumped from the highest bale of hay to the platform by the ladder exit, a height that could have easily resulted in a broken bone or sprained ankle.

"That's not the wind," he said. "That's a snake moving around up there. We better get out of here!" Donna and I hustled across the bales of hay, staying close behind Paul as he hurried down the ladder.

Wesley was working pretty close to the barn when Paul ran toward him, shouting as he went. "Wesley, there's a snake in the barn! There's a snake in the barn!"

Wesley threw down his garden tool. "Are you sure?"

"Yeah, it's hanging from the rafters above the hay." Paul's excitement and the petrified expression on our faces prompted Wesley to take us seriously.

Wesley called to Ronnie and, with pitchforks in-hand, the two of them disappeared into the loft. We heard them talking, shouting, and laughing, but couldn't understand what they were saying. About ten minutes later, we watched them walk out of the barn with Wesley holding his pitchfork high above his head. A big, long black snake was attached.

By this time, Dad and Ginny (holding Gary on her hip) had wandered nearer to the barn, wanting a better view of the show. With a quick dip of his pitchfork, Wesley flung the snake to the ground at Ginny's feet. Startled, she jumped back.

"Wesley, that ain't funny!"

The men laughed at Ginny as the snake started to slither away. Wesley caught it by its tail and, in one quick and smooth motion, snapped it hard like a whip. Death was instant.

Wesley tossed the snake carcass into the garden not far from the path to the house. Dad clapped his hands shouting, "Okay, okay, the show's over! The day's half gone, and there's a lot more work to be done. Ginny, you and those kids get on back to the house!"

During the next week or two I passed by the dead snake and, each time, took note of its slow decomposition into the earth—therein contemplating (for the first time) the complexities of life, death, and mortality.

Living and working on a farm provides many opportunities for fun and adventure. It can also provide many opportunities for mishaps.

Being a stud and draft horse, Bob was very dangerous. Like I said before, no one was allowed to ride him. Keenly aware of this, Wesley, 15, had been working with Bob for several weeks trying to break down the horse's resistance. To build trust, Wesley gave him vegetable and sugar treats, along with comforting talks and rubdowns. He also placed weighted-down blankets and saddles on his back to simulate a rider.

After a rainy spell in the spring of 1956, Wesley and Ronnie had Bob harnessed to a swinging tree and chained for pulling logs. Their chore was hauling cut logs from the woods to the sawmill near the edge of the property where Dad was waiting. On a trip back for more logs, my brothers stopped by the house. In one of his rebellious moments, Wesley decided it was the right time; come hell or high water, he was going to ride Bob back to the woods to collect more logs, even though the horse was still chained and harnessed to a swinging tree.

As Wesley prepared to mount Bob, Donna screamed as she ran into the house. "Mom, Wesley's trying to ride Bob! Mom, Wesley's trying to ride Bob!" By now, Ronnie had nicknamed Donna "Blabber-mouth." The name stuck.

Bob, being a draft horse, was very tall. To make it easier, Wesley prepared to mount him from the front porch steps.

"Mom, Wesley's climbing on Bob!"

He slowly slid down onto Bob's back.

Donna's screeching had finally gotten Mom's attention, and she arrived at the porch in time to see Wesley's equestrian attempt.

"Wesley, you're gonna break your neck trying to ride that animal!"

"I'm okay, Mom!"

"If you hurt him, your dad will beat the life out of you!"

"Mom, Wesley's riding Bob!"

Poor Bob. Donna's loud and shrill voice plus a rider on his back was more than Bob could take. In a state of panic, he reared up and dashed down the front yard with Wesley barely hanging on.

Wesley hung on for life as the horse headed for the four-foot tall fence. Surprisingly, Bob jumped and cleared it. While Bob was still airborne, Wesley dismounted the beast, somehow landing unhurt. When Bob touched ground on the other side, his front hooves sank deep into the muddy garden while the rest of him completed a forward flip through the potato plants.

Luckily, neither horse nor rider was injured, and there was only minor damage where the chain and swinging tree had caught the fence. Wesley, counting his blessings, picked up Bob's harness and led him back to the woods where more logs were waiting.

As Bob and my two brothers approached Dad at the mill, Wesley shouted, "I rode him Dad! I rode him!" It was a proud moment for Wesley.

A few days later, Ronnie and Wesley were leading Bob to the barn. They were wondering if the previous incident had broken some of the horse's spirit and maybe, just maybe, Bob would be a little more accommodating.

Wesley held Bob's reins while Ronnie climbed onto his bare back. Bob's reaction was immediate. His skin twitched and convulsed. Fearing for his life, Ronnie panicked and vaulted from the horse's back.

"Ronnie, why'd you do that? Now he knows you're afraid of him."

"Didn't you see the way he was behaving?" Ronnie asked.

"Oh, come on Ronnie! Here, let me try it."

Ronnie held Bob's reins while Wesley mounted the horse. Right away Bob's skin began twitching again, but Wesley insisted on ignoring the signals. Bob's tail began to whip back and forth, and his eyes grew bigger and began rolling about in their sockets. Bob was about to go crazy and Ronnie knew it.

"Look at his eyes Wesley! Don't you see his eyes?"

By now Wesley was looking bug-eyed, too, and he slid from the horse's back. Wesley had chickened-out just in time. Bob reared up, broke free from Ronnie's grip on the reins, and galloped down to the fence. I don't think Bob was ever mounted again, let alone ridden.

No one knows why our father didn't discipline his sons for going against his wishes. Maybe Dad thought Wesley was too big for a whipping, or maybe he saw his own impetuous youth reflected in his son's silly, but dangerous, stunts.

Not too long after that, Wesley was playing on top of the sawdust pile at the neighbor's mill. He and a friend were competing to see who could jump the farthest from the mill shed's second floor doorway into the pile of sawdust. Wesley won, but in the process broke the tibia bone in his leg. He spent two days in the hospital, followed by several weeks in a cast. Using crutches, he was forced to install fence posts while wearing the cast and never followed up with the doctor. Instead, when the time was right, he used a hacksaw and removed the cast himself.

I had my own share of mishaps down on the farm that year.

The first happened when Paul rolled a bicycle tire rim up the tongue of a piece of farm equipment stored in one of the sheds. Then he carelessly allowed it to drop ten feet onto my head. When Mom saw my bloody head, she said, "Paul, how the hell did this happen?"

"Mom, I told him to move out of the way, but he wouldn't listen."

On another day, Ginny was pulling Gary and me in our neighbor's little red wagon. I became upset when she made me get out. She said the wheel was loose and I was too heavy. Pouting from sheer stubbornness, I refused to get out of the way when asked, thereby allowing the wobbly wagon wheel to roll over my bare foot. The wheel hurt but didn't do any damage. The axle, however, separated from the wheel, came crashing down, and buried its sharp end deep into my foot. It cut a major blood vessel, creating another serious medical emergency.

Ginny's explanation? "Mom, I told Tommy to stay out of the way."

At this point in my very young life, my family was beginning to wonder about me.

Revenuers

I'll reiterate: working the farm was hard work, especially for Wesley and Ronnie. At the time Ginny thought Ronnie was mean and picky. But years later, she realized that a good part of his mood was frustration due to a "stressful position of responsibility." Looking back, she recalls, "Ronnie had to be a man too early. He tried to teach Paul and me how to help get some work done."

Ginny also explained: "It was better for all of us when the mean overseer (Dad) wasn't at home. I never saw Dad work very hard for very long at anything. Also, at that time, I didn't know that the corn on top of the mountain could be used to make moonshine."

When supplies were running low one day, Dad decided to dash out and purchase some food and ingredients for making his moonshine. Since the truck was torn apart for repairs, Dad had to harness Bob to his sled and drive him up the valley to the supply store. Using our kitchen stove top, he had just made and sampled a fresh batch of brew and, before he left, Mom opened a few windows to air out the odors.

Ginny was playing in the front yard with little Debbie when two men in brown suits strolled up to the front gate.

"Hey little girl," the strange voice blasted, "where's your daddy's still?"

Ginny was startled but recovered well.

"What's a still?" she replied naively.

Without answering her question, the men identified themselves as revenuers and presented their badges as proof.

All of a sudden, Ginny felt a surge of adrenaline. She ran to the porch and yelled into the house through the screen.

"Mommy, the police are here!"

Mom dashed to the front porch with the usual flock of children close behind her.

One of the men asked: "Are you Mrs. Dixon?"

"Yes I am."

"Mrs. Dixon, we're from the Department of Treasury, and we have reason to believe that some illegal whiskey production may be going on near these premises. Would you mind showing us the locations of any water holes on the property?"

A convenient, high-quality, and plentiful source of water was necessary when setting up a whiskey still, and water holes were the usual locations for illegal whiskey production.

Mom told Ronnie to show the men around the place. Ginny and Paul went along too. Ronnie was not concerned about getting his father into trouble, because he knew Dad was using the kitchen stove to make his brew. So Ronnie showed them every water hole he could think of. By the time they left, the men were pretty tired of walking.

Later in the day, Mom caught Wesley walking about the house.

"Wesley, your dad should have been back hours ago. I want you and Ronnie to go see if you can find him."

My brothers had barely made it to the barn when Wesley called out, "I think I hear Dad and Bob coming!" Sure enough, in the distance you could hear the distinct clip-clop, clip-clop of Bob's hooves as they pounded the road.

"Yeah," Ronnie said, "and they're comin' awful fast!"

Ronnie and Wesley ran to the fence by the barn just in time to open the gate and let Bob and the sled through. However, for some strange reason, Dad was missing.

"Look, Wesley, the groceries are still in the box on the sled. Dad must have fallen off!"

"Ronnie, I'll unhitch Bob. You go and see if you can find him. If we're lucky, you'll find him lying dead on the side of the road somewhere."

Ronnie ran into Dad about a mile up the road. Dad said he had stopped to have a drink with Hank, an old Negro friend who lived along the way.

"I think we might-of had too much to drink," Dad said. "We got awful loud." He said Bob was spooked when Hank fired his gun into the air, causing Dad to fall off the sled. "Bob headed for home and wasn't about to stop for nothin'," Dad added.

When Dad got back to the house, he was told about the Revenuers nosing around. The timing of his return couldn't have been more perfect. Had the revenuers smelled the whiskey on his breath, their suspicions would have been even more aroused.

"Shit! Those bastards are sure to come back. I better get rid of some of this stuff."

Dad's stash of mash, a major ingredient for whisky, was hidden in the chicken house in a barrel covered with plastic and potato sacks. He took the mash, mixed it with the pigs' slop, and fed the mix to the pigs and chickens.

The next morning all the pigs and chickens were hung over. We thought he had killed them, but most, if not all, survived.

Brownie, Round One

One day early into our second year on the farm, a friend from the Elgood area gave Wesley (and the family) a dog. He was a six-year-old brown collie and sheep dog mix. Appropriately, he was called Brownie.

The friend said Brownie was a stray, but we soon found out that he belonged to our neighbor more than five miles away. The dog loved Wesley, and seemed to love the farm and family just as much. So much so, that every time we returned him to his true owner, he would always find his way back to our farm.

Our neighbor finally gave up. "You might as well keep him," he said. "He won't stay here anyways."

Wesley promised Dad that Brownie was a huntin' dog. "Humph," Dad grunted, "I ain't never seen a dog worth his keep. I'll believe it when I see it." He wouldn't have to wait long.

Less than a week later, some of us were awakened early in the morning by Brownie's barking. Afraid the noise would anger Dad, my brothers dashed to the back porch to put a stop to it.

"Brownie, quiet," Wesley whispered. As he petted the dog, he noticed something odd lying near the end of the porch. As he looked closer, it became obvious. "Holy cow, it's a dead groundhog. Brownie got us a groundhog!"

Ronnie was just as proud and excited as his brother. "It's fresh kill too, Wesley. Let's tell Dad."

They told Dad what Brownie had dropped off on the porch, what a good dog he was going to be, and that we could eat groundhog for dinner more often now.

Dad said, "Oh yeah, we'll see about that."

Mom wasted little time cleaning and preparing the fresh wild game. She cooked groundhog stew that night, with her special seasoned gravy. She added some scallions and fried potato slices on the side, and threw in a big batch of gravy-sopping biscuits to make the meal complete.

A man wouldn't have to consume much of Mom's homemade, country cooking to appreciate it—or its source. Once Dad finished his meal, he scooted his chair away from the table. Leaning way back in the chair, he pointed a toothpick at his oldest sons; and, in between smacking his lips and sucking air through his rotting teeth, he gave a wink.

"Well boys," he said, "I reckon we have us a huntin' dog."

We all cheered. That was what many of us—and especially Wesley—wanted to hear. Brownie was already earning his keep.

Skullduggery

Early in June 1957, Wesley and Dad were visiting the Butlers when, around two in the afternoon, someone in the family sounded the alarm.

"Hey Mom, there's a black car parked over by the barn." Mom and a bunch of us kids ran to the front porch to see who it was.

The black 1949 Chevy had passed the barn and was now stopped near the middle of the creek. A man and woman in their late twenties stepped out, looked under the car, and began to argue with the driver, a slightly older man. Ronnie jumped from the porch railing to the ground.

"Mom, do you want I should go down there and see what's going on?"

"Ronnie, you get your butt back here! We don't know them people or what they're up to."

"Ah Mom," Ronnie moaned, "you never let me do anything." Mom had to watch him like a hawk, because he was "sneaky" and often getting into trouble.

The couple stopped arguing, and we noticed the woman walking toward us. She stopped at the front porch steps close to Ronnie, who was eyeing her suspiciously.

"I'm sorry to disturb you and your family, ma'am, but I was wondering if we could borrow some lye soap. We'd like to use it to stop a leak we found in our gas tank."

"Ginny, run to the kitchen and fetch us that cake of lye soap your dad's been using."

At this point the two men could be heard talking beside the car. The woman continued on, explaining how the car had kicked-up a rock a few miles back that appeared to have damaged the gas tank. Ginny returned with the soap, and the lady thanked us and walked back to the car. Ronnie, in his sneaky mode, tried to stray after her.

"Ronnie, you get back here or I'm gonna put a switch to your behind!" Ronnie dropped his head, kicked the ground, and shuffled his way back toward the house.

Mom made herself comfortable in one of the rocking chairs on the porch. She was with child again and feeling a little tired. "Ronnie, go fetch the shotgun," she said, "and put it behind the front door—and make sure it's loaded."

We continued to watch as the visitors argued and tried to repair the car's fuel tank.

Minutes later, from the porch, we saw that Dad and Wesley had returned from the Butler's and were having a discussion with the two men by the barn. Wesley broke away from the group, and we watched him as he sprinted past us and the farmhouse to the corn crib out back. Boy, could Wesley run! Everyone but Mom and Ronnie was wondering what the dickens he was up to. When he reappeared carrying a quart size mason jar of Dad's whiskey, most of us knew. In two shakes of a lamb's tail, Wesley was back at the barn handing over the devil's firewater to one of the men. The man gave something to Dad; and whatever it was, probably money, he stuffed it into his pocket. The two strangers returned to their car and, in between sips of whiskey and drags from a cigarette, continued their lazy attempt at repairing the tank. Wesley and Dad remained at the barn watching them. There was little doubt they were concerned about the men's behavior.

With half a jar of whiskey left, the three strangers once again began to argue. This time it was very intense. Our family was on edge.

Now upset with her husband for selling alcohol to strangers of questionable character (and intellect) Mom had lost all her patience. She was considering using the shotgun to send a signal for Dad and Wesley to chase them away when … Kaboom! There was an enormous explosion. Smoke and flames were shooting high in the sky. They had set the car on fire, and all three were running toward the barn where they were confronted by Dad and Wesley. They seemed to be apologizing for what just happened. We saw Dad point to the Butler's property just before they started running in that direction. It was odd though; Dad and Wesley were following them, but at a distance.

Mom had to practically tie Ronnie to the porch to prevent him from rushing down to the creek to put out the blaze. She said it would die out before nightfall, and by then Dad and Wesley would be home. The rest of that afternoon we went about our business, as we kept checking the car and waiting for Dad and Wesley's return.

They arrived around dinnertime, and many of us kids joined them down by the smoldering car. It was the first time I had ever seen such an ugly mess. It was completely black and charred and smelled just awful.

The family appeared mortified as Dad and Wesley gave us the scoop: Evidently, the three people were looking to buy some of Dad's moonshine when they realized their car was damaged. After they set fire to the car, they ran toward the Butler's house to use the phone. On the way, they argued some more and began to fight. Wesley and Dad rounded the corner just in time to see one of the men fall into the roadside ditch and the other man throw something into the hay field.

Wesley said the man was out before he hit the ground—stabbed through the heart. The assailant collapsed from exhaustion at the side of the road. He was in tears. The young woman was hysterical, most likely trying to revive a dead man. Wesley ran to the butlers leaving Dad there to try and comfort them. After calling for an ambulance and the police, Mr. Butler and Wesley returned to the crime scene to witness the woman cradling her friend's head to her bosom. Having lost so much blood, they were certain he died in her arms before the ambulance arrived.

The next day, the police arrived and questioned Dad, Wesley, and Mr. Butler about the murder. They found the killer's knife exactly where Wesley said it would be: fifty feet from the road in the hay field.

Several days passed before the burnt car was towed away. Meanwhile, Ronnie took Paul and me for a walk along the road to the Butler's place. When we reached the crime scene, Ronnie pointed at the dirt bank by the side of the road.

"Look, there's still some blood on the rocks and dirt from that man who was stabbed." For a few seconds we studied those red patches, and I struggled to imagine what had transpired there.

Brownie, Round 2 and 3

One morning that summer, after an early breakfast, Wesley decided to take Brownie and a few of his brothers hunting. It was the first time that Wesley, Ronnie, Paul, and I would hunt as a team. I remember much of the hunt because it was also the last time the four of us would hunt together. Since I was only five and a half years old, Paul was told to keep me close and not let me out of sight.

Wesley picked up the 12-gauge and a handful of shotgun shells. He said we wouldn't have to go far because there were several groundhog burrows over in the clover fields behind the house. We walked across our backyard, heading south.

From my young perspective, the backyard simply slid into a rocky and shallow stream in the foreground with little or no northern bank. The southern bank of red clay was about a foot high, presenting a serious obstacle were it not for my big brothers' help. They carried me across the small rocky creek, up the steep bank, and onto the clover and weed-covered southern shore. Brownie barked and headed eastward along the creek bank. I looked south, where my eyes were drawn to a huge field of clover and what seemed like a scene from the western Great Plains. The only thing missing was the wagon trains.

With a jerk of my hand, Paul redirected my thoughts. Brownie and Wesley blazed the trail, with Paul and me behind them and Ronnie bringing up the rear. As we walked, the grass became taller than me blocking out the clover, and shrubs and trees began to crowd the horizon.

About a mile from the farmhouse we spooked something and heard it scurry through the grass. Brownie was right behind it. By the sound of it, Ronnie thought it was a groundhog and Wesley agreed. Following Brownie was easy. Although we couldn't see him, we heard him clearly and followed his fresh path through the clover and weeds. After tracking him for a couple of minutes, we found him barking and growling, head buried in a groundhog burrow. Brownie seemed pretty worked up over the prospect of killing a hog.

Wesley, however, thought our dog wasn't enthusiastic enough. "Brownie—sic him, boy, sic him!"

With Wesley's urging, we all joined in.

"Sic him, Brownie! Sic him, boy! Sic him!"

Brownie became enraged, digging and throwing dirt from the hole. He was like a machine. Pretty soon, we had trampled down the tall grass to form a clearing about twelve feet in diameter. Half of Brownie's body was buried in the hole, his barks and growls muffled. Then he got quiet and started to back out. Ronnie was as worked up as the animal.

"Holy shit! He's got him, Wesley! He's got one!"

Wesley knew what Brownie was about to do and shouted a warning: "Paul, you and Tommy get back!"

To our astonishment, Brownie pulled out one of the biggest groundhogs we had ever seen. The two animals were in a death grip, violently shaking each other. The hog had its teeth clamped onto Brownie's tongue and lower jaw. Brownie had an opposite and even tighter grip on the hog's snout. His canines had penetrated the roof of the hog's mouth, smothering the beast and making it nearly impossible to breathe. Blood splattered both animals' faces and the adjacent grass and weeds. Even though they were in great pain, neither beast would let go.

Ronnie became afraid for Brownie.

"Shoot him, Wesley, before he tears up his tongue!"

Taking careful aim, Wesley pulled the trigger. Boom!

Brownie's face was now covered with blood, but he was free. The hog was dead.

"Wow! Man, that was something," Paul said.

I, on the other hand, was too shaken to say anything.

"Good boy Brownie," Wesley said, stroking the dog's head. "Good boy Brownie. Now, let's take a look at that tongue."

In spite of having a torn tongue and a few other minor wounds, Brownie wore a huge look of accomplishment. Wesley was so proud of his dog. His wounds would heal just fine. Exhausted from the fight, we headed home with fresh game for Mom to prepare.

But Brownie wasn't finished. A lot of the fight may have been taken from him, but most of the chase was still there. On the way back he flushed something from the weeds nearby and cornered it in another hole. As we approached the dog, he let out a loud "Yelp!" and backed away.

I said, "What's that smell?"

Ronnie knew right away. "Oh my God, it's a skunk!"

"Brownie, come!" Wesley commanded. "Come here, Brownie!"

But he didn't need a command to retreat—he had been sprayed by the skunk. Everyone rushed from the area, trying to keep Brownie at a distance.

We had a good laugh when we got home, but Wesley's laughter was cut short when Mom ordered him to give Brownie a bath.

The next day Ginny gave him another bath. She said she felt sorry for him because no one wanted to pet him. This time we had better results using a solution of vinegar and detergent in water. Still, it was difficult to get rid of the skunk's scent, and most of it just had to wear off. During the next week or so, everyone avoided getting too close to Brownie.

I'm sure Brownie had never lost a fight before that day. However, after having received a good dose of its defense mechanism, I'm also sure Brownie never bothered another skunk.

Alcohol, Guns, and Abuse

Dad's violent tendencies began to increase in frequency and intensity in the summer of 1957. Although there was never any excuse for Dad's behavior, his heightened hostility was most likely due to his continued alcohol consumption and the pressures of working the farm. Dad was difficult to live with even when he was sober. Now, when he drank, he would blow every little thing out of proportion.

Dad was notorious for screwing things up and blaming the resulting mess on his wife. He would often say, "Every time things get to going good, Shortie wants to tear down my playhouse." He often screamed at his sons, telling them they were lazy and not working hard enough. Apparently, he also felt that Mom wasn't keeping us kids clean enough. "Shortie, give them damn kids a bath; they look filthy!" Even Mom's fantastic cooking was attacked. "You call this food? Why, it tastes more like shit to me."

When sober, I'm sure he realized his behavior could get the family booted off the farm. He was right in that thinking. Our family was running out of time and chances.

Now, add Mom's twelfth pregnancy to the mess. Timing and circumstances now precipitated the worst series of violent episodes we had ever seen.

One day, drunk and pissed off about something, Dad caught Mom in the hallway and pulled her into their bedroom. For near an entire minute, he pistol-whipped her with his .22 revolver and didn't stop until he had cracked the weapon's ivory grip. When Dad interrupted his assault to lay the pistol on the nightstand (probably to lock the door so he could continue the beating in private) Wesley put the barrel of the loaded shotgun to his father's face.

"If you even try to hit her again, Dad, I'll shoot you."

A sudden change came over Dad. His contorted, wrinkled, and angry face relaxed into the countenance of a pathetic human being, and he fell to his knees.

"Go ahead and shoot me, Wesley," Dad pleaded. "I deserve it for what I did."

Ginny saw the bloodstained revolver lying on the table, but her thoughts of retribution were brushed aside when Wesley stepped between her and the handgun.

"Just get out, Dad! Now! Get out and don't come back until you're sober!"

Dad rose from his knees and sat on the sofa in the living room. After composing himself for a few minutes, he went outside, started the pickup, and drove away.

Wesley and Ronnie helped Mom walk to the Butler's for help. James Ruble, a neighbor who happened to be driving by in his pickup, took them to the hospital in Princeton. Mom was treated there and released. The next day her face was so swollen and bruised we could hardly recognize her. Dad was arrested and jailed for several days.

Since all our crops were doing well enough, Wesley left the farm to spend some time with our Aunt Clara and Uncle Robert in Falls Mills, Virginia. Dad would be home soon enough, and Wesley relished the chance of getting away from the farm. With Dad and Wesley gone, it meant Mom, Ginny, Ronnie, and young Paul had to work even harder.

Paul sadly remembers his second summer on the farm in Elgood. He, Ronnie, and sometimes Ginny were forced to spend hours in the hot sun, hoeing the corn and potatoes. The afternoon heat was scorching, and they had little relief until late summer, when the corn was tall enough to provide a little bit of shade in the early mornings and late afternoons. Even with the shade, the chore beat them up.

Paul felt lost and insignificant standing in the middle of a thirty-acre cornfield. His cramped and aching muscles, parched mouth, and blistered hands left him wondering why they were there in the first place, since the tall corn prevented any significant weed growth. At nine years old he didn't understand many of the things his father and mother forced him to do. His only relief came when Ginny finally found him somewhere in the corn. She brought lunch, a refill of his water jar, and welcome—albeit brief—conversation.

In early August Dad and Wesley returned and, working together with Ronnie and Paul, they spent the next two weeks bringing in most of the crops. As soon as the harvest was gathered, Wesley returned to Falls Mills. He had no desire to remain on the farm with his father.

It was late August. Mom was busy canning a batch of vegetables and fruit for winter. As the smell of pickled chow-chow wafted about, Dad slouched in one of the kitchen chairs. His head was cocked way back as he stared at the tobacco stained ceiling. Shaving cream covered his face, and a towel was wrapped around his chest, neck, and shoulders.

Ginny, straight razor in hand, approached her father with caution.

"You sure you want me to do this, Dad?"

"Why not, girl, ya need the practice. Go on, now. Get going before the cream cakes up."

Ginny began shaving her father as he directed, starting with his sideburns, as her mother monitored the progress. She was doing a fair job until she came to her father's neck and throat. Dad's Adams apple was well pronounced and about one of the ugliest imaginable. Impatiently, Dad began to fidget, causing Ginny to slip and cut the prized appendage. It was a nasty cut that drew a good bit of blood. Realizing what Ginny had just done, Mom said, "Ginny, I'm going to whip your behind."

"No, you're not going to whip her," Dad said. "It was my fault; I shouldn't have moved my head."

Among his daughters, Dad may have favored Ginny the most. He often said, "Ginny's the only one that don't sass me."

Later that morning Dad said he was "going for a drive." A few hours later he was returning in his pickup and another carload of drinking buddies when the pickup stalled. Unable to restart the truck, they left it by the side of the road. Dad rode with his friends to the farmhouse where they bought and shared some of his moonshine. A party had begun.

Boy, were they having a good time! Unfortunately, after so many drinks, they were beginning to have a good time at my mother's expense.

Mom was an impressive dancer, very good at what they called "flat footing" or "country shuffle" dancing. Back then, it was mostly a quick-stepping dance where the beat of the music is kept by tapping and shuffling the feet. It wasn't unusual for her to entertain friends by showing off her fancy shuffle footwork. Most of the time Mom didn't mind dancing for company either, but on this day she had already danced once for the men. She was about three months pregnant, too— and tired. But Dad didn't want to just impress his friends; no, he also wanted to show them and his wife who wore the pants on the farm.

"Myrtle, you'll dance for us again or I'll make you dance with my pistol."

"Harold, I've done enough dancing today, so you can go to hell."

Dad bolted from his chair, headed for his revolver. Mom was now forced to retreat. With Dad in pursuit, she ran out of the house and down the front yard, headed for the hayfields. Dad got off two rounds that missed their target before the gun jammed. He continued chasing Mom toward the hayfields with Ginny close behind. Seeing Mr. Nash in the distance, Ginny screamed for him to come and help.

Us little ones were beside ourselves. We didn't know what to think or do. We were just afraid for our mother. So, when Donna began to cry, we all cried.

Meanwhile, Dad chased Mom around the haystacks, first one way, then the other. He finally caught her and started to beat her over the head with the gun. Fortunately, Mr. Nash was there in time to pull Dad away. He bravely stood up to Dad that day, sending him back to the house before escorting our mother to the hospital. Ginny thought Mr. Nash saved Mom's life.

The farmhouse was quiet that afternoon. Having witnessed Sleepy Dixon's drunken fury, his drinking buddies had wasted little time vacating the premises. As usual, Ginny was out in the front yard playing with Donna and Debbie when Dad awakened from his drunken nap. He sat upright on the edge of the living room sofa, rubbing his eyes and shaking off the cobwebs. His notorious .22, its cracked ivory grip now wrapped in sticky black electrical tape, was resting on the end table beside him. Suddenly, Dad must have remembered what happened earlier in the day.

"Where's your mom?" he shouted.

No one was in the room, but many of us heard him.

"Where's your mom?" he shouted again, much louder and angrier.

Ronnie ran to the hallway, stopping just outside the living room door.

"Did you call me, Dad?"

Paul came out of the kitchen and joined his brother.

I was upstairs taking a nap or playing with Gary when I heard my father's shouting and demanding. Being very young and inquisitive, I hustled down the stairway until I was standing on a step directly behind Ronnie. I heard Dad repeat his demands, but louder: "Where's your mother, dammit?"

"I don't know," Ronnie said.

"Ronnie, if you don't tell me where she is, I'm gonna shoot ya!"

"I really don't know where she is, Dad."

Bang! The gun exploded.

To Ronnie, it felt like a sledgehammer had knocked his foot out from under him. He tried to stand, only to collapse again, screaming in agony.

Confused and alarmed, I watched my brother fall to the floor. Mouths agape, Paul and I stared first at our brother, then at our father.

"See! I told ya I was gonna shoot ya!"

Blood leaked from Ronnie's shoe forming a small puddle on the floor.

Hearing the gunshot and Ronnie's screams, Ginny came running into the hallway. Ronnie called for Paul to help him out of the house. Ginny struggled to hold on to Debbie and at the same time help Paul with Ronnie.

"Ginny," Dad said, "if you help him, I'll shoot you too."

Hearing that, she let go of Ronnie and stepped back against the wall. She watched Paul struggle to help Ronnie off the front porch and down into the yard. A puddle of blood here and a drop or two here and there, marked the way. Ginny choked back her tears and performed a quick head count of her younger siblings. Like baby chicks to a mother hen, we all huddled close to her side. She knew her brothers needed help, and Paul was way too small to carry his big brother very far. Now paralyzed with fear, she was reluctant to leave us four little ones alone with our father. Just when she thought she would explode from indecision, she watched her father disappear into the kitchen.

Taking her chances, Ginny handed Debbie to Donna.

"Donna, you be a big girl now and look after the little ones."

She then met her brothers at the gate where she helped Paul carry Ronnie down the road to Mr. Butler's house. To slow the loss of blood, they stopped by the barn and tied Paul's t-shirt tightly around Ronnie's foot. Ginny prayed that God and Donna were watching over Gary, Debbie, and me, and that Dad wouldn't commit another unfathomable offense.

Ronnie had lost a lot of blood, but thanks to Mr. Butler he was treated in time. His wound was cleaned at the hospital, stitches applied, and the foot bandaged. For some reason the doctors thought it best to leave the bullet wedged between the bones of Ronnie's foot.

Within a matter of hours the hospital reported Ronnie's injury to the police, and Mr. Nash also reported Mom's beating. The next morning two police cars arrived at the farm. They placed Dad under arrest and hauled him back to the county jail.

Soon after the shooting Wesley returned home. September had arrived and, except for Wesley, all my older siblings had returned to school. Two weeks later he decided to quit school. He was almost 16 now and there was still plenty of farm work for him to catch up on. Wesley thought his presence on the farm, once Dad returned from jail, would be a good way to keep an eye on our mother and inhibit our father's abusive tendencies. Besides, it would be a few weeks before Ronnie was well enough to do any major chores, so that burden fell on Wesley.

Unfortunately, Wesley did not remain on the farm for very long. He tried to talk Mom into leaving Dad for good, but found the effort useless. He wondered how many disasters it would take before our mother would give up her insane addiction to, or fear of, our father. Domestic friction between Wesley, Mom, Ronnie, and Ginny soon became unbearable. Gathering the remainder of his belongings, Wesley left the farm again.

On October 7, 1957, Dad was indicted for "maiming" his son. He swore it was an accident. Two weeks later, on October 22, the maiming charge was dismissed when he pled guilty to a lesser charge of assault and battery. Dad began serving the remaining four months of his six-month sentence in the county jail.

After these violent incidents, Mr. Nash told our mother we had to leave the farm before Dad returned, or as soon as we could find a suitable place to live—whichever came first. He didn't want to see our father on his property again.

I'm surprised he allowed our family to stay as long as we did.

Country School and Store

During the time we were looking for a new place to live, I was invited to join my older siblings at the Elgood Elementary School. I'm not sure, but I think it was a special one-day session to introduce preschoolers like me to the school routine. It was a quaint little school situated at a three-way intersection way out in the country, with mostly farms and a few houses scattered about. Just across the road was a small, rustic country store, built with heavy-duty wooden planks applied vertically as siding and covered with advertising for Coca Cola, Sunbeam, and Texaco.

The thirty minute bumpy roller-coaster bus ride through the country, with its hills, valleys, and switchbacks, was my first—and it was fun. On the way we passed Dad's pickup truck. Someone had driven, or pushed, it off the side of the road into a deep ditch. That was the last place any of us can remember seeing it.

When I arrived at the school, I was introduced to some of the students and teachers. Donna, 7, and I stuffed our winter coats into her locker, which happened to be very close to our classroom door. Next, I sat in class beside her for most of the morning. Since this was all new to me, I can remember being very shy and easily embarrassed with all the strange kids looking at me.

I was relieved when the class was dismissed for lunch and recess. Mom had packed two or three lunches for us all to share. Ginny divvied up the food and we consumed it ravenously before putting on our jackets and heading outside for recess.

Ginny took charge of Donna and me and led us across the road to the country store. We waited at the steps as some other kids went in ahead of us. Then Ginny led us inside and down the aisles of the store. Never in my life had I seen so many nice things in one place. Ginny said she had two nickels and asked Donna and me if we wanted some licorice. Of course we said yes.

As we waited at the counter for our candy, I saw something that looked mouthwatering familiar. It was a cream-filled, coconut and

93

marshmallow-covered, chocolate snowball cake, and I couldn't take my eyes off it. I knew I had experienced this delicacy somewhere before. There they were, eye-level on a shelf right in front of me, and they were beckoning me: Take me. You know how delicious I am. So take me and eat me.

Placing my finger on one of the cakes, I said, "Ginny, can we get one of these?"

"No, Tommy, I don't have enough money for that. A piece of licorice will have to do you today."

I was so disappointed. With so many of the cakes on the shelf, I thought they wouldn't miss just one of them.

So, with everyone in the store milling about and not paying any attention to me, I stuffed one into my coat pocket. Ginny paid for the licorice and we ate it on the way back to the playground. No one had seen me take the cake.

During recess I somehow devoured one of the two snowballs without anyone noticing. If not for the rush, the experience would have been as I had imagined it would be—heavenly. The bell rang to end recess, and I stuffed the remaining snowball into my coat pocket.

Donna and I met at the locker to hang up our coats. As she helped me with mine, the remaining snowball fell out of my coat and landed on the floor in front of us. Donna picked up the half-eaten cake, stared at it with an open mouth, and looked at me in horror. She realized that the dark ring around my mouth wasn't from licorice but from chocolate cake.

"Tommy! I'm going to tell."

Donna ran down the hallway with the cake in her hand. She stopped Ginny before she entered her classroom and showed it to her. By then I was ready to cry.

Ginny walked back to me and saw how upset I was.

"Don't cry, Tommy. It's all right. We'll take care of this after school."

The rest of the afternoon seemed like an eternity. The next two hours were filled with classroom drawing and coloring projects. What would normally have been a fun time became agonizing as my mind kept returning to thoughts of impending doom.

After school Ginny rushed me back to the store, so that we wouldn't miss our bus. She showed the partially eaten cake to the proprietor, apologized, and told him that she would return tomorrow with the money to pay for it. The man told her not to bother, but Ginny insisted. And before we left, Ginny said, "Tommy, tell the man you're sorry, and it won't happen again."

Pouting and embarrassed, I said, "Sorry."

While riding the bus home that afternoon, Donna badgered me over and over. "Boy, are you gonna get it when you get home. Mommy is going to whip your behind real good, Tommy Mack."

When Donna, Paul, Ginny, and I got off the bus, it happened. I was so afraid of what Mom was going to do to me, I wet my pants.

Barging through the front door, Donna ran to Mom.

"Mom, Tommy stole a cake from the store, he ate half of it, and he peed his pants." Mom just looked at me, and I started crying again.

My mother took pity on me that day. She figured I had suffered enough and learned a good lesson.

Debbie and Gary shared the remaining snowball cake, and because she was such a pesky blabbermouth, Donna didn't get any reward. The following day at recess Ginny paid the store clerk ten cents for the cake. She gave another sincere apology, saying it wouldn't happen again.

However, what should have been a good lesson was only half-learned.

V

THE COLD
SHACK
c. 1957-1958

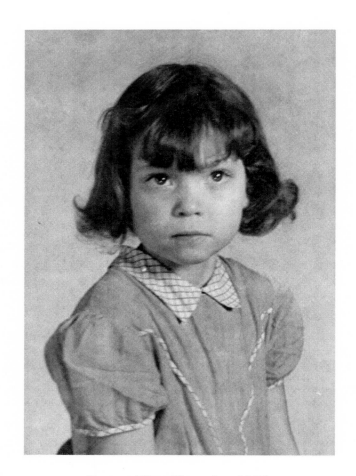

Donna (6) at Elgood c. 1956.

Big Vein, a dog-tail hollow curled-up between two mountains, was our family's next stop. Located on Boissevain Road and about one mile northeast of Tank Hill Road, Big Vein was sparsely populated and showcased several small farms and a scattering of houses. Several of the houses, ours included, were bordering on dilapidation.

It was fall, and since Dad still had about three months to go on his six-month sentence, Mom was able to talk Wesley into returning home to help us move, prepare the new home, pigpen, and chicken coops.

There were three things I hated most about Big Vein.

One was the snow, which seemed to linger much longer than in the surrounding hills and valleys. Not a lot of snow, but just enough to create the second thing I hated most—ice. Because of it, someone in the family was always falling. Fortunately, the little ones didn't have very far to fall. When the ice melted we had mud, which caused more slipping and falling, along with heavy laundry chores for Mom.

The third thing we all hated was the cold. This holler had to be the coldest hollow for mountains around. I guess it was the combination of mountains blocking-out the sun and little or no insulation in the walls of the house. Or, maybe Mom and our older siblings weren't proactive in dressing us little ones properly for the cold.

There are few good memories to share about our brief stay at Big Vein. As always, our mother struggled to make the best of our roller coaster family life. The most impressive thing about these times was our persistent ability to shrug off the bad, and to allow life and the wonders of nature to consistently plant smiles on our dirty faces.

Wesley and Ronnie were like bloodhounds when it came to locating free coal. I used to think they could smell it. But that wasn't true. They could simply read a mountain's terrain and make a good guess. More often than not they would guess right and find a suitable seam for the taking.

Being natural scavengers, my older siblings had searched the hills and valleys around Big Vein long before we lived there, so they knew where the coal was located. Some locations were in plain view, but few families were as desperate to mine them.

Sometimes we found coal by accident. One time Ronnie, Ginny, and Paul were picking wild strawberries on the side of a hill. Ginny had almost filled her quart jar with berries when the ground underneath her opened up. If she hadn't grabbed a nearby root, she would have fallen into a mineshaft and probably would have been seriously hurt.

After clearing away the vegetation and opening up the entrance, the abandoned mine provided most of the coal we needed then and well after our short stay at Big Vein.

Scrounging up wood and coal for cooking was a year-round chore, and I was sometimes allowed to tag along.

Once, while digging for coal, we stumbled upon an abundant supply of wild mushrooms. Ronnie decided to surprise our mother by picking some. It was a day or two after a good rainfall, and we were walking along the southwest slope of the mountain amid rotting trees and stumps. My brothers told me to be careful where I stepped.

"Pick only the pink ones and brown ones," Ronnie said.

He told me the pink ones were small and flat on top, and the brown ones were larger and dome shaped. He also said that milk inside mushrooms was a good sign and clear liquid was bad. Big Vein became an ideal location for collecting edible wild mushrooms.

When we brought them home, Mom checked each one carefully to make sure they were good. None of us ever became ill from eating them.

However, I should inject a note of caution here. Unless you have a mother like mine, I recommend proper training in mushroom picking. Becoming familiar with the physical characteristics of edible mushrooms, where and when they grow, how they bruise, and how they smell should prevent any harmful consequences.

You can't slop (feed) hogs very well when the slop freezes solid. Therefore, late fall or early winter was a good time for butchering. We had brought a handful of animals from the Elgood farm to Big Vein. During our last year in Elgood, we had castrated a male hog and spent a lot of time fattening "it" for just this purpose. Butchering unneutered hogs and females in heat will leave the meat with an unpleasant after-taste.

Slaughtering a hog is something you wouldn't want your average six-year-old to witness. But I did—at least some of it. It was pure curiosity on my part.

There was a lot of commotion in the hog pen that day. Two separate fires were being tended, and three large galvanized tubs of water were being prepared. One tub was left unheated while each of the other two straddled its own fire, the steam vapors trailing away with the brisk winter breeze. For some strange reason, I was watching a man from our front porch as he was spreading straw about the ground when Wesley walked by carrying Dad's familiar .22 revolver, its cracked grip still wrapped with tape.

Yep, a big dose of curiosity overwhelmed me, and that's when I followed him to the pigpen. Staring through the holes in the fence, I watched my big brother stun the animal by placing a well-aimed bullet between its eyes. The small caliper weapon was ideal, since they didn't want the heart to stop pumping too soon. I can still hear the bone-chilling squeal that came out of that hog's snout.

The hog snapped to military attention, stared straight ahead as if in a trance, and crumpled to the ground. While it was lying on its side still kicking, two men struggled to elevate its body above the head. Another man quickly severed the carotid artery with the skillful plunge of a very sharp knife.

Now down and out, the hog was ready for bleeding. The hind legs were bound to a wooden pole, and the carcass was lifted into a hanging position. This allowed the remaining blood to drain from the body and provided easy access for butchering. The straw was essential for soaking up the blood and mud and keeping the mess down.

Next, the hog was dipped into the tub of scalding water for cleaning. Mom, Ginny and Aunt Helen, using sharp knives, scraped the loosened hairs from the animal's skin. Germs and hair were rinsed away by splashing several buckets of fresh scalding water over the carcass. At this point, the hog was degutted, partially dismembered and hung to chill overnight.

Fortunately, I don't remember much more of the process. I had already seen enough. The decapitation had turned me away, and when I returned to witness the sausage making process, I became nauseous and stumbled away for the last time.

Not only was the cold winter air sufficient for preserving the meat, it also enhanced the unique and unpleasant aroma of the animal's blood and intestines. Little goes to waste at a good hog butchering.

Mom was strict with her children and especially strict with the girls. She was old-fashioned in her ways and rules, which sometimes led her to be unfair.

Daisy had suffered a few hard times and scary situations after leaving home, but now she was working and making her way. One night in early February 1958, Daisy stopped by unexpectedly to see the family and introduce us to her new boyfriend, Chester Wright. She had driven two hours from Pilot, Virginia.

Daisy was surprised, disappointed, and somewhat embarrassed to see Dad back at home and not suffering in jail. He had been released a week or two early due to good behavior. Reluctantly, Daisy had to make her visit brief. What little conversation she and Dad had was strained, and he made the point of telling her that he would be moving the family again, probably within a week or two. Dad almost always moved the family whenever he returned from any significant jail term, and he seemed exceptionally excited about moving back to Boissevain

Mountain. The places Mom picked never seemed to be good enough for him.

Dad practically begged Wesley to stay and help plow and seed the gardens once we moved back to Boissevain. Knowing how important the crops were to our survival Wesley gave in, but not without conditions. Dad had made an agreement with him—if Wesley would use the big white mule Dad had purchased from Uncle Jessie to plow the fields, Dad wouldn't bother him anymore, and Wesley could go back and live at our cousin's, the Millers, on Jenkinjones Mountain.

Daisy excused herself from the conversation with her father. The clock was ticking, and she wanted to play with her new baby sister. It was Debbie's second birthday, and Daisy wanted the day to be pleasant and special. Plus, she hadn't seen me since the scalding sent me to the hospital. Daisy had also brought along some of her old clothes for Ginny to try on. My two sisters retired to our parents' bedroom to check out the clothes.

"Lord God almighty, Ginny! What's that on your back?"

While trying on the clothes, Ginny had forgotten about the welts on her back and arms from a whipping Mom had given her.

"Oh, Mommy whipped me the other day," Ginny replied, with embarrassment and shame in her voice.

"What did you do to deserve that?"

Ginny said she had been unfairly punished for something one of her brothers had done, but she was too embarrassed to provide Daisy the details. Now, looking at Ginny's damaged skin, Daisy was reminded of why she had left home.

"Ginny, I'm going to have a private talk with Mom."

"It won't do any good, Daisy. Mom's mean."

With Dad hanging around and eavesdropping, Daisy was afraid to broach the subject of discipline with her mother. Having her new boyfriend present didn't make it any easier. Dad and his nasty mouth were an embarrassment, and she ended her visit without discussing many of the things she had wanted to.

I can remember becoming ill near the end of our stay at Big Vein. No, it wasn't from eating bad mushrooms. I was feeling miserable due to a fever, and I'm sure I was acting out and crying in a very unpleasant way. Since most of the family slept in one bedroom, my crying kept everyone awake.

Mom, Ginny, and Paul had tried every way they could to quiet me down. Ronnie, 14, would normally have complained about not getting his rest. Instead, he surprised the family with a new strategy, perhaps out of sympathy for my illness, or perhaps from his selfish desire to sleep. Ronnie reached into his pocket and pulled out a key chain with a single key attached.

"Don't cry, Tommy," he said, "here ya go." I took the gift and immediately stopped crying.

As I recall, the most attractive feature of the key chain was the piece of tanned leather attached to the metal ring. It was smooth to the touch with some type of embossed logo. And it was new enough to retain a slight chemical odor from the tanning process.

Pretty soon I curled my tiny body into the fetal position and, with the leather in my hand and my thumb in my mouth, fell asleep.

Ronnie was so proud of himself.

VI

BOISSEVAIN
c. 1958

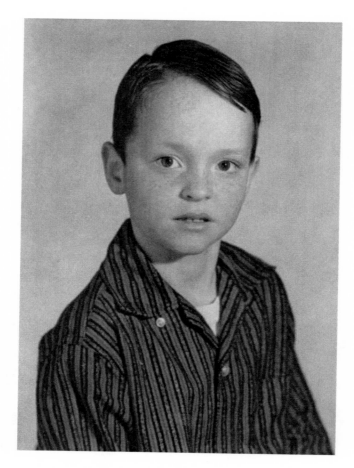

Tommy (6) first grade, Boissevain, c. 1958

A Cabin on the Mountain

Late in February of 1958, we moved to a small log cabin on a piece of property possibly owned by the Pocahontas Fuel Company and previously rented by my Uncle Jessie and his growing family. It was near the top of Boissevain Mountain on Tank Hill Road.

The road onto the mountain was nicely maintained at the time with a top coating of a few inches of gravel. About half way up the mountain, on the right, was Mama's house and property with the plain brown and white trailer where our Aunt Tini lived. Other neighbors were few and scattered about. At the top of the mountain, the gravel ended and a dirt road branched into two directions. Tank Hill Road turned left and wound its way for another half mile across the mountain, finally ending at Lenore and Elmer "Gabby" Franklin's property. You only needed to continue on this dirt road for less than a quarter of a mile, and you would see our new home about two hundred feet to the left. From our front porch you could view the progress of our garden as well as see or hear anyone approaching the house or traveling further across the mountain to Gabby's place.

Our residence here was still within a twenty minute walk from both Tipple Hollow and my birthplace under the hill. Except for Elgood, living on the mountain was a big improvement from living on the side of a mountain or in a hollow. Most of the property immediately

107

surrounding the cabin was fairly flat. The front of the house faced southeast onto a one acre lot which provided a healthy batch of summer crops. Directly east of the front of the house was the driveway (or road) to our house. Our back yard, or the west side, was fairly flat for the first quarter acre. Beyond that was some of the mountain's most fertile soil, three acres of sloping hills and valleys, now poised for Wesley, a horse, and a plough to transform into a patchwork of art that would provide more than half of our summer crops.

Near the middle of March, Mom started having labor pains and was rushed to the hospital in Bluefield. A few hours later, she gave birth to her twelfth and final child, **David Keith**. Unusually quiet and reserved, David was a healthy child with straight light brown hair and big brown eyes. His birthday was unique as it was the same day of the month our dad was born.

Four days later, while the newspapers and radios were touting Elvis Presley's induction into the Army, Dad drove his wife and the newborn home. He felt so proud sitting behind the wheel of his recently-purchased 1946 Chevy.

Later that day, Daisy visited us at our new home on the mountain providing several pieces of clothing for the newborn. She also brought a small portable record player. To brighten our mother's spirits, she began playing some of Mom's favorite country songs. Tex Ritter's "Rye Whisky" and "Wayward Wind" along with Hank Williams' "Hey Good Lookin" and "Your Cheatin Heart" were a few. Some of us danced and sang to celebrate the occasion.

Before the songs and singing were finished, Dad walked into the house to see what all the commotion was about. He said, "Daisy, stop playing that darn thang; you're gonna run up our lek-trik bill."

Daisy couldn't stand her father. She wanted to spend the night with her mother and siblings, but Dad made her so angry and afraid that she left around dusk.

Early one morning, I sensed excitement in the air. I also noticed more than the usual traffic coming from Gabby's place further out the mountain. "Where are them people going Mommy?"

"They're going to the horse trading show down the road, Tommy. In a little bit, I'll be taking you, Paul, and the baby to see your Aunt Tini. On the way, you'll get to see some of the horses. As a matter of fact, I think Ginny is down there with your aunt right now."

Strange as it may seem, our walk that day marked a unique transition point in my life. The world about me had invited me to a party—a party where all of my senses seemed to breathe with a renewed and richer vitality.

Traveling by foot was our usual mode of transportation when visiting family and friends—or just seeing the sights. The event wasn't far from the cabin, but you would think it was near the end of the world from the way I complained.

"I'm tired. How much farther is it?"

"Just a little bit, Tommy," Mom promised.

"Paul, can I have a piggyback ride?"

Complaining and asking too many questions was normal behavior for me then. I also remember the sunken muddy road, reddish colored clay dirt, and high, root-laden dirt banks supporting numerous moss-encrusted trees. Sometimes the trees and banks boxed us in from both sides of the road. In those days I wondered a lot and asked many questions as to why this and why that.

After two quick piggyback rides from Paul, we arrived at the split in the road. This was the place. At the gathering, I gained even further understanding as to why the roads were always in such bad shape:

Traffic from people, autos and trucks, and horse-drawn farming equipment were major contributors to the bad road conditions. However, none were as big a factor as the heavy horse-drawn wooden sleds that were not only used for farming, but were often used for transportation as well.

There must have been about twenty men, twenty or more horses, and very few women to be seen. I had never seen so many horses in one place. There were big horses and little ones, old horses and young ones, not to mention a donkey or mule thrown in too. Many owners were pressing the animals into various races and pulling contests to prove the animals' worth to one potential buyer or another. It was a good thing the event was held outdoors, because the odor and noise would have been nearly unbearable if conducted indoors.

We weren't there more than five or ten minutes, when we saw my dad. He was looking our way too. I think it was the look that he gave Mom that prompted her, with a jerk of my arm, to say, "Come on boys, let's go see your Aunt Tini." Was visiting my aunt what she had planned from the beginning? Or maybe, she wanted to check up on Dad too.

I stood in my aunt's bedroom watching her dress and undress in front of a mirror. She had just smothered me with several kisses, her breath rank with the smell of alcohol. While my aunt and mother talked, Tini was keeping Ginny and my cousin, Garnell, busy ironing various garments for her.

"Myrtle, why don't you try on some of those floats there? Lord knows you could use some new clothes."

"I'm doin' fine with what I have Tini. I don't need to go to the places you go. Besides, I think they're a bit too small for me."

For some strange reason Tini would try on a fresh ironed garment, wrinkle it up, and toss it back into the clothes hamper. Aunt Tini didn't seem to like any of the dresses or skirts that Ginny and Garnell had taken such great pains to iron just right for her. In spite of it all, Ginny was sporting one of the biggest smiles; she was just happy to be with her cousin and feeling that she was helping out.

Soon, I was happy to be outdoors with Paul and the younger cousins. We usually played tag or dodge-ball, something athletic, to prove how fast we could move or how high we could jump.

Later in the afternoon, we all headed back up the mountain toward home. From a distance we could see and hear that the horse trading was still going on. A few more minutes of walking and a closer look told us that something was different this time. The crowd was gone, but a handful of men and a couple of horses with harnesses and plowing gear remained. My father and three other men were playing cards, smoking cigarettes, and drinking moonshine from mason jars. Two other men, over by the dirt bank, were shooting pistols at cans and bottles. Some were joking and laughing while others were yelling and arguing over something. There was little doubt they were in various stages of intoxication.

I remember being petrified with all the commotion. Paul, four years older, didn't seem to be as bothered. He may have actually seen it as entertaining. Ginny looked a bit nervous too, albeit for another reason: there were too many hungry eyes looking her way, she thought. Mom walked up a bank at the side of the road and leaned across a barbed wire fence near Dad. I gathered she was having words with him. Then, I remember the sudden explosion of powder from Dad's pistol followed by a cloud of dirt when the bullet hit the dried clay near Mom's feet.

With ringing in my ears, I heard my father shout, "Take those damn kids and get your ass home, woman!"

And, that's what we did. Mom said she darn-near peed her pants.

The rest of the trip home didn't seem as tiring, and I don't think I asked any questions. Well, maybe I did ask for a piggy-back ride.

<u>Boissevain Post Office and Company Store c. 1940's</u>

<u>Retribution</u>

My brothers and sisters weren't much different than many siblings of large families. I may have mentioned it before, but I'll say it again: Sibling rivalry was subtle and rare. Picking and arguing, on the other hand, were most common; and by now, Ronnie had become the king of pickers.

One morning our mother, Dad, and Wesley drove to Pocahontas to sign up for and receive the family allotment of Government Surplus Food Commodities. While she was away, Ronnie was left in charge of the house and kids. Ronnie took advantage of our parent's absence by bullying and picking fights with his younger siblings. Ginny and Paul usually received the brunt of his transgressions, and unfortunately for Ronnie, things didn't work out quite like he had anticipated that day.

"Hey, stop it! What are you two doing?" Ronnie screamed.

"We're going to give you a dose of your own medicine," Ginny said, as she helped Paul wrestle him down to the back porch floor and onto his stomach.

While they both sat on Ronnie, they managed to pin his arms behind his back. It took both hands and most of Paul's strength to keep a tight grip on one of his brother's arms. Struggling for control, Paul said, "Do you give up now?"

Ronnie refused to buckle-under. "I'm going to tell Dad."

They both chuckled as Ginny leaned closer to Ronnie's ear: "Even if you did, he won't believe you," she said.

Ginny, looking around for ideas that would make the best of the situation, noticed a mop leaning against the wall. She knew Mom had recently used the mop to clean the kitchen floor, and since it hadn't been rinsed very well—if at all—the mop had an extra-special appeal. Ginny and Paul proceeded to mop Ronnie's face with the tool.

"Ouch! Pew! Hey, that's dirty … and it stinks!"

"Will you quit picking on us now," Paul asked.

Ronnie struggled while babbling incoherently. Ginny and Paul continued working the dirty mop around and around and up and down their brother's face and neck.

"Stop! If you don't … stop … I'm … I'm gonna puke!"

Again Paul said, "Do you quit now?"

"Okay … Okay … I give up!"

Paul and Ginny were still wary of their big brother. To see what Ronnie would do, they released him and scampered out of his way. This was the first time they had ganged-up on Ronnie, and they braced themselves for retaliation.

Reasonably hurt and humiliated, Ronnie did nothing. He just walked through the house and out the front door, mumbling as he went. As he crossed the front yard, he looked back at Paul and Ginny, now laughing, and gave them a warning: "Wait till Dad comes home, I'm going to tell."

Later that day, Ronnie told Dad what had happened. Thinking it was quite a story, Dad just laughed and laughed. It was probably the hardest our father had laughed in a long time—at least while sober. Dad especially liked the part where Paul and Ginny "mopped the floor" with Ronnie.

After that day, Ronnie rarely picked on his siblings; and when he did, it was brief and much more considerate.

Prior to 1958, Dad had made it a point to always be with Mom when she cashed the monthly welfare check. That's when he usually took most of the money and blew it away on alcohol and gambling. But things were a little different since his last incarceration and since we had moved into the log cabin on Boissevain Mountain. Wesley was stepping up and taking on an even bigger role for the family's welfare. Now that our big brother was old enough, big enough, and bad enough; he was determined to take [family] matters personally. He felt that he had to be the responsible man around the house by standing up to his father and not letting him continue to abuse and take advantage of the family.

In addition to staying home and working around the house and gardens, Wesley boldly told Dad that, from now on, he would be escorting Mom to Pocahontas to cash the welfare check and buy the family groceries. Obviously, that didn't sit too well with our father.

"Oh ... so you're the man of the house now, are ya?"

"No Dad, I'm not. I just think it would be better if I did."

"Well ... we'll see how long that works."

Wesley was well known and liked by many people in the Boissevain, Jenkinjones, and Pocahontas areas. Mr. Love down at the post office was one of those people. Wesley and Mr. Love had worked out a plan: whenever Dad stopped in to pick up the welfare check, Mr. Love was supposed to tell him that the check hadn't arrived yet. That way, Wesley and Mom would have plenty of time to grab the check, rush to town, cash it at the bank, and buy supplies. All before Dad knew what was happening.

Around this time, Dad brought home a young man named Billy to help with various chores about the house and gardens. In exchange for his labor, Billy would earn his room and board. It was the first time Dad had welcomed an outsider to work with the family, and just as he had promised his father, Wesley hitched up the mule every morning and started plowing the fields. Everything was set, and it worked well—for a while.

As time went by, Dad began to resort back to his arrogant and overly demanding ways. He would constantly pick and nitpick over most of their work, and he would keep pushing and pushing the three young men until they were frustrated and exhausted.

One morning Ronnie was having difficulty placing the harness on the big and cantankerous white mule. Dad, Wesley, and Billy were laughing and teasing him about it. When Ronnie turned away from the mule, it bit him on his shoulder. This was no friendly nip. It wasn't just a little nip either; the mule had pealed away an unhealthy chunk of Ronnie's skin. Furious and in considerable pain, he ran into the house and grabbed the shotgun. As Ronnie crossed the porch and was leveling the loaded gun at the mule, Dad snatched it from Ronnie's grip. "What were you planning to do with this?" Dad asked.

"I'm ... I'm gonna shoot the son-of-a-bitch!" Ronnie boasted.

As Ronnie beckoned for his father to give him the gun back, Dad said, "No, you won't either. I'll be the one doing the shoot-n around here—just you remember that." The mule was lucky that day. If Dad hadn't grabbed the gun, Ronnie really would have killed the animal.

Several days later, Dad approached the three young men as they sat on a grassy bank in the shade by the newly plowed field. "Wesley," he shouted, "why aren't you kids work'n?"

"I've finished the plowing, Dad. My job's done."

"No it ain't. There's sowing and plenty of other things to be done."

"That wasn't part of our agreement, Dad," Wesley said, raising his voice in agitation.

"That's too bad. I need you here."

Standing up, Wesley said, "Bull shit!" and started stomping his way across the mountain.

"Wesley, you get your ass back here!"

Before Dad could do or say anything else, Wesley had disappeared, and Ronnie was running after him.

My brothers sat in the shade of an old oak tree that looked down upon the grave of our grandparents. After talking for an hour, they decided that it was more important for Ronnie to stay at home while Wesley made sure that Mom was able to safely cash the welfare checks, secure transportation, and shop for and bring home food and clothing. Ronnie returned to the cabin that afternoon.

After spending the night at Aunt Helen's, Wesley returned the following afternoon to collect his clothes and personal things. He was glad to see the Chevy was missing—and Dad with it. He didn't want another argument with his father. Wesley had just walked in the door when Mom gave him the bad news. Not only had Dad hidden Wesley's clothes, he had also smashed his Guitar against the footboard of his bed. Dad had done such a bang-up job; Wesley had to sweep up the pieces. Dad told everyone to leave the pieces as they were for Wesley to see. And, we did too.

"Son-of-a-bitch!" Wesley was furious.

He had upheld his end of the promise; and Dad hadn't. Taking his clothes and breaking his guitar was as low and as "down-right dirty" as his father could get.

Now, the only thing he could think about was getting even. It didn't take him long. Wesley gathered-up his father's latest batch of homebrew and hid it in the woods.

Mom said, "Wesley ... I don't think you should do that."

"The hell I can't! You tell Dad that I said two can play that game."

Now, the feud was on.

But, Wesley wasn't finished. He ran to the back porch, and scanning left and right, he said, "Mom, where's the mule?"

"Ronnie has him. He rode him down the mountain to see your grandma about something."

Wesley was extremely agitated as he headed for Mama's place. When he arrived, he found Uncle Jessie and Ronnie talking as they stood beside the saddled mule. Wesley jumped into the saddle, saying, "He's mine now, and I'm taking him."

Jessie stepped in front of the mule and secured a firm grip on the harness's cheek strap.

"Where do you think you're going?"

"Jessie," Wesley warned, "this don't have anything to do with you."

Ronnie was grinning. The day before, he had watched his father smash Wesley's prized guitar into tiny pieces. Now, he was sympathetic to Wesley's method of exacting revenge.

"Ronnie, I want you to tell Dad he can have the mule back when he gives me my clothes back."

Jessie said, "Wesley ... I think you best leave the mule here."

With that, Wesley spurred the mule hard, and it bolted, ripping the harness from Jessie's grip and almost knocking him down. Jessie could only watch as the mule and his nephew rounded the curve on Tank Hill Road and disappeared from sight.

Come early June, the feud was still on. Wesley had spent most of the afternoon sitting on a knoll just within sight of the cabin, waiting and hoping for his father to leave. He had been wearing his cousin's clothes for days, hoping to get his own back, yet afraid to confront his father about it. Around two in the afternoon, Wesley was awakened from a light doze when Dad started up his Chevy. His day seemed to brighten a bit as he watched his father drive off the mountain.

Mom had Wesley's clothes waiting for him. She said it took a while; but with Ginny, Ronnie and her searching, they finally found them under some loose floorboards in the attic. Dad hadn't seen his mule and may have given up on ever seeing it again.

Gabby Franklin had been waiting at his home for Wesley to gather-up Mom. Now, just as he'd promised, Gabby drove them to the Post Office to pick up the check and again to Pocahontas where she could cash the check and buy groceries.

It had been a long day for Mom, and even longer for Wesley. In spite of his afternoon nap on the knoll, he was dog-tired. With so many boxes of groceries and no other way of getting them home, they had to pay for a taxi to drive them back to Boissevain Mountain. Wesley and Mom grew nervous as the taxi clawed its way up Tank Hill Road. They were wondering how Dad's ego was handling this new way of securing the family supplies. This was the second month in a row.

Halfway up the hill, the taxi was approaching Mama's place when Dad surprised them by running down through the yard and flagging the taxi. Angry, cursing, and spitting tobacco, Dad opened the taxi door and jerked Mom out onto the side of the road. By the time Wesley could get to them, Dad had knocked her into the ditch.

Grabbing Wesley's arm, Dad said, "Come here boy; I have a score to settle with you."

Dad proceeded to pull Wesley into the yard where he sucker-punched him—real hard—in the jaw. Wesley looked stunned as he rubbed his jaw and stared back at his father. When Dad gave Wesley his best and cockiest grin, it was all that our big brother needed—Wesley just went crazy. Anger from years of emotional and physical abuse rose up inside Wesley, pumping him full of adrenaline. He became a tractor trailer headed for a crash, and his father was the guardrail. Wesley didn't hear Jessie's or Irene's screams until well after Dad was bloody and unconscious. Even then, he wouldn't stop pummeling Dad until my aunt and uncle dragged him away from Dad's limp body. It was fortunate for Dad that my aunt and uncle had been visiting Mama at that time of day.

Minutes later, Uncle Jessie helped his dazed brother into their house where he [Dad] was treated. Wesley, Mom, and Irene gathered down at the taxi where the driver offered to be a witness to the abuse. Aunt Irene said that, earlier in the day, Dad was angry at Wesley over something and wouldn't tell her what it was. She said Dad sat in the house sharpening his knife and threatening to kill Wesley. Upon hearing that, Wesley and Mom climbed back into the taxi and hurried home with the groceries. Wesley rushed back to Aunt Helen's with his own clothes—clean, folded and packed neatly in two pillow cases.

Wesley felt secure staying with the Millers on Jenkinjones Mountain. He was pretty sure his father wouldn't risk his life by transgressing upon the Miller property. Uncle Burl and Aunt Helen had already made it clear that five shotguns and five itchy trigger fingers were waiting for him if they ever saw him on their property—uninvited. They all detested Dad for the way he treated Mom and us kids.

Mothers usually don't like to hear about their son getting his ass kicked—especially when their grandson is doing the ass-kicking. After hearing the news about her son's beating, Mama reported the incident to the sheriff. She expected him to arrest Wesley, but the taxi driver had already reported the incident. The sheriff only snickered, saying, "Mrs. Dixon ... I'm sure Sleepy got what he deserved."

Meanwhile, back at the farm; Dad, Ronnie, and Billy were left with the bulk of the crop work. With Dad having been beaten and humiliated, many thought he was probably plotting some kind of revenge. All the beating accomplished was to agitate my father even more. It didn't take long for him to start taking it out on our mother. Again, Mom was beaten. Fortunately Dad was weak from his drunkenness, and she was able to escape to a friend's house.

A day or two later, Ronnie hiked across the mountain and told Wesley, Aunt Helen, and Uncle Burl that Dad had beaten Mom again. This angered them all, especially Wesley. Wesley had warned his father about hitting Mom. My brothers rushed home to check on Mom and confront their father. When they stepped off the Miller's porch,

Uncle Burl said, "Be careful Wesley. If you get the chance, give your old man one for me." Of course, neither one of our parents were home. Ginny knew where Mom was hiding, and she told Wesley where he could find her.

Cupping her face in her hands, Mom sat sobbing quietly on her friend's sofa. Her hands were hiding some of the black and blue bruises Dad had inflicted earlier.

"I've seen him beat you for the last time, Mom," Wesley cried in anger. "Either you leave him for good or I'm leaving for good."

Seconds passed and Mom said nothing.

"Well?" Wesley demanded.

"Go ahead and leave Wesley," she cried, "Daisy left … you might as well leave too."

Mom didn't realize it, but she was laying some serious guilt on Wesley.

"Damn both of you!" he shouted, storming out of the house.

Weeks would pass before any of us saw him.

Most August days on the mountain were hot and sunny; the nights were still surprisingly cool. On the second Saturday of the month, Ginny, Donna, Gary, and I were outside the house cooling off. To keep cool we would sometimes take a dip in one or more of the rain barrels that were kept beside the house. We had recently had a good amount of rain and the barrels were almost full of rain water collected from the cabin's tin roof. As usual, Ginny was left in charge of her younger siblings. Donna was wearing a pair of shorts while Gary and I were wearing our underpants. Ginny was sporting a yellow, two-piece bathing suit. It was new and her first time wearing it.

Meanwhile, Dad and three of his drinking buddies, Cat, June, and Billy, were shaving and cleaning up in our kitchen. They were just getting wound up. It had been almost three years to the week since Dad and June stood before the judge for drinking and manufacturing alcohol. Now, they were still drinking buddies, and they were preparing for another night of drinking in Pocahontas. Mom was still staying with her lady friend who was helping with the two youngest, Debbie and

David. It was too early, if ever, for our dad to forgive his son for beating him up. And his attitude showed it. Dad was still behaving badly—at his drinking worst—and Mom just wanted to stay away from him. Wesley was on the other side of the mountain staying with Aunt Helen. Plans had not changed; Ronnie and Wesley had determined that their younger siblings needed an older brother to be at home. Ronnie was the chosen one, and he and Paul were in the house eagerly waiting for the grownups to leave.

June and Billy finished cleaning up first. They came out of the house, walked by us kids, and lit up a cigarette while greeting us. Ginny said hello back to them, and they walked over to Dad's Chevy beside Tank Hill Road to smoke their cigarettes and wait for Dad and Cat.

Ginny was almost thirteen years old and looked very mature for her age. I believe this was a major reason for her discomfort around Dad's friends, especially when they were drinking. She also did not like the way June and Billy were staring at us while we were playing. That's when she decided that it was time for us to dry off, go into the house, and climb out of our wet clothes. About the same time, Dad and Cat walked outside.

Dad said, "You girls get in the house, you've been out here long enough."

That night, knowing from past experiences, Ginny was expecting one or more of these men to return with Dad in a drunken condition. She did not want to be around when they came back. So, she came up with the idea that it would be better if we all camped out in the attic where none of the drunken men would bother us. As a six year old, I though the idea sounded like fun.

Once Ginny told Paul and Ronnie about the plan, everyone helped in gathering all the pillows and blankets we needed for the camp-out. While we were carrying our beddings outside and around to the right side of the cabin, Paul couldn't help but notice that Billy and June were still standing across the road staring at us. When they saw us staring back, they left to catch up with Dad and Cat.

The only way to get into the attic was through the outside attic window near the chimney. The window was hinged with an old-fashioned latch that could be opened from outside or inside the attic. We used a wooden ladder built specifically for access to the attic or roof. The ladder was so long and heavy that Ginny and Ronnie struggled a bit to put it in place.

After several trips up and down the ladder, we had transferred all we needed to comfortably snuggle in for the night. We also discovered, much to our disappointment, that the attic light was not working and we would have to use candles. Paul and Donna would be sleeping together on one mattress while I slept on the other mattress with Gary. That left the bottom bunk of a bunk bed for Ginny. Ronnie would be the only one not sleeping in the attic.

It was about nine o'clock and darkness had set in. We all ate some of Mom's delicious sweetbread biscuits as snacks by candlelight and washed them down with some water. Milk would have been great but it was expensive and we didn't have a working refrigerator at the time to keep it fresh. For an hour or two we chatted and played silly games that you would expect for kids our age:

Paul said, "I went around behind the outhouse and saw a dead skunk ... I one it."

Ginny said, "I two it."

The seconds began to tick away, signaling to Paul that too much thinking was going on. Paul said, "Come on ... quick ... somebody keep it going."

Quickly, I added, "I three it."

"I four it," Donna replied.

Gary shouted, "I five it!"

"Okay ... I six it!" Paul shouted.

It came back to Ginny, who said, "I seven it."

Knowing my turn was after Ginny, I didn't hesitate: "I eight it."

Paul and Ginny broke into loud laughter. "Yuck," Paul bellowed, "Tommy ate the dead skunk!"

"Oh no," I cried, realizing how I had been tricked.

"That's disgusting," Donna moaned.

"Why did Tommy have to eat the dead skunk?" Gary asked.

"Okay Gary," Ginny said. "Listen … I walked down the road and saw a fresh … a … a fresh baked apple pie cooling on Aunt Irene's porch … I one it."

Donna was quick: "I two it!"

Paul said, "I three it!"

We finished the game and replayed it over and over several times until we were tired of it and Gary began to understand. Around eleven o'clock, the games stopped and Ginny told us that it was time to be quiet and go to sleep.

Donna and I wouldn't shut up, so Ginny yelled at us saying, "If you don't be quiet … you're gonna have to sleep downstairs." Well, that was all it took to keep us quiet. Pretty soon we all were sound asleep.

A little while later I awoke. It was still dark; after midnight I would guess. And, it seemed rather unusual for me to be awake so soon after having fallen asleep. Maybe it was the strangeness of the attic. Just fifteen feet to my right, I could see the faint glow of the moonlight shining through the bare attic window. It was quiet, except for the breathing and occasional rustle from those sleeping. For some reason the crickets I had heard before I fell asleep were much quieter.

Still, very sleepily, I closed my eyes. I thought I heard a muffled voice from the ground below. My heavy eyelids strained and opened ever so slightly. I must be dreaming, I thought. My eyelids closed for only seconds before opening again. What's that? I asked myself. I had heard something again. Somehow my peripheral vision caught a movement to my right, and it wasn't one of my siblings.

There, in the frame of the open window, was the silhouette of a human form. At first I thought I heard it moan. Then, it seemed to struggle quietly to pull itself into the attic. I wondered: Is it a shadowy figure of a man—or is it a ghost?

I lay motionless and began to sweat. Just as fast as they had formed, the tiny beads of sweat had penetrated my clothing—soaking my garments. I wondered again, Could this still be a dream?

I could not scream. I couldn't blink. I could barely breathe. I watched in horror as this black ghost-of-a-figure penetrated the window opening and melted to the attic floor.

It was a step that couldn't be heard or felt, for at this point the shadow wasn't walking. Instead, it seemed to be floating. I was beginning to wonder where this dream—if it was a dream—was taking me. I felt that I should be waking up now—anytime now. But the shadow continued. It was among us.

Is it coming for me? I thought. No. It had stopped and was now hovering near Donna and Paul. I kept asking myself questions: What was it doing? What does it want?

Seconds passed that seemed like hours. The shadow paused briefly near Paul and Donna, moving on to the bunk bed where Ginny was resting. I kept wondering as to its intension?

With sweat soaked clothes, I held my breath. I was afraid to move for what seemed like an eternity. Then, when I could no longer hold my breath, I gulped a breath of air and quickly thought, or did I shout: Please don't take my sister!

It was at this time that I heard Ginny's screams. Paul and Donna joined in. Their screams shattered my dream and nightmare, propelling me into a sense of reality and urgency. This is real. This is happening. I thought.

Now, revealed and shaken by all the noise, the shadow became human. It was a man. He was cursing, grunting, and stumbling, as he tried to quickly make his exit back through the window. In an instant he was gone, and I felt that he must have dove head first out the window. This was a dive or leap that must have been ten feet or more to the ground.

We all gathered ourselves closer together to comfort each other. No one slept well after that. Dozing briefly now and then, my wait for sunrise seemed to last forever.

Right about dawn we were rousted by June, Billy, and Ronnie. Apparently the intruder had removed the ladder from the window, but the men found it and placed it into position for our exit. We didn't tell them anything about what occurred, just that the ladder must have fallen down. That's when Ginny noticed that June still had beard stubbles, and hadn't shaved, unlike the rest of the men the day before. The two men also told us that Dad and Cat hadn't returned home because they were locked up in the Pocahontas jail for public intoxication.

After June and Billy left, Ronnie and Paul prepared gravy (lumpy due to not paying attention), and Ginny made biscuits (brick-hard when she forgot to add the baking powder) for breakfast. It was during the preparation and consumption of our odd-tasting breakfast that we all had the time and freedom to discuss what had happened in the attic.

Paul said he was awakened by a hairy hand caressing his leg. Donna said the same. Ginny, on the other hand, said that she felt the rough stubbles of the intruder's beard and whiskers on her face seconds before she was dragged from the bunk bed. She thought he had done this in order to have more room to lie on top of her. But Ginny was able to get away and hide in the closet. That, plus all the noise we were making forced the intruder to give up and dash out the window.

Ginny wasn't sure about the identity of the intruder. But she had her suspicions. Whoever he was, she knew the man was older and hadn't shaved recently. She and Ronnie also knew that when Dad found out what had happened, there would be trouble ahead.

When Dad returned home the following Monday, someone told him about the intrusion upon the family and the assault upon his daughter. No one was surprised when Dad grabbed his loaded twelve-gauge shotgun, a handful of shells, jumped into his Chevy, and went hunting. "I know who it is," Dad said, "and I'm gonna make him pay for it."

Dad called on June at his house around four in the afternoon. His wife answered the door and told Dad that her husband wasn't at home. Dad shouted from inside his car, "Why did John break in on me?"

"I don't know what you're talking about," she replied.

Dad asked the woman to come down to the car and talk with him. She refused. Dad drove away slowly, saying, "Junior needs a good beat'n and I'm gonna give it to em."

Later that evening, Dad accosted June when he found him on the road just below his house. "Sleepy, I don't want any trouble with you," he said.

Dad followed him, arguing with him until June joined his brother, Fred, on his porch. June and Fred spoke briefly there. Unusually relaxed, Fred sat in a chair on the porch as June walked into his living room and settled into a chair just inside the open front door.

Only seconds after exchanging words with Fred, Dad aimed his shotgun at June; and from only twenty-five feet away, fired a round through the open doorway. The center of the blast struck June near his right temple—knocking him from the chair into the floor. While trying to warn his brother, Fred had moved into the line of fire receiving pellet wounds to the right side of his face. Even June's wife was nipped in the arm by two of the pellets. As the victims' blood pooled onto the wooden floor, Dad and his Chevy sped away into the dark.

Fred and his family, as witness to the shooting, contacted the law right away. By midnight, Dad became the subject of a wide-spread police dragnet that eventually led to him being chased by a deputy in a Model-T Ford truck. The hub caps spun off the deputy's truck during the chase, but the law couldn't catch Dad and his Chevy.

Two deputies had our cabin staked out during the early hours of Tuesday morning. They were expecting Dad to return. About eleven in the morning, the sheriff and another deputy "slipped down the mountain" and captured Dad while he was hiding at a friend's house in Tipple Hollow. Dad offered no resistance.

On the nineteenth of August, Dad appeared in court in the custody of the county sheriff and was appointed public legal counsel to defend him against two felony charges. Two weeks later, on September second, his lawyer asked—and was granted—an order of continuance to move the trial to a later day in November; stating he had not had time to prepare a proper defense on behalf of [Dad] the defendant. In November, Dad pled "not guilty" to the felony charges of "malicious wounding" and proceeded to trial-by-jury. With the evidence stacked against him, the jury found Dad guilty and he was sentenced to eight years in the state penitentiary. Our father began serving—by far—the longest prison sentence of his life. Dad's drinking and abominable attitude had finally done him in.

The two men and the woman survived the shooting, but June, having been seriously wounded, paid the price of one eye for whatever he did to piss-off Sleepy Dixon. It could have been the alleged breaking and entering of our attic along with molestation and attempted rape. Maybe, it was something else. Or, maybe, it was many things.

Neither Mom, nor anyone else in our family would have condoned such senseless violence. We have always hoped that Dad was—at least—correct in his assumption of June's guilt.

The Union Mission

It wasn't until several days after Dad's arrest that Mom found out about what her husband had done and that he was in jail. All of us kids: Gary, me, Donna, Paul, Ginny, and Ronnie were alone making-do at the cabin on Boissevain Mountain. Someone, most likely Mama or Aunt Irene, rushed to inform the proper authorities that there were six children living alone without any adult guardian.

The State Child Welfare agency wasted little time in determining that Mom was physically and emotionally incapable of taking care of all us kids. So, near the end of August, the state took us to The Union Mission, an orphanage located high on the side of a steep hill near Scott and Commerce Streets in Bluefield, West Virginia. It was a grand, impressive, and awe-inspiring structure for anyone to behold—especially a young child.

I remember good and bad times at the orphanage. When we first arrived, the mission director wanted to separate the Dixon boys from the Dixon girls. However, the little ones cried, complained, and made such a ruckus that they gave up and left us all in one room by ourselves. While in the orphanage, we played and socialized with kids from other broken and dysfunctional homes. The food was good, and we were given nice clothes to wear to school that fall.

The Mission had very strict rules that had to be followed. Some kids broke the rules by accident, and even necessity (i.e. fighting in self-defense). Some were deliberate. Breaking the rules sometimes resulted in spankings and, for the older ones, severe beatings.

One day Ronnie broke the rules and was lucky he didn't get caught. He and another kid had sneaked out to see a movie in Bluefield. While my big brother was enjoying the movie, I received my first memorable beating at the hands of two older kids in the orphanage. They were simple bullies, probably about ten years old. Normally I would stay close to Ronnie, who was almost fifteen, or sometimes Ginny or Paul. On this occasion, they caught me alone near the bathroom holding a juicy, bright red apple in my hand.

"Give me the apple," one of them demanded.

When I refused, they pounced on me, smacked me about my face, and kicked me. Then they pulled the apple from my hand, laughed, and walked away. Damage was limited to a bloody nose and a few bumps and bruises. Someone had witnessed the two boys' assault on me and reported them. They were caught and disciplined with a wooden rod.

After a while, we all became very unhappy about having to live at The Union Mission. Some of us prayed and prayed that someone in our family would be able to rescue us.

While we were counting the days at the orphanage, Mom was living with our Aunt Clara and working hard to convince our case worker that she was ready and able to retake custody of the rest of her children. Mom had filled out and signed numerous welfare forms and the family was about to receive a well-deserved family sustenance check from the state.

Around the middle of September, Mom finally received the necessary papers to collect her children. We were so happy to see her and our case worker, Ms. Sugar, standing on the porch of the orphanage. Ms. Sugar and her Chevrolet station-wagon provided transportation back to our cabin and home on Boissevain Mountain. On the way, we stopped at a supermarket in Bluefield, Virginia. Most of us waited in the car while they bought some food for us.

Soon after we arrived at the house, we all pitched in to help carry the groceries from the station-wagon into the kitchen. When Ronnie approached the porch, he noticed that all the crops that he and Billy had stacked on the porch were gone. Ronnie guessed that our Uncle Jessie had taken them. It was just as well, seeing as most of the crop would have gone bad had they not been consumed.

As Mom was putting items away, she asked, "What happened to all the flour, sugar, and baking powder we had stored on top of the cabinet?" Some of us, with blank faces, looked around the kitchen and at each other. Nobody knew.

Since the house had been left unattended for weeks, someone had also cleaned the entire kitchen of everything eatable and of value. Now, Mom would have to return to the store to purchase and replace many things that were taken or stolen. They had even taken the beat-up old axe that we used for chopping wood.

Shenanigans

The nights on Boissevain Mountain were beginning to get a little chilly come October. While our father was settling into the prison routine, Wesley came home to live with and help the family. With very little money to buy coal or wood, Wesley, Ronnie, and sometimes Paul returned to the laborious process of storing-up coal for the winter. This time they were digging coal not too far from the cabin in one or two abandoned mines on the mountain. On one occasion, my older brothers had worked most of the day digging and piling up coal to be carried back to the house. They laughed and clowned around to dull the pain from achy muscles and blistered hands. Having access to Dad's Chevy made their work a lot easier. It was almost dark when the Chevy, loaded with coal in buckets and burlap bags, headed home. The rest of their diggings would have to wait till morning.

When they returned the next day, the pile of coal they had worked so hard for was gone. Wesley and Ronnie were furious. As they returned home they thought about the missing coal. Then they thought about the missing food, crops, and axe. They even fell asleep that night wondering who could be mean enough to be doing these things.

My brothers returned to the abandoned mines a few more times that month. Twice they happened upon our uncle and cousins carrying coal from the same abandoned mines. But, they had learned their lesson. From then on, they dug-out only what they could carry home, leaving little coal for someone else's easy-picking.

After the orphanage, Ginny, Paul, Donna and I attended grade school at Boissevain. Ronnie started his first year at Pocahontas High School.

One afternoon, in mid-October, some of us saw Ronnie returning from school. He walked into the yard with his school books and a mysterious looking box tucked under his arm. Paul, Ginny, and I gathered around and questioned him about the box.

"It's my birthday present to me," he said. "If you promise not to tell Mom, I'll show you what it is?"

Of course we all agreed not to tell. Ronnie said, "Okay, but I can't open it here. Let's go to the attic where Mom can't see us."

So, the four of us climbed up the ladder and entered the attic. Alone there, we watched Ronnie open the box revealing a dozen or more fancy looking cigars. "Oh my," Ginny said. "Where'd ja get them?"

"I stole em from the old Negro man that lives across the road from Grandma. I'm gonna smoke one right now, and all of you have to smoke too. Or else, I'm gonna think you'll tell on me."

"No, we won't tell," Ginny promised.

With that, Ronnie pulled out a box of matches, bit the tip off the butt end of a cigar, put that end into his mouth, struck a match, and proceeded to light-up the larger exposed end of the cigar. After several hard puffs and turns of the cigar to get it started, he handed it to Ginny. She puffed once and blew out the smoke. She passed the cigar to Paul and he puffed and blew smoke. Paul handed it to Ronnie again, and he began taking a few more puffs. Then Ronnie handed it back to Paul.

I was beginning to feel snubbed. "What about me," I asked, "don't I get to puff on it?"

"No Tommy," Ginny said. "You're too young. It'll make you sick."

But Ronnie thought we should all be in this together: "Oh ... go on, Paul; give him a puff. See if he likes it or not."

Paul took a puff and held the cigar to my mouth. I puffed once, coughed, and began choking. Ginny and Paul started patting me on my back until I caught my breath. While I was composing myself, my siblings continued repeating the puffing sequence several times. Ronnie, as a tease, offered to give me another attempt. I was already feeling nauseous and disgusted with the weed and proceeded to turn away from his offer. Soon the attic was full of smoke from the cigar. No one, except maybe Ronnie, inhaled or even knew how to inhale the smoke. But, because we were breathing in so much secondhand smoke, we were—in effect—actually inhaling the cigar smoke. Within minutes everyone except Ronnie was nauseous or very sick.

After a few more minutes of breathing in that attic, Paul and I were heaving our last meal. Ronnie was doubled over, laughing his guts out.

Standing up from the bunk bed, Ginny said, "Oh God, if Mom finds out about this—she'll kill us."

"Come on," she said, grabbing my hand then Paul's, "let's get to some fresh air before we die."

As we stepped from the ladder to the ground, we could still hear Ronnie laughing hysterically inside the attic. I don't recall anyone cleaning up the mess. But I'm sure Ginny returned later to do just that.

The smoking we did in the attic that day was my first and last. I suspect it was the main reason I never developed the habit. And, I can't imagine that I ever will.

Our Uncle Jessie paid a visit to our house. He said that he wanted to make sure that we were doing well. As he was leaving and walking to his pickup, Ronnie saw him nonchalantly take our brand new axe from the chopping block and put it into the back of his truck. He started his truck, but before he could drive away, he saw Ronnie take back the axe. Our uncle got out of the truck to confront his nephew. Ronnie challenged him by cocking the axe in a defensive position; whereby our uncle decided to get back into his truck and leave.

Uncle Burl and Aunt Helen convinced Mom and Wesley that it was time to leave Boissevain Mountain and all of its shenanigans. She had found us "a nice place" in Jenkinjones.

These were hard times for many, and a sad day when family preys on family. It only foments anger and resentment.

VII

JENKINJONES
c. 1958-1960

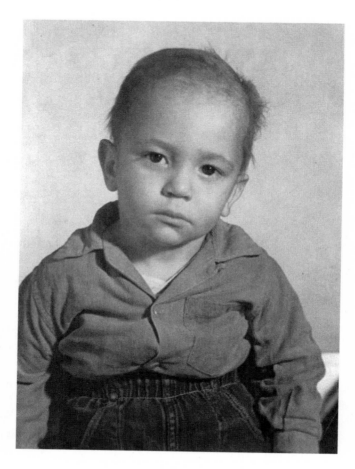

David (1) at Newhill Road, April 1959

The Company Home

Fall's late October splendor had arrived at the grubby little mining town of Jenkinjones, West Virginia. The Jenkinjones mining operations, having seen bigger and better days, were winding down. I remember nothing about the move; it seemed like I had just awakened from a nap, and we were there. Well, who knows, maybe that's what really happened.

Some of my older siblings only wished it were that easy. Our heavier furniture was delivered by truck; some of the lighter stuff was delivered by hand and foot. Paul remembers carrying chairs, boxes of clothing, and nick-knacks across two miles of the dusty backwoods terrain between Boissevain Mountain and Jenkinjones. At least twice he made the trip.

Our house, owned by the Pocahontas Fuel Company, was a single story structure with a wooden clapboard exterior in need of a good paint job. The roof looked good, but during our stay the company had to address a few minor leaks. Facing northwest, the house sat beside Newhill Road, which wound its way around Jenkinjones Mountain and terminated as a switchback at Trestle Hollow Road. From the front porch you could look across Newhill Road to the valley below and see Trestle Hollow and Trestle Hollow Road, where most of the poor Negro families lived. Many referred to it as "Nigger" Hollow, a word I was uncomfortable with then and have refrained from using most of my life.

We accessed our home near the coal bin beside Newhill Road. Gary and I were scolded for playing around the coal bin with our plastic toy soldiers and Indians. I guess little boys just love to get dirty, and coal black was about as dirty as we could get. Come winter, the bin needed to be filled every month, but many times we didn't have enough money for coal, and digging coal was no longer a viable option. That's when Ronnie and Ginny would cut and drag dead wood off the mountain to keep the stoves going.

They were a great team using a two-man bow saw. Since Ginny was two years older, they were about equal in strength and could make quick work of some rather large logs. Sometimes when Ginny wasn't available to help Ronnie, Paul stepped in. Not quite 12, Paul was verbally and physically abused by Ronnie, like when he shoved the saw's wooden handle into his stomach.

"Come on, you weakling! I don't want to be here all day! Ginny makes you look like a sissy!"

Within a year, though, Paul would be carrying his weight at the task.

From the coal bin, sturdy wooden steps climbed a four-foot dirt bank. A plank walkway led across a small front yard to the front porch, then continued along the right side of the house where it connected with the kitchen and back porch, turned left again and ended at the outhouse in back. Mom loved this walkway and encouraged all us kids to use it whenever we could. Since our yard was frequently muddy, it kept our clothes and shoes cleaner. Anything that helped make the house less dirty and reduce the laundry load was appreciated.

Behind the house was a seven-foot wide breezeway. Here the walkway continued between the house and a four-foot tall stone retaining wall. Instead of a backyard, we had a steep hill that ascended to the top of the mountain.

Our front porch was the family's favorite hangout. We spent many hours there, watching and waving at people coming and going. Mom snapped green beans, peeled potatoes, and chatted with the women. Whenever possible, we gathered to hear Wesley play his guitar and sing. Since our front porch faced northwest, we loved watching storm fronts roll across No. 8 Mountain. Due to the coal company's brutal strip-mining process, No. 8 had been scalped, thus devoid of some of its natural greenery. Nevertheless, it was still a beautiful sight.

While watching the storm front close the distance, we took advantage of the fifteen to thirty second warning to stop whatever we were doing and move to shelter. Further warning came in the form of pea-sized water droplets and sometimes hail as big as marbles that pounded the paved road, wooden walkway, and roof. Finally, a wall of water swept across so hard and fast that it would take your breath away if you weren't sheltered. Donna, Gary, and I sometimes took summer showers in the rain. Clad only in underwear, we lathered our bodies and hoped the rain didn't stop before we rinsed. Mom and the older ones enjoyed watching our showers-in-the-rain, wishing they could be so free.

The timing of the move to Jenkinjones interrupted our school year. Switching schools in-state would have been easier than going to a different state, so what I had started in first grade in Boissevain, Virginia, I now had to resume as a first-grader in Jenkinjones, West Virginia.

The Jenkinjones Elementary School was a quaint, two-story brick structure situated at the bottom of the mountain within the shadow of the railroad trestle at Trestle Hollow Road. It was only a 20-minute walk down Newhill Road. Or, you could cut the time in half by: 1) walking four minutes along the road, 2) a minute sliding downhill on your butt, 3) half a minute crossing the railroad tracks, 4) another minute sliding downhill by the seat of your britches, and 5) a final two-minute walk to the school. If it was good weather and we didn't have too many books to carry, we took the shortcut.

You'd never see a school bus on Newhill Road. The curves were too sharp and the switchbacks were downright suicidal. Only cars and small trucks could travel this road. Eighth graders, like Ronnie, had to catch the bus at the bottom of the mountain, to be bused a few miles to the high school in Anawalt, West Virginia.

On October 27, several days after we had settled into our new home, the radios and newspapers were announcing bad news. The Bishop #34 mine had another explosion. This time it was probably a misplaced dynamite charge that killed 22 miners. Surviving Bishop #34 miners would have to be pretty desperate to return to work after that, but they did. For many men it was all they knew and, despite the hazards, new blood continued to seek out the mines. There were few jobs in those mountains that could feed and clothe a family, and even fewer that paid as well as mining coal.

I remember little about the first winter on Newhill Road, only that it was very cold with very little to do. We seldom used our sled; although there were plenty of hills, they were suicidal in their steepness. One chilly morning Paul wanted his younger siblings to take the shortcut to school. But our well-worn path was coated with snow and ice, and we didn't want to end up unconscious or dead, sprawled-out in the ditch beside the railroad tracks at the bottom. We balked at Paul's invitation, choosing the long and safe way. After a couple of close calls, Paul adopted a more responsible attitude and joined his siblings on the longer, winding road.

The Company Store at Newhill Rd. in Jenkinjones, WV.

Inside The Company Store at Newhill Rd. in Jenkinjones, WV

The Company Store and Post Office

Pretty soon, my siblings and I were visiting the company store and post office located near the foot of the mountain.

These company stores were large buildings that sold candy, food, clothing, radios, tables, and chairs, along with big ticket items like furniture, stoves, washing machines, refrigerators, and even catalogue orders for automobiles and trucks. Freight trains, loaded to the brim, docked weekly at the stores. They were the only places for miles around where you could buy things that weren't home grown or home brewed.

Once or twice each month (especially when Mom received the welfare check), we made a pleasure excursion to the store and post office with Mom, Ronnie, or Ginny. Usually I'd be given a nickel or dime to buy candy. At my age, most kids would be begging and pestering for all they could get. I, on the other hand, somehow knew how scarce money was to the family and was content with what I was given. I would seldom ask, let alone pester, for more.

Unlike the company store, the post office featured a poolroom, along with a tobacco, candy, and ice cream store in its basement. It wasn't as busy and therefore provided its patrons, especially young boys and girls, with fast and efficient service. You might ask: why would a business sell candy with tobacco? Many men and women, my mother included, were smokers. Many smokers were also tobacco chewers, and they usually had their little ones in tow when they stopped for their weekly supply. When the children saw all the delicious candy and ice cream on display, they would sing their songs of wanting. Their parents would usually fall victim to the songs and give in.

I usually bought a box of Cracker Jacks or a small colorful box containing various pieces of candy and gum. Either way, I was rewarded with a surprise inside. Or I'd buy a few pieces of licorice or a box of Animal Crackers with a string attached for carrying. I'd sit on a bench enjoying my sweets, while Mom and the others did their shopping across the road at the company store. Sometimes Donna or

Gary sat with me, and it was a requirement that we share with each other. What a treat!

Daisy's letter was forwarded to Jenkinjones from our P.O. Box in Boissevain. It announced that on March 10, 1959, she had become Mrs. Chester Wright. Daisy and Chester had eloped to South Carolina and were married by a justice of the peace. Daisy was the first born, and it was only fitting that she would be the first to be married. It must have been a very happy time for her, but I'm sure that she would have preferred her family to be there, especially Mom.

In no time, spring was upon us. The mountains had morphed from the gray barrenness of a Newhill winter into the various greens of sprouting grasses, lilies, and leaves. Forsythia was abundant, especially on the steep banks along Newhill Road. The surrounding hills and hollows were teaming with dogwood and fruitwood blossoms, and the sweet aroma of honeysuckle nearly overpowered the senses, albeit for too short a duration.

Brownie was about nine years old then, and was beginning to suffer seizures, acting unpredictably and foaming at the mouth. Mom insisted he be chained to a tree in back of the house, where he was fed and watered for several days. Eventually his condition became so hopeless and dangerous that we had the dogcatcher take him away and put him down. The Brownie we knew and loved was very affectionate, eager to please, and a country dog through and through. He was almost like family and was missed by all.

The Millers

When recalling the times in Jenkinjones, I can't help but heap praise upon my Aunt Helen, Uncle Burl, and my cousins Betsy, Bruce, and Brian. Helen would make frequent visits with our family when she traveled to the company store and P.O. Some of my cousins would ride their horse, Dixie, from the top of the mountain where they lived, to the top of Trestle Hollow Road where it met Newhill Road.

If a large amount of supplies were needed, Dixie pulled a sled. They would unhitch the sled where the dirt road ended and the paved road began. From there, they'd ride Dixie to the store. After shopping, the supplies were tied to the horse's back, and she would be walked back to the edge of the hollow, where the supplies would be loaded onto the hitched-up sled for the trip home. The trip took the better part of a day, so their visit with us had to be brief if they wanted to be home before dark. Even with the moon shining, it was pretty dark on that mountain.

The family tales say old Dixie was struck twice by lightning as she made the trip across Jenkinjones Mountain. Nevertheless, she died from natural causes at the old age of 20-something.

Helen was my favorite aunt back then because she made herself more available. When I was about seven, I remember spending some time at her farm on the mountain. My aunt and Cousin Bruce picked me up at our place for one of their return trips with supplies. I remember riding on old Dixie's back most of the way. The smell of her sweat, the squeaking of the saddle, and the sound of the sled scratching the road along the way still linger in my mind.

The Millers let me pick fruit and vegetables from their gardens. One day I ate so much I got a bellyache. After that, I was more careful about making a pig of myself. I also got to sleep in my own bed, which consisted of a canvas mattress stuffed with leaves and a pillowcase full of chicken feathers. Hanging on the wall above the bed were pictures of the Cisco Kid and his sidekick, Poncho, well known cowboys of that era and two of my favorites. When I went to bed, I was so proud to have them looking over me. But that would change.

That first night, Aunt Helen and Cousin Betsy took my small hand and led me to the bed. They sat me down and proceeded to wash my dirty feet. The washcloth and water felt warm and soothing as they talked for a moment or two about nonsense. Bruce and Brian came into the room, smiled at me, said good night, and left. Cousin Betsy planted a warm kiss on my cheek before she turned out the light.

Normally I slept through to morning, but because of the unfamiliar bed and bedding, I woke up early in the night. As I lay there trying to get back to sleep, I noticed a faint glow of moonlight casting an eerie shadow upon Cisco and Poncho. My cowboy heroes suddenly seemed alive as they smiled down at me. But their smiles were menacing and impish, not a bit friendly.

I became fearful and broke into a feverish sweat, before finally turning my eyes away from their burning stare. A few seconds later, I summoned the courage to peek at them again. Their stares seemed closer now, more intense. Their eyebrows wrinkled and moved up and down, as if frowning at me. I turned away again; my clothes soaked in sweat, and covered my head with the blanket. After what seemed like hours, I finally went to sleep.

I awoke at daylight to see Cisco and Poncho frozen motionless in their frames. I never slept in that bedroom again.

Aunt Helen's kitchen always promised the sweet smell of home cooking—spices, yeast, and the latest batch of biscuits. I recall the pleasant meals during my summer stay at the Miller farm. I joined my aunt and uncle and three cousins at the table, and although we spoke little, the conversations were always pleasant, unlike some of the mealtime conversations at home.

Evening meals normally consisted of beans and cornbread, along with scullions and tomatoes from the garden. Or we'd have rabbit stew with salads made from turnips, beets, lettuce, and tomatoes. Oil and vinegar was the common dressing. For dessert we'd have canned fruit on homemade biscuits, or homemade cakes and pies. Breakfast was usually eggs or gravy and biscuits, with bacon or homemade pork sausage. When lighter appetites prevailed, the rooster crowed from a big box of Kellogg's Corn Flakes sitting on an open shelf. Occasionally they'd throw in some corn fritters with jam or Karo syrup. I don't remember anything about lunch; maybe they were too busy to eat anything except for an apple or left-over biscuit on the run.

The Millers lived way up on the top of Jenkinjones Mountain. Few people made the trip via automobile, usually traversing the mountain by foot or horsepower, but occasionally someone would venture forth with an old four-wheel-drive Jeep and conquer the terrain. The road leading to my cousins' home was long and especially unpleasant for a young man like me. Older adults making the trip with young children had to provide several piggyback rides.

From our house on Newhill Road, the trek to Aunt Helen's consisted of a three-quarter mile hike up a mountainous trail, a two-mile walk across a flat, strip-mined section of the mountain, followed by a half-mile hike up several switchbacks. The trip ended with a quarter mile downhill stretch past the cornfields to the vegetable gardens and, finally, the farmhouse yard. That's a three and a half mile trip that someone in my immediate family made at least once a month.

Each of my cousins had plenty of chores to do every day. Bruce and Brian had the responsibility of making sure the cows came to the barn for milking. They had to do a lot of walking and listening for cowbells in the distance. The cows knew when they were to be milked and headed for the barn without being told. From the top of the hills you could sometimes see them in the distance, as well as hear the cowbells. Occasionally a cow would stray due to illness or injury, so my cousins had to be vigilant.

They also had to saw, cut, drag, and split wood for heating and cooking. Since they lived near the top of the mountain and not far from a depleted strip-mined area, they sometimes gathered coal for heating. Uncle Burl and his boys hunted a lot, too. Deer meat was rare, since they had been hunted-out years before, but small game was plentiful. Most of all, they had the seemingly endless chore of tending and weeding the gardens.

Like settlers of old, the Millers were good and simple people who—from scratch—carved roads, built their home and farm, and worked the land with pride. With strong backs and determination, they pretty much lived off nature from the 1930s through the early 1960s. Although many would consider it a hard and meager existence, I think they were rich beyond money. They did more than survive on Jenkinjones Mountain. They did well.

Terror, by Night and Day

Not too long after moving to Newhill Road, our family became good friends with several of our neighbors. Wesley developed close ties with Roger Bright next door and Eddie Weaver up the hollow. Ronnie hooked up with the younger brothers Ricky Bright and Jessie Weaver. Paul, 11, became friends with Larry and Judy Bright.

As sneaky teenagers, Ronnie, Ricky, and Jessie wanted someplace private to hang out, smoke cigarettes, and sneak a nip or two of moonshine and not get caught. The three decided they were going to build a log cabin in the woods above our house. Paul and I witnessed the cabin's progress. For a bunch of skinny teenagers, I was amazed at how confident and skilled they were.

Building the cabin took several weeks that summer. They cut, notched, and laid logs to form a 10-by-16 foot cabin. By the end of August the exterior was complete, including a sturdy front door with a padlock for keeping out strangers and kids like me. The last bit of construction I remember was the installation of flattened, brown cardboard boxes on the inside walls.

Mom was so busy with us kids that it took months before she learned about the drinking and smoking that went on at the cabin. By then the boys had found more convenient locations to let loose.

While the three young men were busy building their little house, Wesley was busy tearing down big houses. For a good part of the year, The Company paid him and another man to demolish and clean out the debris from three dilapidated houses along Newhill Road. One of the demolitions was the house next door to ours. The job paid well and kept him close to home and out of trouble.

During the day, most of the family was busy playing and doing chores. At night there was little to do except talk, read, and argue or fight about this and that. We were often tired by nine o'clock and many of us would go to bed around that time.

One night the entire family was awakened by someone's terrifying screams. It was nine-year-old Donna. Mom and some of the kids ran to her bedroom to see what the matter was. She was sitting up in bed screaming hysterically, her eyes glazed over as if in a trance. She clawed at the air as if defending herself from some invisible attacker. She kept screaming that the Devil was in the room and would not leave without her. Donna had apparently developed a fever and was hallucinating.

By using soothing words and cold compresses applied to her forehead, face, and neck, Ginny and Mom eventually calmed her down. The next morning the fever was still high. Upon examination by Dr. Murray at Jenkinjones, it was suspected that Donna had been bitten by a tick and developed a case of Rocky Mountain spotted fever. Mom essentially confirmed the diagnosis, remembering that she had removed a tick from Donna's scalp several days earlier. Donna was given antibiotics and began a gradual recovery that lasted about three weeks. We were told that if her treatment had been delayed two or three more days, she could have suffered permanent paralysis and maybe even death.

It was around the time of Donna's nightmare that the family endured another event that would scare the dickens out of us.

I had just crawled into my bed and was doing the usual tossing and turning to get comfortable. I placed my hand under my pillow and felt a very sharp burning pain in my thumb. I screamed and sat up in the bed.

Just as with Donna's nightmare, the family came to the rescue. I screamed and cried in pain as I held my thumb. Mom and the others tried to calm me down so they could ask me questions After several minutes, we could see the thumb was beginning to swell, so Mom used cold compresses to reduce the swelling. Ice would have been great, but in those days a working refrigerator was rare. The cold compresses were of little use and my thumb swelled way beyond its normal size.

Someone guessed that a bee had stung me but nobody knew for sure. Mom, Ronnie, and Ginny looked for a bee but couldn't find one. I was given some aspirin and cried until the wee hours of the morning when the pain subsided enough for me to fall asleep.

The next day Mom took me to Dr. Murray's office in Jenkinjones. I remember waiting a long time in his office before he finally called us into the examination room.

"Well, young man, it looks like you got stung by a bee," Dr. Murray said as he looked at my thumb.

Mom was curious. "How do you know it's a bee sting?"

"I'm guessing," he said. "But I won't know for sure until I remove the thumbnail."

I couldn't believe what I had just heard.

I said, "Remove what?"

"Yes, I'll have to remove your thumbnail in order to find and remove the bee's stinger. That will also reduce the swelling and prevent any infection."

I can remember asking the doctor if it was going to hurt. He said it would hurt some, but he also thought that I was a big boy now and could handle the pain.

Well, I did cry a little when he stuck me with the needle. Considering all my previous cuts and scrapes, I didn't recall having suffered through such a distinctive pain. But removing the nail was almost painless once my thumb was numb. The doctor cut my thumbnail all the way back and removed the stinger without any problem. To protect the tender skin I wore a bandage for a few days. My thumb sure felt strange—lighter and naked—and it seemed like months before Mom was able to trim my thumbnail.

By September 1959, Ronnie and his friends had stopped visiting their log cabin. They had found a more accessible place—one with electricity, water, and fewer spiders and cobwebs.

Early one morning, just a few days before school started, Donna, Gary (now 5), and I decided to take the ten-minute hike up the mountain to visit the cabin. The first thing we did was check to see if it was locked. Indeed it was, and we wouldn't be able to play inside among the spiders. The three of us milled around until Donna got bored and wanted to go home. But I wasn't ready to leave.

"Come on, you guys," I said, scampering up a young sapling. "Let's have a contest to see who can climb the highest."

As he started to climb his tree, Gary shouted, "Okay, I know I can climb higher than you, Tommy!"

From my perch I watched Donna look for a good tree, but she seemed to be having accessibility problems. Several dead tree limbs blocked her way and she had to move them aside.

I was about twenty feet off the ground and planning to climb higher. Gary was below and to my left, about fifteen feet high in his tree. Donna was about to start her climb.

"Ayeee, aayeeee, eeeeeee!" she screamed.

Stunned, Gary and I looked down and saw Donna doing some kind of fancy dance—spinning, stomping, flapping her arms, and fluffing her curly hair. I was about to tell her to stop fooling around when I realized bees or hornets were attacking her. She ran out of the woods and down the path for home, screaming and flailing her arms.

"Gary, don't leave your tree!" I shouted.

I was too late. Gary had panicked, slid down his tree, and dropped to the ground. Unfortunately, he ran by the same area where Donna had been attacked.

"Ouch! Ouch!" I heard him yell as he danced and swatted away. Within seconds Gary too was gone. I was left alone, high up in my tree and scared to death.

While Donna and Gary were being attacked, I had climbed another five feet higher. Instinct told me that higher was safer. So far I had been right. About four minutes had passed since the attack and I strained my eyes to look for bees. I thought I saw some near the ground, but wasn't sure since they were so far away. Then one or two buzzed within a yard of my feet. I started to panic. I couldn't decide whether to stay or slide down.

I had been stung only once before and had to have my thumbnail removed. What would the doctor remove if I were stung many times, like Donna? And what if I was stung so high up in the tree? I thought I might lose my grip and fall to my death.

There were no branches to stand on. I had my legs wrapped around the skinny sapling in a serpentine manner. Ten minutes passed and I was getting tired. I was gripping the only branch that could support my weight and it was beginning to cut into my hand. I was losing my grip. The good thing was that I had not been stung. Not yet, anyway.

Again I scanned the surrounding area for bees. Seeing none, I slid slowly down the tree, stopping about ten feet from the ground. I thought I saw some bees circling near the base of Donna's tree about thirty feet away. This meant that the nest was between the exit and me. Tommy, I thought, you're going to have to take the long way out.

I slid to the ground and slowly circled in a clockwise direction, keeping thirty feet between the nest and me. I made it safely to the edge of the woods and then waded through the tall weeds, brush, and briars, until I joined the path that led down to the house. As I headed home, I breathed a sigh of relief and wondered how Gary and Donna were doing.

Still sobbing, Donna was sitting at the kitchen table. Gary watched as Mom tended his sister's scalp and hair. I knew he was trying to act tough, because he stopped sobbing when he saw me.

"I was only stung two times, Tommy," he said. "How many times were you stung?"

"None," I bragged. "I didn't get stung at all."

"I don't believe you," he said. "Let me see."

Gary began inspecting my face, neck, and arms, while I watched Mom pick dead insects from Donna's hair with tweezers and toss them onto a plate. I could tell from their black and yellow markings that they were indeed hornets. Donna had managed to kill several of them by smacking her head.

Finding no red welts on my exposed skin, Gary looked surprised and disappointed that I had been spared. So I told him, "You wouldn't have gotten stung either, if you had stayed in your tree."

"You were just lucky, Tommy," Mom said. "All you youngins need to be looking out for bees anywhere you go. And for heaven's sake, stop charging through the woods like a bunch of wild animals! Maybe this will be a lesson to you."

Donna had taken a real beating that day. In addition to being stung a dozen or more times on her face and scalp, her ankles and calves were scratched by briars from her mad dash down the mountain. Fortunately, none of us were allergic to hornet stings.

That afternoon, Donna was still feeling some discomfort. Mom thought she needed something to occupy her mind and soothe the pain, so she asked Donna if she wanted anything.

Mom normally yelled at us younglings—or youngins as she would often say—if she caught us messing around with the woodstove or fireplace. She became especially angry if she saw us messing with her cook stove. But on the afternoon of the attack she made an exception. Mom gave Donna, Gary, and me permission to prepare our own lunch treat on the stove.

Mom first made sure there was a good, hot fire burning below the two front burners (or stove eyes). Then she peeled and sliced three potatoes from our garden. Working from a small wooden stool, Donna and I sprinkled the stove eyes with salt and placed potato slices upon them. A minute later we flipped them with spatulas. Pretty soon we were enjoying homemade country fries.

Wesley (17) at Newhill Rd., April 1959.

Friends and Neighbors

As far as our neighbors went, the Bright family was one of the best. We were close with Ricky, Larry, and Sheila, and they continued to stay in contact with my older siblings. During the summer of 1959, my family had the honor of being graciously included in the festivities for one of their family get-togethers. The event was held on their property next door, with some games taking place in our yard.

It was a fun time. The Brights had set up a large, military-style tent in their yard. Plenty of food and beverages were provided, and there were games for the kids. Dozens of friends and family were milling around inside and outside the two houses for most of the day. It had been a long time since I had seen so many people at once.

We played softball that afternoon. I was seven years old and this was my first time swinging a bat. It was probably the first time for some of the other kids as well.

Paul and Larry supervised our ball game, conducting a bat toss to determine who chose sides first. The pitcher tossed the bat to the catcher, who caught the bat with one hand. Then the pitcher grabbed the bat above the catcher's grip, the catcher grabbed the bat above the pitcher's grip, and so forth and so on until only one was left holding onto the knob at the end of the bat. A final hard push by the loser to dislodge it from the winner's grip determined the final winner of the bat toss. If he held on and didn't drop it, he got first pick of the players. The team losing the bat toss got to bat first.

Before playing the game, all the kids five years and older were given several chances at bat. I was having a lot of difficulty seeing the ball and, being unaware of my budding competitive instincts, I wasn't satisfied with my allotted time at bat. I made contact only once and struck out twice.

Other players were shouting at me: "Tommy, it's not your turn anymore!"

When I refused to step out of the batter's box, Paul said, "Tommy, I'll give you three more pitches, then you're taking the field."

"Okay."

On the first pitch I swung and missed. I got a foul tip on the second. I was so angry and frustrated that I could have kicked a cat.

I got a good look at the third pitch coming my way. It was my last chance, and Paul had tossed me an outside pitch that I didn't want to waste a swing on.

In desperation, I lunged for it and swung hard. The bat flew from my grip and struck Paul in the groin. I covered my mouth with my hand as my brother groaned. I was petrified and expecting swift retribution. I had never struck my big brother before, and now I was sure he was going to kill me. I waited in shock to see what he would do next.

"I'm sorry, Paul," I finally said, "it was an accident."

Paul wasn't seriously hurt but he sure was angry with me.

"Tommy, go sit down on the walkway and don't move until you're told."

As I took my seat, Donna walked over to me.

"Paul's gonna kick your behind, Tommy Mack," she whispered.

"No he ain't," I said. "He knows it was an accident."

"Oh yeah, well just you wait and see, Tommy."

For the next half hour I worried about what she said. I also had to watch everyone else have fun.

Later that evening, just before dark, I found out that some of the Bright family and friends would be sleeping in the tent that night. I thought this would give me a chance to watch the older kids interact. I kept my distance from them, to not inhibit their socializing. I felt I was on probation after what I had done to Paul, and didn't want to be accused of spying.

As the evening wore on, it seemed that Ginny had made a new friend. George Taylor was about 15, muscular, and short in stature. He wore thick, black eyeglasses with Coke bottle lenses. George was doing everything he could to impress my sister. As I watched, I learned something about flirting and showing off.

I could see why Ginny was smitten by him. Not only likeable, George could run faster than anyone I knew—including Paul—and was eager to prove it. He had already won several foot races that day. He reminded me of the Roadrunner in the TV cartoon as he dashed around the yard.

"I bet I can do something you've never seen anyone do," George boasted.

Teasingly, Ginny replied, "Okay, Georgie Porgie, what can you do that nobody else can do?"

"I can run up a tree just like a cat," he boasted.

"No you can't!" I shouted, jumping out of the shadows.

George ignored me.

"Ginny, I'll bet you a quarter."

"We don't have any money, George. Just prove it or be quiet." Ginny was getting real sassy.

With his new sweetheart challenging him, George chose to show off one last time. "Well, okay," George said. "Give me a minute to change my shoes. I'll need the other ones for traction."

He ran to his father's car and put on his special shoes. As we gathered around the catalpa tree in our front yard, I noticed his shoes had tiny metal spikes. I studied George's movements as he stepped off a distance from the tree. I had my doubts. Shucks, I thought, only cats or squirrels can run up a tree.

The sun was dipping below No. 8 Mountain when George charged the tree. About four feet away, he leapt into the air and landed about three feet high on the tree trunk. The bark flew as his feet churned. When he was about five feet up, George vaulted from the tree and performed a backward flip in the air. We gasped. Landing feet first, he stumbled backwards but was unable to catch himself. George's behind hit the ground hard.

Still full of piss-n-vinegar, he jumped to his feet.

"How'd ja like that!" he cried. "Pretty good, huh?"

I think Ginny was impressed. I know I was. My mouth was still open in disbelief.

George said that he could run up a tree like a cat and that's exactly what he did that evening. I've only seen Hollywood stunt men do such a thing since.

During the next year or so, George stopped by the house several times to call on Ginny. Mom restricted their dating to short visits at the house and a few school functions. It wasn't surprising to see them drift apart, for Ginny wasn't even 14.

Later that night, just before Mom called Paul and me into the house for bed, we overheard the older kids saying they were going to play Post Office in the tent. Before I fell asleep, I said, "Paul, how do you play Post Office?"

He didn't answer me. Surely he's awake, I thought. I wondered if he was still mad at me. Tired and reluctant to repeat the question, I soon fell asleep.

Nighttime wasn't always boring. I had attended second grade for less than two weeks when our family received its first invitation to watch a show on our neighbor's television. At this point in time, the family had very few opportunities for this type of entertainment.

It was a pleasant Saturday in September. We all had eaten dinner, and Ginny was left cleaning and putting away the dishes as well as watching the three youngest. Mom had baked a cake to share. She gathered me, Donna, Paul, and the cake, and grabbed a flashlight.

The Weaver family lived up in the hollow past the end of Newhill Road. The walk took about twenty minutes and we arrived a little before dark.

The TV show that night became the family's favorite—Bonanza, starring the four Cartwrights, Ben, Adam, Hoss, and Little Joe. Not only was it our first time seeing the show, it may also have been the debut of Bonanza. The show first aired (in color) on Saturday, September 12, 1959. Sitting with family and friends, eating cake, and watching the Cartwrights became one of our family's best memories of evening entertainment.

After the TV show, Mom thanked the Weavers for their hospitality and gathered us kids for the walk home, which was longer and more difficult than expected. The road was rocky and we had only one flashlight for all of us in the dark. Even though the road hurt my bare feet, I fondly recall that return trip through the hollow. The night air was cool, and the crickets, frogs and other critters were putting on a show. Occasionally the flashlight would malfunction, which left us nervous and a little afraid. But once we were out of the hollow and on Newhill Road, we had enough moonlight to see us home.

We returned to the Weavers and Bonanza several times that fall and winter. Sometimes, by the time we got home, our clothes and hair would be soaked from the damp air. We learned it was better to wear our shoes, dress warm, and bring an extra flashlight. Shivering and stumping our toes in the dark wasn't fun.

Come springtime, we acquired an old black and white television with rabbit ears. The picture was snowy with poor horizontal and vertical hold, but the sound was good. From then on we seldom had to walk through the hollow at night.

We had great neighbors on Newhill Road. In addition to the Brights and the Weavers, the Walks family lived down the road. When our television was out of commission, we'd watch Saturday morning cartoons with the Walks kids who were close in age. Mighty Mouse, Woody Woodpecker, and Popeye were at the top of our list. Mom especially loved the cartoons and worked hard to make the time to join us.

The Partition

October brought sad and scary times to our home on Newhill Road.

Ronnie, 15, caught a cold that was severe enough to prevent him from attending school. By the end of the second day he had a high fever and was vomiting. Mom tried to bring down his temperature, with no luck. Ronnie was sweating, moaning, and crying for hours.

After a quick visit to Dr. Murray's office, a neighbor drove Mom, Wesley, and Ronnie to the closest hospital, in Gary, West Virginia. Mom stayed with him for two days until he was strong enough to return home.

Back on Newhill Road, Ronnie soon became too sick and weak to even walk to the outhouse. Mom said it was time to call the doctor again. Dr. Murray arrived with his black bag, greeted my mother, and acknowledged the kids milling about. Since we had two bedrooms, each with two beds, Mom had rolled Ronnie's bed into the living room for everyone's comfort and the doctor's examination. The doctor leaned over and asked Ronnie how he was doing. He could only reply with a moan. The doctor stood up, looked at all the kids gathered about, and said, "I would like for everyone except Mrs. Dixon to leave the room."

Mom waved her hands at us. "Out! Out! You kids go on outside and play!"

About thirty minutes later we watched the doctor get in his car and leave. In a flash we were back in the house and huddled around Ronnie's bed.

"From now on, I don't want any of you hanging around this bed," Mom said. "Your brother might be contagious, and I don't want you catchin' what he has. You hear me?" We all acknowledged her request and reluctantly walked away.

Mom and Ginny put up a partition of blankets and sheets, hung from a clothesline to give Ronnie privacy. I thought I overheard Mom telling Ginny that Ronnie might have meningitis (did she say spinal?), a not-so-common childhood disease. The doctor had also said that there wasn't much else he could do for Ronnie. I assumed that he meant the rest was in God's hands.

Mom debated moving Ronnie back into one of the two small bedrooms on the northeast side of the house, but changed her mind. She thought it would be better for his spirits if he stayed on the southwest side. His bed was repositioned facing the windows, so he could take in the afternoon sun setting over the mountains.

During the next two days Ronnie drifted in and out of consciousness, and his neck muscles protruded in a disturbing manner. Mom summoned Dr. Murray, who gave Ronnie another shot and some pills, and told Mom he was taking him to the hospital in Gary again. He told Mom to keep the faith and to stop by the hospital in a day or two.

After he left, Gary asked, "Tommy, do you think Ronnie is going to die?"

"Naw, Ronnie's too young," I told my little brother, "and too strong."

But it was just wishful thinking because I had my doubts.

"Mommy, is Ronnie going to die?"

"I don't know, Tommy. Only God knows."

Mom wasn't much for beating around the bush. She'd either say what was on her mind or say nothing.

Ronnie's condition stabilized and he returned home a week later. Mom, Ginny, and sometimes Paul worked hard at messaging his legs and arms to prevent muscle deterioration. We all tried to go about our business as usual, but I kept peeking behind the partition, hoping to see my big brother sitting up in bed and eating food again. I still wondered if he was going to die. The doctor asked Mom to call him if Ronnie took a turn for the worse.

Thank God that never happened. About a week later Ronnie was sitting up and eating. And even though he wasn't strong enough to walk to the outhouse, he could manage the potty near his bed.

As Thanksgiving in 1959 approached, the clothesline partition came down.

A day or two before Thanksgiving, word was out that volunteers from the company store were delivering food baskets for the needy around Newhill and Trestle Hollow Roads. Most of us kids were playing around the front porch that day, hoping to be the first to spot the food basket delivery truck. Mom was in the kitchen showing Ginny how to shave her legs. It was Ginny's first attempt, and she was concentrating so hard that she didn't see Wesley walk in.

"Don't do that!" Wesley shouted, causing Ginny to drop her razor and almost cut herself. "If you do, big black hairs will grow back!"

It was an old-fashioned country exaggeration that no one but the most innocent and naïve would believe, but it scared Ginny so much that months passed before Mom was able to convince her otherwise.

Around noon Gary came running toward the house, shouting, "It's coming! It's coming!" He had apparently snuck around the side of the mountain to get a heads-up on the competition.

"No fair!" I cried, as he scurried up the porch steps. "You cheated!"

We watched the truck round the bend of the mountain. It stopped at the Walks' house down the road, bypassed the Brights next door, and then stopped in front of our house. One of the men sitting in the pickup's open bed asked, "Is this the Dixon residence?"

"Yeah!" we cried in unison. By now Mom had joined us on the porch.

Another man asked, "How many in the family, ma'am?"

Pausing to count her fingers, Mom replied, "Ten. There's ten of us."

The man looked at his list, shook his head, wrote something down, and then started picking up brown bags full of stuff and placing them into two large cardboard boxes. The men carried the boxes to the front porch and placed them in front of Mom. I tested the box and one of the bags; they were quite heavy. I also noticed the large turkey in one of the boxes. Mom signed a receipt and the men headed for Trestle Hollow.

Each child had been given a large bag of mixed goodies that included candy, nuts, apples, bananas, and oranges. The family was given a big bag of assorted nuts and a large turkey ready for cooking. These nutritious items helped Ronnie's speedy recovery and allowed us to enjoy what I remember as one of our better Thanksgivings.

By the end of 1959, Wesley had completed the demolition and cleanup of all the houses and property on Newhill Road that didn't have renters or squatters. Knowing that he would soon be unemployed, he enlisted in the Army and looked forward to beginning basic training the following spring.

It was a sunny but chilly December day when someone decided to take a few pictures of Wesley. He stood in our front yard with Dad's black Chevy and a big chunk of No. 8 Mountain in the background, wearing a well-ironed and starched pair of black slacks that accentuated a sporty pair of polished white shoes. He wore a colorful, striped shirt, with sleeves rolled almost to the elbows and hands tucked into his pockets for warmth. Elvis and rock-n-roll were topping the charts, and whether Wesley used a dab a of Brylcreem or splash of Vitalis, his hair and shoes were looking the part. It was one picture among many that I came to enjoy while flipping through the family photo albums.

Shame

It was the spring of 1960 and the school year was winding down. I was leaving school with Paul and Donna one day when we came across a young Negro boy riding a bicycle. We were standing near the entrance to Trestle Hollow Road, between the Jenkinjones Elementary School and the United Methodist Church, known as the old Negro church.

"Hi there," Donna said. "What's your name?"

"Henry."

Paul said, "That's a nice bike you have there, Henry."

"Thank you," Henry said politely. "My mommy and daddy gave it to me for Christmas."

We all introduced ourselves to Henry and told him where we lived. He said that he lived in Trestle Hollow. Of course we knew that. He was about a year younger than me, very friendly, and we seemed to hit it off. Thanks to a century of Jim Crow laws and racial segregation, it was my first time talking with a Negro. I'm not sure what held my fascination the most. Was it Henry, the little Negro boy? Or was it his new bicycle with the training wheels?

Paul and Donna turned away and continued walking.

"Tommy, don't you be long now or Mom will be worried," Paul warned.

"Okay."

They took the shortcut home while I stayed chatting with Henry. I told him I had never ridden a bicycle before and didn't know if I could. He said it was easy, especially with the training wheels.

Then he surprised me by offering to let me ride it. I eagerly climbed on and started pedaling along the sidewalk, up and back a couple of times. I felt somewhat insecure, and had it not been for the training wheels I would have toppled over. I thanked Henry for the ride and said that I should be getting home. I watched him ride out of sight, disappearing under the trestle and up into Trestle Hollow.

Having no books to carry, I automatically took the shortcut home. I scrambled up the steep bank on my hands and toes, headed for the

165

railroad tracks. After crossing them, I climbed another steep hill before arriving at Newhill Road.

While attending school at Jenkinjones, I learned to play marbles, a popular game at the time. It was the perfect poor boy's sport—if you were good, it didn't take long to accumulate a lot of marbles. Paul was really good. He won the majority of his contests, taking marbles from first through the sixth graders. Paul didn't discriminate. If a kid was foolish enough to challenge him, he didn't hesitate to take his marbles. "I won these fair and square," he'd say. Paul left for school in the morning with one pocket half full of marbles, and returned with both front pockets brimming.

Paul was my supplier. He fed me enough marbles to play a few games each week. In the beginning I lost them all, and he threatened to cut off my source if I didn't start winning. Pretty soon, Paul had me playing him in practice games at home. By the end of the school year I was winning enough matches to accumulate and maintain a small stash of my own. I no longer needed to borrow marbles from my big brother.

Like I said before, I didn't always take the shortcut home. Sometimes, especially when it was raining, muddy, or when I had a nickel or two burning my pocket, I took the paved road home. This was the winding part of Newhill Road that passed between the post office and company store with a switchback or two. I spent those rare nickels or dimes on candy, chewing gum, or whatever. After leaving the store, I walked the quarter mile along the road chewing my gum, looking for discarded pop bottles, and, if it was the season, picking fruit from trees. The apples and pears were delicious, but pear season brought special precautions, as the rotting fruit attracted dozens of yellow jackets. I learned that if I moved carefully and slowly, I wouldn't be threatened.

After eating food from our brown-bagged lunches at school, some of us tucked the empty bags into our pockets to be reused. On the walk home we'd fill the bags with fruit, eventually gathering enough cooking apples for Mom to make apple pie, apple butter, and applesauce. Mom had wonderful canning skills. My older siblings say she canned for so many years that she could pick boiling hot tomatoes from the water with her bare fingers.

Early one morning, a couple weeks before summer vacation, Paul grabbed my shoulder, spun me around, and said, "Tommy, I think there's someone out front who wants to see you."

Paul was smiling with a cat-that-ate-the-mouse look on his face.

"Who is it?"

"Go see for yourself."

I ran onto the front porch and was shocked to see Henry. He was riding his bicycle up and down Newhill Road, directly in front of our house. This was quite daring and bold. It was rare to see a Negro on Newhill Road, let alone a little Negro boy alone on his bike. Even at eight years old, I knew this visit was out of the ordinary.

Heck, it was only a year or so earlier that Brownie had chased a Negro off Newhill Road, and the man didn't stop running until he was safe in the hollow below. At first we thought Brownie didn't like the smell of Negroes. But we soon realized it was because our dog was in the early stages of the disease that eventually claimed his life.

Did Henry ask for me? I wondered. Had he been waiting for someone to talk to him? Maybe he just wanted to get my attention.

Whatever the reason for his visit, I was happy to see Henry. It was the first time anyone had stopped by to see me. I was excited and I ran down to greet him.

"Henry, what are you doing here?"

"Hi Tommy. I wanted to see you and let you ride my bike again."

Henry dismounted.

"Oh! Okay. Thanks, Henry!"

Excited, I climbed onto his bike and took off on a wobbly spin down the road.

"Don't go too far!" he shouted.

I stopped at that point, turned around, and headed back toward Henry and the coal pile. I repeated the ride a couple more times, and then Henry took a turn. As he rode back and forth, I noticed he was pedaling standing up.

"Hey, can I try it standing up?"

"Sure," he said.

I hopped onto the bike again and sped away. On the way back, I was standing tall and pedaling past Henry when one of the training wheels came loose. Henry and I gathered to assess the damage. Paul, seeing we were having a problem, joined us for a look at the bike. After removing the training wheel, he told us we had lost the nut holding it in place and couldn't use it.

"You can still ride the bike without it." Paul said.

"No, I don't think my daddy would want me to do that," Henry informed us.

"I'll try it," I said. I mounted the bike and, with a good push from Paul, pedaled a few feet before crashing into a ditch.

"Keep trying," Paul said. Then he left us alone.

I tried riding the bike again and again. Henry wouldn't attempt it without both training wheels. Once or twice I almost rode the bike off the edge of the mountain.

Just when I thought I was getting the hang of it, Henry said, "I have to leave now, Tommy."

I pleaded with him. "Just two more times, Henry. Please."

"No, I have to go home now."

Henry and I were soon engaged in a tug of war over his bike. I would ask for another try. He'd say no. I'd ask again. He'd say no again. I'd pull on the bike. He'd pull it back.

Finally, I pushed him and his bike to the ground.

"Okay, nigger," I shouted, "take your bike and go home!"

Henry picked up the training wheel and started pushing his bike home. As I watched him grow smaller in the distance, I felt something strange and powerful deep within myself. It was similar to the feeling back in Elgood when I was caught stealing the snowball cake. In a few short years, I would come to fully understand what it was.

I turned around and walked past the coal bin and up the wooden steps to the porch. Mom was standing there, leaning against a pillar with her hands tucked inside her apron. She was staring at me with strange, sad eyes. I didn't know how long she had been there, and wondered how much she had heard or seen.

"Tommy, you should be ashamed of yourself. If you don't treat your friends right, you won't have any."

I guessed she had seen enough. I turned my back on her and walked into the house.

It was June and we were moving again. Wesley was gone, and Mom had secured a less expensive rental in Falls Mills, Virginia, a small unincorporated community near Bluefield, Virginia.

Despite the wild and crazy things that happened there, Jenkinjones had turned out to be a healthy and inspiring home for the family, and especially for a young man like me. The lessons and fond memories would provide ointment for my growing pains.

While Ginny and Mom were organizing things at the new home, our dear friend and previous neighbor, Gabby Franklin, helped us move our furnishings. Our house on Newhill was empty by the time Paul and I climbed into the back of Gabby's old and battered pickup. I can still recall the smell of hot rubber tires, leaking gasoline, and burning motor oil. With Ronnie and Gabby in the cab, we situated ourselves as best we could amid the last pieces of furniture and other belongings.

As we headed across the winding mountain road, the hot summer air seemed cool as the sweat evaporated from my skin. I recall a unique sadness, as if deserting a friend, but also a feeling of wonderment of what adventures might lie ahead.

VIII

FALLS MILLS
c. 1960

The cape on the hill had seen better days c. 1985.

The Cape on the Hill

"Wow! Look Paul, there's waterfalls over there!" I was pointing toward the creek that snaked its way between the railroad tracks and the paved highway.

"That's why they call this place Falls Mills, Tommy. Didn't you read the sign back there?"

Before my thoughts could ramble any further, Gabby slammed on the brakes, pulled the truck off the road, and stopped. Ronnie hopped from the truck's cab to the ground.

"Oh boy!" I shouted. "Are we going to see the falls?"

"No, we're not going to the falls," Ronnie said. "Paul, you and Tommy get out of the truck. Gabby said this clunker might not be able to get up the hill with all three of us in it."

"What hill?" I asked, as Paul and I jumped to the ground.

"That one," Ronnie said, pointing.

Gabby had very little room to maneuver, so we stood on the side of the road watching him struggle to turn around. Ronnie, Paul, and I followed the truck as Gabby drove it to the bottom of the hill.

This was no ordinary road; not even by Tazewell County standards. Instead, it was very steep with large areas of exposed flat rock and loose stone scattered about. The truck had difficulty climbing, constantly spinning its wheels. But we were making progress. Ronnie was intent on making us stay away from the tires so we wouldn't get hit by loose rock. "Don't walk behind the truck!" he shouted.

About eighty yards from us, I saw Ginny and Mom waiting for us on the front porch of our new house. It was Cape Cod style with two front dormers and seemed quite large looming above us.

As the truck pulled into the front yard, I scanned the terrain by doing a complete 360, noting that we had several neighbors. On the way up the hill, there were three houses and a small trailer on the left. On the right, for most of the way up the hill, there were only cliffs, trees, and a steep drop-off to the highway below. Standing in our front yard, which forked off to the left of the road, I could see that the road, Kevin Lane, continued on up the hill with a big white house situated on the right side of the lane. A day or so later, I would discover that the lane ended about a hundred yards further up the hill, just past the barn belonging to our neighbor in the big white house.

The family spent the rest of the day organizing furniture and establishing designated bedrooms. All I could think of was the falls that was just down the lane and across the highway. The roar of its rushing water, faint in the distance, beckoned me. Mom said there would be plenty of time for play and sightseeing later, and she warned all of us that the falls were very dangerous and that a few children and grownups had drowned there. Upon hearing this, my curiosity was somewhat dampened.

Our house at Falls Mills had a small living room, a large kitchen, and a large bedroom downstairs, plus two medium-sized bedrooms upstairs. Only the farmhouse at Elgood was bigger.

Our living room contained an old, rusty pot-belly stove with its flue and chimney shared by a quaint fireplace (seldom used) in the first of two upstairs bedrooms. An open metal grate on the ceiling above the stove allowed radiant heat to pass through to the second floor rooms. I could tell the stove was quite old, and its first firing that fall provided the proof. Barely noticeable at room temperature, the three-inch long crack near its belly, shaped like a Y, seemed to grin whenever the stove churned out a good bit of heat. Naturally, the magnitude of the grin was proportional to the amount of air being sucked through the crack and, as long as the fuel supply was maintained, the grin expanded with an increasing supply of fresh air and oxygen. Whenever the area surrounding the crack became red-hot, the grin melted into a yawn, providing a good view of the glowing embers inside. In the dead of winter, Mom and Paul were persistent at maintaining a robust fire, the main reason the crack eventually expanded to a dangerous degree.

Some of us enjoyed rubbing a stick of firewood against the red-hot spot just to watch the sparks fly. Mom would get upset when we did this.

"Tommy, you're gonna set the house on fire doin' that. If you don't stop mess'n with that stove, I'm gonna make some sparks fly of my own."

Mom would often invoke some of her old-fashioned superstitions in an effort to restrain her children's behavior: Breaking a mirror would get someone seven years of bad luck, handling frogs could "stick" us with a "passel" of warts, and—in this case—"Gary, if you keep playing around with that fire, you're gonna wet the bed. Now put the wood down, and get away from that stove!"

The warnings didn't do much good. Playing with fire or not, some of us would wet the bed anyway.

The back and front porches extended the width of the house but didn't wrap around. A four-foot tall, hand-operated water pump was anchored to a wooden platform surrounded by a concrete pad. The water was a little rusty at first when Mom pumped it, but within seconds it became clear and turned out to be very tasty. I was in awe; I thought our new water system was the best we ever had. I reached up and gave the pump handle a pull and it wouldn't budge. I gave it a push, then a pull, and it still wouldn't budge. I jumped up and laid my entire body across the pump handle, whereby it slowly lowered me until my knees touched the concrete pad. The pump handle had almost supported my weight.

"Maybe you'll be able to work it next year, Tommy," Ronnie said encouragingly.

In the back yard, about sixty feet from the pump, was our outhouse. I heard Mom tell Ronnie that first night that he and Paul would have to dig and rebuild a new one before winter. Since we had arrived so late, she also said we would be "breaking ground in a hurry" to put in a vegetable garden in preparation for her late summer and early fall canning.

To the left of the house was a narrow strip of yard that contained a small pile of coal for heating and cooking. A steep bank led down to an overgrown lot that was once a garden.

The next day was a very busy one. Everyone, except the youngest, had chores to do. At eight years old, my chores were mostly to stay out of the way. All I wanted to do was explore the terrain. Again, Mom said we weren't allowed to do any exploring until Ronnie or Paul was finished with his chores and one of them was available to go with me.

So, before further exploration of my surroundings, I met and said hello to some of my new neighbors. I found out that Edgar and Eve Wells were responsible for informing Mom and Wesley that our house was available. I also learned that our Aunt Clara had been living here just a few months earlier. Many years earlier, my mother had tended to the Wells children—Lloyd, Willard, and Janet—as they played in their baby cribs along with Wesley, Ronnie, and Ginny. All of them were still friends. Now, as our new neighbors, they were kind enough to offer their help when needed.

While surveying my immediate surroundings, I noticed a large crawl space underneath the house. Access was easy at the coal pile. I was exploring deep under the house, when I heard family voices through the floorboards.

I took a rock and tapped it against the floor above my head. *Thump-thump a thump-thump*! I could still hear them talking. I repeated my knocking. *Thump-thump a thump-thump*!

Then, I heard a reply. *Thump-thump*!

"Yes!" I said with excitement, before scurrying out from under the house. I ran into the living room, thrilled that someone had acknowledged my presence under the floor. Mom and Paul were standing there.

"Did you hear me?"

"Yeah, was that you banging Tommy?" Mom asked.

"Yeah," I said, "where was my banging coming from?"

Paul said, "It sounded like it was coming from under the stairway, there."

As we looked over at the stairs, we noticed a small hinged access door located under the stairwell leading to the upstairs bedrooms. We opened the door to find an empty crawl space for storage. No one had noticed it before.

As I squatted inside the compartment, Paul stuck his head inside and looked around, saying, "You know, we could cut a trap door in the flooring here, and make it a secret escape hatch."

"Wow! When can we do that?"

Paul said the secret hatch would have to wait. Mom was lining up chores for us all. Yeah, maybe chores that involved more exploring, I thought.

Early the next day, Gary and I were milling about our front porch when I heard the freight train whistle blowing. The family and I had heard the whistle the previous day, but we were so busy moving in that we didn't pay much attention to it. On the other side of the hollow and falls below, I saw the train come in to view. I counted four engines churning at the pace of a plow horse. Even at my age, I understood they were hauling a heavy load. I watched as box cars, flat cars, and coal cars (heaped high with coal) passed by. It was a long trip with many winding turns that began at the Bishop mines southwest of Falls Mills, to Bluefield, West Virginia, and on to who knows where else. I had watched freight trains before, but never one this long.

"Hey Gary," I called out, "let's count the railroad cars to see how many there are."

Gary said, "Okay. One, two ..."

"No Gary," I interrupted. "Not out loud. Let's count them to ourselves and see what number we come up with."

"Oh," he said. Gary pointed his fingers at the train and began his counting all over.

I had counted to twenty eight when Gary jumped off the porch. "There's too many, Tommy. I'm going out back to see what Paul is doing."

Gary's unbridled energy and short attention span would prove to be a source of mild consternation by many in the family.

Rain and thunderstorms were some of the best times to count cars. While I was counting cars, Ronnie or Paul swung the little ones (David,

Debbie and sometimes Gary) around one of the porch columns into the rain and back onto the porch again. Heck, even I was strong enough to give two-year-old David a somewhat reckless whirl about the columns and into the rain, which he loved. But, after almost hurting him, I was told not to try it again.

I counted five engines and 49 cars by the time the two red cabooses came into view. I had no sooner joined my brothers in the back yard, when we heard the loud rumbling of an automobile coming up the hill. I ran back to the front yard to see if we had visitors. Paul and Gary joined me, and we waited for the first glimpse of the unusually loud vehicle. By the time it had crested Kevin Lane, the entire family was standing by the porch to watch it coast to a stop just inches from the steps.

"Well, it still runs and it sure can climb a hill," Ronnie said, stepping from the car.

Ronnie had driven home—without a license—Dad's 1946 Chevy. Sitting in our front yard, it looked bigger than usual.

"Where on earth are we going to keep it?" Mom asked.

"I was thinking we could park it by the side of the house near the coal pile," Ronnie suggested. "If we give it a new muffler and adjust the valves, it'll almost be good as new."

With Mom's permission, Ronnie maneuvered the Chevy back and forth several times to get it backed into place beside the house. He then locked the car and walked inside. Gary and I just stood there looking at the car. Before following her son into the house, Mom said, "I don't want you kids messing around or playing on that car. It's not a toy." Duly warned, we walked away, redirecting our thoughts.

The Chevy stayed parked beside the house for several months. The following winter, Ronnie and some of his friends finally decided to repair it, but their effort was too late. The engine block was cracked. Evidently, someone had forgotten to put enough antifreeze in the radiator for winter storage. We eventually had to pay someone five dollars to haul it to a salvage yard.

Unlike some of the properties around Tazewell County, Mom wasn't about to keep a junked car sitting in the yard.

Pocket change was scarce enough for our mother, let alone us kids. The word allowance was rarely spoken. However, pennies were available to be earned (on-the-bottle). My hankering for Tootsie Rolls and licorice sticks and the latest edition of my favorite comic books led me to take regular walks along Falls Mills Road. We always found plenty of discarded pop bottles there. Each regular bottle fetched me two cents, and a quart sized one brought a nickel. We redeemed the bottles at Ward's Market, a small country store on Falls Mills Road, just a hundred yards from the bottom of Kevin Lane.

I would usually cash in enough bottles to buy a ten cent comic book. Superman was my favorite hero. Three years later, around March 1963, Superman would be dethroned by the first (#1) issue of Spider Man—and it only cost me twelve cents (12¢). If it was a good week, I would have enough to buy a box of Cracker Jacks and a comic book. Like most kids, I especially liked the toy prizes stuffed inside the box. Once I got a miniature plastic bowling ball and pin set. The ball and pins came in halves which had to be detached and snapped together to form a complete unit. Before that day, Gary and I had never bowled. This small toy provided weeks of amusement until we lost it through the many cracks and knot holes of our bowling alley (the front porch floor).

A few years later, due to new child safety regulations, only paper surprises were found inside a box of Cracker Jacks. Many in my age group weren't too happy with that.

Ward's Market was a convenient stop-off for those living nearby. In addition to common food items, Ward's offered access to a telephone for families like ours that had none. A table and chairs were supplied for the regular customers, guests, or anyone driving by and wanting a sip of coffee, soda pop, or just a good old-fashioned jawing or gossip session. Mr. and Mrs. Ward were often the first to be notified of medical, fire, or other emergencies. Our family was among a few local families that had established credit accounts at Ward's, and even though we were sometimes two or three months behind in payments, they never cut off our credit.

Mom almost always sent one or two of us to the store for her. Every week or two she made an itemized list, and the Wards would fill the order and mark the items on our account. I remember the first time I actually read the list before handing it over. Cigarettes were at the top of the list. After Pall Mall's, filtered Winstons were Mom's favorite. She wasn't allowed to smoke her own brand when Dad was around; his unfiltered Camel's had to do. Mom tried her best to limit her addiction to two or three packs per week, which was too often a losing battle for her. Not knowing about the cancer threat, I didn't mind aiding her in her habit.

However, looking further down the list, I was embarrassed to see the fourth item. Kotex—I knew what that meant. Purchasing cigarettes for my mother was one thing, but having to pick up my mother's and sister's feminine hygiene products and carry them home was downright unnerving. Before leaving the store, I made sure such a recognizable item was situated as far down inside the bag as possible. Heck, if any of my classmates had seen such a thing, I would never be able to face them again.

Wards Market had changed ownership by 1987.

The Falls & Dam

A day or two later we caught up with most of the chores. Several in the family decided to take a trip to the falls. Mom stayed at home with the youngest, Debbie and David.

Ronnie and Ginny led the way down Kevin Lane. We were given caution when we had to cross over Falls Mills Road to the bank of the creek. Traffic was sparse, but the curve was sharp, blind, and potentially deadly. Falls Mills received its name from the mill that once sat near the falls. Considering the location, it must have been a very quaint and beautiful scene.

We followed the well-worn path from the creek bank to the nearest falls, and as we approached the creek, I couldn't stop the sudden rush of fear and adrenaline that shot cold chills up and down my spine. The sight and sound of the water rushing toward and over the rocks was unlike anything I had ever experienced before. I had no idea it would be so scary.

We counted three major waterfalls, each separated by large rock outcroppings. Gary and I must have stood petrified at the water's edge with our mouths hanging open, until Ronnie's command broke through the roar of falling water: "Follow me, and do as I do!"

As Paul, Donna, and I watched from the bank, Ronnie put Gary on his back. Then he and Ginny, using a wooden plank found nearby as a bridge, walked over the rushing water to the first rocky outcropping about ten feet away.

Once there, they turned around and beckoned for the rest of us to follow their lead.

"Come on, just look at where you're stepping and not at the water," Ronnie shouted.

"Yeah, it's easy," Ginny said.

Donna and Paul scrambled across the plank with ease. Now it dawned on me—I was the only one left on the bank. Not wanting to be the little coward, I swallowed the lump in my throat and walked the plank to the

182

other side. I felt excited and received some praise for my accomplishment.

"Well, that's the easy part," Ronnie said. "Look where we're going next."

He pointed to a log that had washed downstream from a recent flood. The log had stopped at the falls creating a 15-foot bridge between the first and second rocky outcroppings. The water flowing under it was even more fierce and intimidating than the first leg of the journey. I stood there looking at the log, the cascading water, and the 20 to 30 foot drop-off below.

"I'm not crossing that," I said.

Donna said, "Me neither."

"Oh, come on you guys!" Ronnie shouted in frustration. "This is easier than the plank. I know you can do it! Just watch me!"

As before, Ronnie picked up Gary and carried him across the log with Ginny not far behind. As Gary slid from his back to the dry bedrock, he called across, "See how easy it is!"

Paul, Donna, and I stood motionless staring at the water while Ronnie waved at us with encouragement.

"You all can do it too," he shouted above the roar of the falling water. "This log's dry and not slippery! You're both too big to carry! Now come on across, or you're forever going to be a chicken, and I'm not going to bring you here anymore!"

Even Paul, at 13, seemed intimidated for a few seconds. Then, Paul said something that made a lot of sense: "We've walked across many smaller logs and trees without slipping or falling. This one shouldn't be any different just because it has running water under it. Come on!"

With that, Paul, me, then Donna, slowly and carefully inched our way across. We finally made it and were close to the center of the water falls. We stood upon large rock formations that provided a great view of the surrounding area. I could look a hundred yards directly upstream (in a southerly direction) and see the crossing bridge at Wards store. To the east were another falls and a steep bank that led to the railroad tracks above. Facing north, or downstream, I saw treacherous rocks directly below my feet and churning whitewater that leveled and pooled before winding its way downstream for Pocahontas, Bramwell, and other small towns.

Near flood stage water at the falls in Falls Mills, VA.

As we admired the view, I noticed that one more crossing would put us onto the opposite bank of the stream. But, this one did not seem to have any plank or log to use.

A few minutes later, Ronnie and Paul decided they would challenge the rushing water at the top of the falls to reach the eastern bank. I wondered how they were going to do it. Was I listening to two crazy people? While Ginny kept an eye on us younger ones, Ronnie and Paul rolled up their pants to the knees, then climbed and crossed a few rocks until they were at the edge of the rushing water.

Facing the far bank, Paul jumped upon Ronnie's back, and they entered the rushing water as one. Now, near double the weight, they would less likely be swept away by the current. Were Ronnie's legs strong enough to support Paul and navigate the swift water and slippery rocks just inches from the edge of a raging torrent? It didn't look easy, and I remember being so scared. Once or twice Ronnie almost lost his footing, but they made it across. I hardly heard the cheers and praise from my siblings. All I could think about was how dangerous their return journey would be.

"No Ronnie!" I shouted. "Don't do it again!"

I was so happy when they decided it was too risky and didn't come back the way they went. Instead, they scampered up the steep bank and followed the railroad tracks to the bridge crossing, and north along Falls Mills Road to pick us up. After what we had just seen Ronnie and Paul accomplish, the return crossing of a tree and plank no longer seemed insurmountable.

Never-the-less, when we got home that afternoon, some of us felt like we had done something special. Donna shouted, "Mom, Ronnie gave Paul a piggyback ride across the water falls!"

Once Mom understood what Ronnie had done, she said, "Ronnie, don't you ever pull such a stupid stunt again. You're supposed to be watching out for the younger ones."

Ronnie was lucky. If he had been a little younger and smaller, he may have gotten the switch.

Our first summer living in Falls Mills was loaded with fun, adventure, and pleasant surprises. In addition to becoming more familiar and comfortable with the falls, we made several explorations into nearby woods and mountains.

Below our house we found steep cliffs with large rock outcroppings we could use as shelter from rain or snow. The sheltered areas contained several small cave-like tunnels often used as dens by foxes or other wild animals. We rarely saw them. Maybe it was just a glimpse or two, but we knew they were in there. Freshly chewed bones provided more than enough evidence of their presence.

We took advantage of vine swings to soar high above the banks near the traffic on Falls Mills Road. We found more vine swings among the cliffs and boulders on the mountain above our neighbor's house. These areas provided endless possibilities when playing cowboys and Indians.

Our neighbor's barn was situated at the end of Kevin Lane and near the entrance to the north woods. Paul thought this would be a great place to explore. Once he, Gary, and I were inside, I reminded them of the snake incident back in Elgood.

Paul said, "You're right Tommy, this looks like a great place for snakes to hang out." We hauled our asses out of there and never went back. Foolishly, we never stopped to think about snakes as we climbed about the rocks and cliffs.

From our back porch and well pump, we could look beyond our outhouse and see a large two acre fenced livestock area that occasionally housed a pig, pony, sheep, or goat, depending on the latest occupier's fancy. A hundred yards further was an empty house. It sat low to the ground near the bottom of a gully and was the last house this side of the mountain. We explored the vacant house and found it could be in better shape than ours with a little tender loving care. What a waste! A few months later, we heard rumors that a murder-suicide had occurred there a decade earlier. I thought, No wonder it wasn't lived in.

About a quarter mile north of the vacant house was the wooded area and cliffs I mentioned earlier. Two hundred feet to the left and southwest were about ten acres of fenced-in hills and valleys used for grazing cattle. We would spend many hours in this cow pasture sliding down the hills on makeshift cardboard box sleds, shooting homemade bows and arrows, and harassing the big black bull that was only trying to covet his cows, all the while avoiding the cow pies. On the rare occasion we wore or tracked cow pie into the house, someone else was fast to notice. Gary and I got the switch, at least once, for doing so.

Very early one morning, Paul and I dug up night crawlers for fish bait. With Mom's permission, we took our single homemade fishing pole and headed for the Falls Mills Dam. By walking across the cow pasture, we cut about a quarter mile off the trip. I recall making up a poem as we walked that morning, sharing it in earnest with my big brother. It was an eight-year-old boy's play on words and sounded something like this:

"The dam boy went to the dam to get some dam water.
The dam man said he couldn't have any dam water.
So, the dam boy went home without his dam water."

When we arrived at the dam, we took a seat under the pavilion and watched people fish from the rented canoes. I wanted so badly to do that. But since it cost money, and I didn't know how to swim, we settled for fishing at the stepped falls below the dam. Heck, even Paul hadn't learned to swim.

About eleven o'clock that morning, Paul and I stepped off the paved road to scramble through the bushes and grass on the steep path that led down to the foot of the dam. There, underneath a heavy canopy of tree branches and leaves, we set about taking turns holding our fishing line in the water. Paul adjusted our last remaining red and white plastic float-ball so that the worm was about ten inches below the surface of the water. We could barely see the small fish nibbling at the night crawler. Paul would occasionally pull up a fish only to toss it back in. "Too small," he'd say. I, on the other hand, wasn't having any luck. The fish could smell me better than I could see or feel them.

Thirty minutes and two tossed fish later, Paul wanted to move to a different location downstream. We exited the tree canopy to discover a darkened sky with storm clouds. Paul spotted what seemed like a good location. We prepared the bait and threw our line back into the water.

To the west, we heard a loud rumble. About that time, Paul jerked his pole and line out of the water to reveal the capture of the largest fish we had ever seen alive. I don't know what type of fish it was but it wasn't a catfish, and it was three times the size of the others.

"Wow! Three more of those," I said, "and we can feed the whole family."

"Yep, probably could," he replied. Paul smiled, baited the hook again, and handed me the pole. "Okay, your turn!"

Thunder boomed followed by a flash of lightening that split the dark clouds like yellow chalk on a blackboard.

"No, I'm bad luck," I complained with shaky hands. "You keep fishing and I'll guard our catch."

Thunder boomed again, but closer. The wind was picking up, and raindrops left ripples on the muddy water. All of a sudden, Paul pulled out another fish. "Looks like another keeper," he said.

"Two more," I said, "and everyone'll have a piece of fish on their plate tonight." Paul prepared the line again and we waited. The rain was picking up now, sprinkling our shirts with wet spots, just like Mom when ironing our clothes.

In Jenkinjones we could often guess when serious rain would hit. But now the tall trees were hiding our view of the main storm front, and I was beginning to get a little nervous.

"Paul, do you ...?"

Before I could finish my question, Paul snapped up another one—big enough to eat. "This is great," I said, as the rain began soaking our clothes.

By now the clouds were opening up on the two of us, and the tiny hairs on the back of my neck started goose-stepping from a half dozen or more vicious lightning strikes.

Paul was concerned too. "Okay Tommy, let's go."

Paul handed me the pole and gathered up the three fish. We ran up the bank to the road where it quickly became obvious: if we didn't find shelter soon, we would be soaked long before we got home. We paused under a tree for shelter, but dashed back into the rain when lightning struck nearby.

"Shit!" Paul shouted. "I should have known better. Tommy, you're never supposed to stand under a tree during a lightning storm."

Paul said he was worried about his wallet getting wet. I, on the other hand, didn't have that problem.

"Paul, what age do you have to be to carry a wallet?"

"I don't think age matters," he said, "people carry wallets to keep their money in."

"Oh. How much money you got in your wallet, Paul?"

"None."

"Well, when I get enough money, I'm gonna buy a wallet to keep my money in too."

"Yeah, you should do that Tommy."

Seconds later, we were soaked. We had pushed our luck and Mother Nature too far. She had gotten the best of us. But at least we were bringing home fish for dinner.

I began to worry if Mom would be upset with us.

"Hey Paul, do you think Mom will put the switch away when she sees the nice fish we have?"

He didn't hear me. The storm was making too much noise.

Mom was so happy with the fish we caught that day. If she had planned a whipping, she must have changed her mind real quick when she saw those fish.

Upper section of The Falls Mills Dam

Dirty Jobs

That summer I participated with the family in planting our first garden. It was located directly behind the house and took up almost half the back yard. Initially it was a big deal for me, since I had been too young to have productive input into any previous family plots. Mom decided to keep the crop area small by not tilling the large lower section of the property until the following year. This meant we could break ground by hand instead of hiring a horse, plow, or tractor. Mom, Ronnie, Ginny, and Paul did most of the bull work. A mattock, hoe, rake, and a spade shovel were their main tools.

My major chore was raking and separating sod and rock from the dirt and depositing these into piles along the garden's fence. In the beginning this was fun and gave me a sense of accomplishment. Minutes later, my hands began to burn.

"Mom, my hands are blistered," I said. "I don't think I can work anymore."

Ronnie and Mom looked at my blisters. Ronnie said, "You're not skipping work that easy, Tommy. You can still do other things."

So, I spent the rest of the first day loading rocks into buckets and dumping them elsewhere. I think that was my first day of real hard labor.

The next day was easier for me. Although I still had to fill buckets and dump some rocks, I was given proper instructions and enjoyed going through the process of planting various seeds. That first year we planted six rows of corn. I remember Mom saying we needed at least four rows of corn for "good pollination" to take place between the rows. No pollination—no corn. We also planted potatoes, cabbage, green beans, green peppers, tomatoes, leaf lettuce, carrots, scallions, beets, and radishes.

For the next several weeks I was required to hoe and weed my part of the garden. I was even given my own special hoe with a four foot (broken) handle that I could more easily maneuver around the corn stalks. At one point, when I stopped getting blisters, I thought I was tougher and ready to take on more responsibilities. I would soon have that chance.

Come October the vegetable garden had been picked, cut, and cleared. The soil had turned out a healthy batch of crops, and most of it had already been through Mom's canning process.

With the arrival of fall, Mom decided that our outhouse was full of it. That meant a new one had to be dug. At the time, I was under the delusion that Mom, with her age and experience, had become an expert on outhouses: She could walk into a new, unused, outhouse and: 1) calculate the total volume, 2) factor in if we were going to have a lean, average, or robust food supply, 3) guesstimate the average volume per visit along with the number of visits per day, 4) divide the total volume by the volume used per day, and finally, 5) multiply that number by the appropriate Human Fecal Decomposition Rate Factor (HFDRF) from the rate tables listed in the American Standard Outhouse Manufacturers (ASOM) engineering handbook, to finally arrive at the lifespan (in days) of the outhouse.

Yes—or so I thought.

With less than an eighth grade education, Mom couldn't even begin to approach a scenario that far-out. But, I'll bet someone, somewhere, has. In jest, the family has handed down mountain rumors saying the average outhouse, when used regularly, will last an average of two thousand and eight days. I'm not sure why or how that number came about, other than the fact that the number equates to exactly five and a half years.

For health reasons, I think it was fortunate for us that the current outhouse was located downhill and more than fifty feet from the well. Looking back, that still could have been too close.

In addition to being full, this outhouse was somewhat unstable. On one occasion, while doing my business there, a heavy wind began to blow and I imagined myself inside an accordion as it was being played. All the more reason for expediency, I would guess.

The privy was about thirty feet from the back property fence. That left plenty of room to move it closer to the property line. Once Mom and Ronnie had studied the terrain for a few minutes, they settled on the right place to dig. Initially we were going to double the occupancy by making the new one a two-holer, but Mom said we didn't have the money to buy extra lumber. Somehow we would have to make do with what we had.

It was on a Saturday morning, about ten, when Ronnie and Paul cleared away the grass, marked and measured the spot, and commenced digging the hole. I wanted to dig too but realized there wasn't enough room for more than one digger at a time.

Ronnie said, "Tommy, you and Gary stand back before you get this pick stuck in your head." In addition to the mattock and shovel, a pick was an essential tool for this job.

Once the hole was about a foot deep, Ronnie and Paul took turns digging and shoveling. They tossed some of the dirt from the new hole to a spot near the back of the old privy. That way the dirt would be close and available for back filling what little remained of the old hole. Most of the soil excavated from the hole would be packed around its perimeter, forming a slight mound to raise the privy's foundation, channel away rainwater, and prevent flooding of the pit and groundwater contamination. Sod and topsoil were saved and later spread about the new outhouse to facilitate the growth of new grass—or more weeds, which was generally the case.

About two feet down, my brothers encountered several large rocks. They also began to sweat and called for Ginny to bring them more drinking water. Even though Donna and I were born Aquarians, Ginny seemed to bear most of the water. A foot deeper, they ran into even more rocks. They contemplated digging at a new location, but decided against that, recalling "a bird in the hand is worth two in the bush." At this point their enthusiasm began to wane, forcing them to take more breaks and allowing Gary and me to do a little digging and shoveling of our own. As it turned out, my hands weren't as tough as I thought. Gary and I got blisters faster than a dog can scratch a flea.

I thought it might be due to the way I was holding the tools, but then Ronnie and Paul showed us their blisters. I let out a jaw dropping, "Oh … my … God!"

I don't know how my brothers finished digging the hole that day. I'm sure they would have liked the convenience of a new pair of thick leather gloves. But money was tight, and the blisters would heal when the job was done. In spite of the pain they kept digging, and using two flashlights they finished about an hour after sunset. The hole ended up being about three feet long by four feet wide and six feet deep.

The next day we poured several bags of lime followed by several shovels of dirt into the old pit to speed up decomposition. We left the rest of the job to Mother Nature.

Next, my brothers used a flat blade shovel and claw hammer to strip away the asphalt siding and provide access to the wood underneath. With the structure's skin removed, they were able to use a sledge hammer and crowbar to separate the planks from the supporting timbers.

Finally, there was work for me. Ronnie handed me the claw hammer and told me to get busy removing the old rusty nails from the planks as they were removed. You should have heard those rusty nails scream; they had been there for so long, they hated to leave. It was a slow process: an hour for me and an hour for them to separate the supporting planks. At this time, Ronnie realized that some of the wood was just too rotten to reuse. We'd have to buy, borrow, or steal wood from somewhere.

Well, it just happened that our neighbor had a few pieces of good lumber from his barn that painted a nice new face onto the structure. In addition to the wood, Willard and Lloyd supplied new shingles for the roof, and none of it cost us a penny.

Reframing and reassembling the new structure took longer than expected. The oak, hickory, and ash planks were old and weathered which added to their hardness. Ronnie and Paul bent more than a few nails trying to penetrate the tough planks, and they let loose more than a few curse words that day, too. It was late Sunday afternoon when they put the last screw into the last hinge of the new outhouse door.

But wait! All the work wasn't done yet. For more than eight hours, a family of nine didn't have an outhouse. During that time the chamber pots inside the house were filling up. Now they needed to be emptied, and lucky Ginny had chamber pot duty. We all laughed as we watched her carry them, one at a time, to the new outhouse. She held the containers (Maxwell House coffee cans) at arm's length and straight in front of her. Each step was deliberate, and her eyes were intense, focused on the sloshing liquid inside. She was being funny with that clothespin clamped to her nose—yet careful not to spill a drop.

Our new outhouse wasn't given any one particular name; instead it was called different names at different times, some dating back to our grandparents. In the dead of winter, it was often referred to as The Shiver Shack. In the heat of the summer, The Toxin Tank or The Stench Bench was appropriate. Or, during other times of the year, The Reading Room was somewhat accurate due to a more tolerable sensory environment, most likely.

Two years later, my first thoughts of a sexual nature occurred in The Reading Room. I was thumbing through the shoe section of the Sears Roebuck Catalogue, admiring and dreaming about the handsome, black leather engineering boots so popular with teenagers and kids around my age, the ones with squared-off toes and belted silver buckles near the upper arch. While deciding which page to tear off for my personal use, I stumbled into the women's underwear section and found myself enthralled by the pictures of the young and attractive models. They had always been there. Now—out of the blue—the catalogue provided a new and titillating appeal. No wonder those pages were the last to disappear.

Rude Awakenings

That fall, Daisy wrote to inform us she had given birth to a baby boy. Chester Wright Junior was my first nephew, and it would be some time before I would see him.

Paul, Donna, Gary and I were still adjusting to the schooling protocol and classmates in Jenkinjones when we were forced to start adjusting all over again at Falls Mills Elementary and Grade School. Again, we were pulled out of a school in one state and placed into a new school in another.

My third grade teacher's name was Mrs. Lawrence. I especially remember the two paintings hanging on opposite walls of her classroom. They were large, well-framed reproductions of Thomas Lawrence's *Pinky* and Thomas Gainsborough's *Blueboy*. I wasn't too sure I was going to like her class. She seemed very strict—and mean.

This stressful adjustment period could have prompted me to experience a series of reoccurring bad dreams. On at least three occasions I dreamt that I went to school missing one or more items of clothing. In one dream, it was my shoes. In others, it was my shirt or belt. The dreams finally produced an undesirable effect.

One morning, Ronnie, Ginny, Paul, Donna, Gary and I were running late as we dashed down the road to catch our school bus. Sure enough, as we approached the bus stop by the little walnut tree at the intersection of Mudfork Road and Falls Mills Road, we saw our bus fading into the distance. We could either miss school for the day, or walk a little more than a mile. On this day the weather was cool, so we walked.

When the principle opened my classroom door for me, I felt so embarrassed. Every eye was upon me. As if being late for school wasn't bad enough, I unzipped my winter jacket to find that I had nothing on underneath but a tee shirt. After visiting the outhouse (Reading Room) that morning, I had forgotten to put on my over-shirt before leaving the house. Wearing a shirt without a collar violated the dress code. In a near panic, I zipped up my jacket and went to my seat.

Mrs. Lawrence and a few classmates asked several times throughout the day why I was wearing my coat indoors. Although I was burning up inside that coat, I insisted on telling them I was cold. That day lasted way too long for me.

I don't have much memory of school that fall. Nature and the wild were always beckoning and distracting me. There were so many places around Falls Mills for a kid my age to explore. Without a little common sense, kids could get into a lot of trouble.

One of those intriguing places was located about halfway between Kevin Lane and Ward's Store. It was a flat concrete wall situated on a small rocky ledge about fifteen feet above Falls Mills Road. The wall was about eight feet tall and faced eastward overlooking the creek, railroad, and bridge at Post Road. Normally covered by vines, poison ivy, and other weeds, the mysterious looking wall became quite noticeable in the winter.

From the moment I saw it, it began to stimulate my wild imagination. The fact that it had an unusual and unnatural looking rectangular recess resembling a door just added to the mystery. As in the story "Ali Baba and the Forty Thieves," I began to imagine it was a secrete passageway that opened to the secret password, "Open Sesame!" For a short period of time, I imagined stumbling through this passageway into a dark cavern containing huge mounds of gold, diamonds, and other gems.

Fortunately, my fantasy was obliterated that first winter when I finally summoned the courage to actually climb the cliff and examine the wall up-close. Once I had scaled the steep cliff to the narrow rocky platform at its base, I poked and prodded every inch of the wall and door-like recess to see if it would open and let me in. When that failed, I called-out, "Open Sesame!" When the wall still didn't respond, I spoke several other commands before cursing it in as many ways as I could think of. After more than an hour of communing unsuccessfully with the wall, I was willing to put the fantasy to rest. I never ventured there again, and I don't recall having anymore dreams about it.

Ronnie entered 11th grade and Ginny entered the 9th at Graham High School in Bluefield, Virginia. For Ronnie, the books were too difficult, the teaching too fast, and the changing of classes too hectic.

So, sometime in November, Ronnie gave up. Barely 17, he dropped his books onto the principle's desk and said that he was quitting.

"Ronnie, don't give up now, you only have two years to go."

"No, I've made up my mind. It's just not sinking in." Ronnie quit school for good that day and never went back.

Now that he didn't have to worry about getting up and going to school, Ronnie started coming home late and sleeping late. It appeared he didn't have enough constructive things to do with his time. He tried getting a job but wasn't having much luck.

One time the Sheriff and his deputy stopped by the house. They asked Mom where Ronnie had been the evening before. Mom stood at the door, red-faced, and told the law her son had been home all night. As soon as the sheriff left, Mom said, "Ronnie, I'm not lying for you again. You better get your act together—or else."

A few days past, and just when Ronnie was seriously thinking of getting his act together, he was awakened by Mom: "Ronnie, wake up! Wake up, Ronnie! Someone's here to see you!"

My big brother opened his tired, bloodshot eyes to see the sheriff standing over him. The sheriff had one hand on his revolver and the other hand clenching his cudgel. It was an eye-opening experience for Ronnie, because a few days later he was in Bluefield eyeball to eyeball with an Army Recruiter. He put his signature to the dotted line and was told he would be leaving for basic training sometime the following February.

I was very young when I gave up on the tooth fairy. (It must have been about the same time I stopped believing in Santa Clause.) I think it was my mother's mother who said, "It's not safe to pull baby teeth before they're ready." The reasoning was, if you pull them too soon, you could leave a hole big enough for infection to set in.

Well, I had been carrying two loose teeth in my mouth for several days, and they were really beginning to bug me. Chewing and eating were so uncomfortable, I began probing and messaging the teeth and the surrounding gums in an effort to hasten their removal.

Once I had one of the teeth good-n-loose, I approached my mother as she sat at the kitchen table. "Mom, I have a loose tooth; do you think it's ready to be pulled?"

Like pieces of a jigsaw puzzle, she had the contents of a bag of pinto beans scattered out on the table. Mom was performing the old-fashioned ritual of separating the bad beans and pea stones from the good beans.

"Tommy, I just washed my hands. You'll haf-ta wiggle it for me so I can see it."

I stuck my index finger into my mouth, pushed down on the loosest tooth, and moved it back and forth for her to see.

"Hum," she said, staring into my mouth. "I don't know, Tommy, can you grab it with your fingers and hold it tight?"

As soon as she saw me grip the loose tooth she smacked my hand. I grimaced and groaned as I staggered back. But there really was no pain, only surprise when I felt the loose tooth rolling around inside my mouth.

As I spit the tooth into my hand, Mom said, "Now, when the other teeth get that loose, you'll know what to do."

My mother had just given me a lesson about pain: the anticipation can be worse than the pain itself.

It was the night before Christmas. Mom had scraped, begged, and pinched all she could to buy at least one present for each of us. While the little ones slept, Mom and Ginny finished wrapping the presents. Ronnie was getting dressed for a night out with his buddies. Around ten o'clock, a car honked its horn out front. It was our neighbors, Willard and Lloyd Wells, letting Ronnie know they were ready to celebrate.

Early Christmas morning, we all rushed downstairs to see what Santa had placed under the tree. I'm not sure what my present was that year. Most likely it was a badly-needed pair of shoes. I remember everyone except Ronnie being there to open presents. That's when

Mom said he had a little accident early that morning and would be sleeping late.

Ronnie came downstairs for a late breakfast wearing a large bandage around his head. Apparently, the bandage was hiding ten stitches in his head, which had been cracked open when it forcefully encountered the unpadded armrest of Lloyd's car after it had gone air-born off the side of the road stopping abruptly in a ditch.

Now, with less than two months to go, Mom was beginning to wonder who—or what—was going to catch Ronnie first: would it be The Law, Uncle Sam, or The Grimm Reaper?

IX

FALLS MILLS
c. 1961

Daisy (23) with little Chester (1) c. 1961.

Discipline and the Third Grade

From the letters we received from Wesley, we gathered he was doing well in the Army. Having escaped the clutches of the surrounding counties, he had traveled about other states, made a few good friends, and was now taking advantage of opportunities to see the world. He was based in Germany since October of 1960 and, since he loved it there, was hoping to stay for two more years. Ronnie was keenly aware of his big brother's military success and was looking forward to his own challenges and rewards from serving his country.

I remember nothing about the day Ronnie left home to join the Army. I'm sure it was a solemn occasion for us all. In spite of their occasional tricks and teasing, I was extremely fond of my older brothers. I looked up to them, respected their wishes, and considered them good role models. Rather naively, I would add.

Ronnie reported to basic training on February 14, 1961. I learned later that he was assigned to Fort Jackson, S.C. where he completed his basic and advanced military training. Sometime in the spring he was shipped to Fort Dix, N.J., and performed two weeks of KP before being shipped to Berlin.

After Ronnie left home, my schoolwork and what little affection I had for my third grade teacher plummeted. I was mostly a shy and somewhat introverted student. Much of my shyness could have been attributed to my father's imprisonment. More than likely, my teachers and other key members of the school administration were the only ones privy to such personal information. However, I couldn't stop thinking otherwise. I thought that everyone knew my father was doing time for attempted murder, and—at least for a while—that made me feel like curling up into a ball like one of those black and brown fuzzy worms that we played with so much. If I could, I would have disappeared.

Class participation is always helpful in getting good grades. However, since I was so obsessed with not drawing attention to myself, I never raised my hand in class. My report card reflected it, too.

How shy was I?

Okay, I was so shy I only raised my hand when I had to go to the bathroom. Even then, it would have to be a stomach-cramping emergency. I was even too shy to blow my nose in class, if you can believe that.

Mom sent all her boys to school with a handkerchief in their back pocket. "Now use it," she'd say, having just shoved a clean one into my back pocket, "and I better not catch you wipe'n that stuff on your shirt sleeves!"

But when a kid blew his nose in class, everyone stared—especially me. I saw it as an embarrassing situation and, like most kids, rarely used my hanky in class. Instead, I did what many of the boys did. I secretly picked my nose. Some of us nose pickers were smooth, or more discrete than others. If our pickings were dry, we'd nonchalantly flick them onto the floor. If they were slimy, we'd massage them into the fabric of our pants until they were dry—then we'd brush them onto the floor. I could always guess the kids who picked their noses. They were the ones with tell-tell booger stains on their pants. If my sinuses were really messed up, I'd just play hooky.

I didn't do well on homework or tests that year. I flunked so many tests, I was a regular on the blackboard line—those unfortunates, averaging about five students, who got a D or lower on a test. Mrs. Lawrence would line us up along the blackboard and, with each of us holding onto the chalk tray, she would paddle us as an example for the rest of the class. Depending on how bad our test scores were, we'd receive up to five hard swats. Believe me, it hurt. My face got real red from embarrassment and my eyes watered-up, but I didn't cry.

Not surprisingly, I received the paddle for other reasons that year. By the time I had gotten the message, it was too late. I had flunked and would have to endure another year with Mrs. Lawrence, Pinky, and Blueboy.

Fortunately, that was a huge wakeup call for me. I became determined to focus more in class, do my homework, and not have to repeat another grade.

CW: Mom, little David, Paul, Tommy, Debbie, Gary, Donna, Ginny.

The Summer of 61'

I'm nine years old, and it's our second spring living on Kevin Lane. With Ronnie gone, Ginny and Paul are now the oldest and strongest. I was assigned more tasks and had to spend more time and energy with the vegetable garden.

Whether I had been working in the garden or exploring somewhere, an afternoon meal would sometimes make me sleepy. With droopy eyes, I'd search for a cool spot to recoup my energy.

Once or twice each week, Mom set up the wringer clothes washer near the middle of the kitchen. When the weather was hot, she would open the front and back doors to allow a breeze to flow through the house while the machine was running. She'd start by gathering all the dirty clothes on the floor next to the washer. Often the pile would be two feet high at its center and more than eight feet in diameter. Once the machine was loaded and running, Mom went about performing her many other chores, giving me the chance to lie down upon the pile of cool, cotton clothing. This was nap time.

Within seconds, a combination of the rhythmic slosh, slosh, sloshing of the machine and Mom's recitation of "Amazing Grace," "The Old Rugged Cross," or "Rock of Ages" would lull me fast to sleep. Sometimes Gary would lie down next to me, and we'd both sleep and drool. I was a young man, and a young man my age didn't need much of a siesta to reenergize.

Our sleeping arrangement worked better than most of the other places we lived. Each of the two second floor bedrooms had a single dormer and window. Gary and I shared the bed situated under the left dormer window, with both bed and window facing the top of the stairway. The foot of the bed was four feet from the top of the stair railing, fireplace and hearth. Paul's bed faced my bed with its right side against the front wall to the right of the window. The doorway leading into the other bedroom was between the head of his bed and the stair railing. The other bedroom had a single bed for Ginny and a double bed for Debbie and Donna to share. Mom and three-year-old David slept downstairs.

It was a warm night in early summer, and I was asleep. A full moon had risen and cast an eerie glow through the open upstairs windows. Like shutters blown by the wind, my eye lids flickered open as a brilliant beam of light awakened me. At first I thought it was dawn, but soon realized it was just the moon. As I lay there looking through the open window, I felt a strange, eerie reminiscence of the night three years earlier, when the intruder entered our attic on Boissevain Mountain.

Then, to my astonishment, a shadowy figure began to materialize within the frame of the window. I knew there wasn't a ladder nearby. Nevertheless, the shadow entered the bedroom, and seemed to float down to the floor. It appeared to be wearing a black cape and a strange looking black hat. Pretending to be asleep, I peered through squinting eyes and was horrified to see that it's dark and empty face had turned my way, as if daring me to utter a sound. Petrified, I fought back, refusing to cover my face or believe that this was real. My eyes followed the figure as it turned left, moved in the direction of the other bedroom, and paused by the side of Paul's bed. It turned left again and faced my sleeping brother. When the figure leaned over and placed one of its hands on Paul, I couldn't take it anymore. I covered my face and rolled over to face the wall. I remained in that position, hoping and praying I would survive what I could not see. Somehow, I fell asleep.

The next morning, I bolted upright in bed. I looked immediately at Paul's bed, noting that it had been slept in. But Paul was missing. I ran downstairs and found my mother.

"Mom, where's Paul?" I asked, fear and excitement in my voice.

"I think he went to the outhouse," she replied. "Why, what's the matter Tommy?"

Somewhat relieved, I said, "Nothing."

Barefooted and wearing only my underwear, I dashed through the kitchen and out the back door, hoping to see Paul with my own eyes. As I ran down the path toward the outhouse, I saw Paul coming toward me.

"Paul!" I shouted. "Paul!"

My pupils must have grown the size of marbles as I stared at him, mouth hanging open. Then to make sure he was really there, I jabbed him in the stomach.

"Tommy! What's the matter with you? Go get some clothes on, boy."

I gave a sigh of relief and joined my big brother for a walk back to the house.

"Tommy," he said, "I worry about you sometimes."

"It's alright, Paul. I was just having a nightmare."

Days later, the same shadowy figure returned, hovering about my siblings as they slept. Even though Mom let me sleep in another bed in the other bedroom, the nightmares continued. They finally ended nights later, when I wet the bed.

The nightmares were as real to me as anything I had ever experienced. I can only surmise that the intrusion into our attic on Boissevain Mountain had disturbed me more than anyone could have imagined. Now, three years later, the emotional trauma of the incident may have been manifesting itself through realistic nocturnal visions.

The fact that my father was in prison and another big brother had left the roost probably didn't help any.

A lot of things were happening in our family that summer. In addition to the usual hustle and bustle, there were special comings and goings.

When Daisy and Chester visited us in June, they brought along little Chester Junior, almost a year old. My Aunt Gertrude (Gertie), her husband Mcginnis Hale, and Mama also stopped by at that time. At 72, Mama's strength was waning, yet she was still able to walk with a cane. Most people who knew Mcginnis called him "Pig," while family called him "Uncle Pig." He and his brother, "Rooster," acquired their respective labels as children, when they frequently sneaked off to a local pig and chicken farm tended by prisoners from the county jail. Uncle Pig and Aunt Gertie were regular church goers and attended services in Falls Mills. On the rare occasion when Uncle Pig visited, he was always the center of attention. His fantastic sense of humor, outlandish jokes, and silly songs were real crowd pleasers. He was live entertainment and, since he refused to charge admission, we all rushed for the front row seats when Pig walked into the room.

It was hot inside the house, so during most of the visit the doors were left open and the family stayed situated just inside the front porch where we could stay cooler. Many conversations were taking place at the same time.

"Tommy, come here now and give your granny a hug," Mama screeched. "You know I won't be around much longer." Mama had been saying that to her grandchildren for years, and she would continue saying it for many, many more.

Daisy was asking Mom if she would allow little Debbie to stay with her in Ohio, at least for the summer. Daisy wanted to help Mom, and taking responsibility for raising her little sister seemed to be a good idea. Mom said it was worth a try.

Many of us were amused and smiling as we watched and listened to Uncle Pig. He was singing about a Billy goat with horns of solid brass: "… one sticks out'a his head and the other one out'a his hocus pocus adudlem adokem, you may think I lied …." I didn't quite understand the song, but it sounded real funny when Uncle Pig sang it.

Many years later, I realized that I had been listening to Uncle Pig's version of "The Darby Ram" song from *The Max Hunter Folk Song Collection*, an archive of more than 1500 Ozark Mountain songs recorded between 1956 and 1976. A traveling salesman from Springfield, Missouri, Hunter took his reel-to-reel tape recorder into the hills and backwoods of the Ozarks, preserving the heritage of the region by recording songs and stories handed down by generations. Hunter recorded (1958) Mrs. Allie Long Parker from Eureka Springs, Arkansas, singing "The Darby Ram" and other songs.

Aunt Gertie said, "Myrtle, you and the kids should attend church services some Sunday."

"Well … I'll see if some of the kids want to go," Mom promised, "but you won't see me there unless there's a funeral in the family."

Shortly after my aunt and uncle left, Daisy asked the family to gather in the back yard to have our picture taken. This was the occasion of our most memorable family photograph. The black and white photo captured Mom, Ginny, Paul, Donna, Gary, Debbie, David, and me.

Mom was holding David. Gary and I were posing bare-chested and bare-footed. Ginny and Donna were looking their best prim-and-proper. Paul, as usual, was wearing a much wrinkled long sleeved shirt. He had just finished some of his chores, and the long sleeves protected his arms as he dragged and carried wood. A portion of our garden and the neighbor's smokehouse were also visible in the background. It was a great family photo, but, like most, not complete; someone was always missing.

Daisy took Debbie with her to Ohio that day. The intent was for Debbie to stay as long as she wanted. We would miss her, but Debbie could have a better life with Daisy's young family.

As it turned out, Debbie soon became very homesick. In fact, she cried so much she actually did get sick. Daisy and Mom decided it would be best to bring her home. In early July, she was reunited with us in Falls Mills.

Later that summer, Gary and I were roaming about the property when we noticed that our fence on the north side of the big garden was ripe with blackberries. We dashed to the kitchen and returned to the berry patch with two of Mom's prized Tupperware containers to hold our pickings. Soon we had picked all the ripe berries on our side of the fence.

"Wait here, Gary, while I check for more berries on the back side of the fence."

To reach the other side, I crawled through a small opening near the foot of the combination barbed and wire-linked fence. Hundreds of rocks from years of combing the garden were piled in a heap all along the base of the fence.

"Gary, come on over! There's a whole bunch of ripe berries over here!" Gary kneeled down and began to crawl through the fence.

Before I could pick my first handful of berries, I heard him scream. Gary was known to exaggerate his pain when hurt, but this time the sound urged me to give him the benefit of the doubt.

I faced Gary from the opposite side of the fence. He was standing upright, crying, and gripping his hand. "What's the matter?" I asked.

"I cut my hand," he pouted.

"Let me see it."

"No Tommy, I can't."

"Why not?"

"It'll bleed."

Frustrated and confused, I crawled back through the fence onto our property. I demanded he show me his wound.

Again, he said, "No, I can't."

I couldn't understand my brother's behavior. He said he cut his hand. Yet I saw very little blood.

"Gary, if you don't take your hand away, I'm going to bust you in the head."

The threat worked. "Okay, but you won't like it," he warned.

Gary removed his thumb from the mystery wound. I stood there looking at nothing. Since I couldn't see anything, I looked a little closer.

"Where is it?" I asked.

My face was about six inches from his hand when blood squirted from the palm of his hand, almost hitting me in the face.

Startled, I jumped back. "What the heck?"

Gary and I stood there looking at the tiny fountain of blood. With every other beat of his heart, a small amount of blood squirted from his palm. He seemed to be unusually calm for someone spouting a fountain of blood.

"This looks serious, Gary!"

That was all it took to set him off crying again.

"Don't let it squirt anymore!" I cried. "Cover it up!"

"What is it?" Mom asked, as we barged through the back door and into the kitchen. "What have you boys done this time?"

When she saw the spurting blood, she said, "Oh, for crying out loud! Ginny, run to Ward's and tell them we have an emergency." Gary began to cry even louder.

Ginny was all out of breath when she arrived at Ward's Market. She kept trying to speak, but only nonsense passed through her lips. A few people surmised that there was another emergency in the Dixon family and tried to calm Ginny enough to get her breath back. She finally communicated the situation, and a young man she knew named Frank offered to drive her, Mom, and Gary to the hospital.

By the time Frank's shiny, new, red convertible reached the hospital, Gary seemed a little weak and giddy from all the excitement and, possibly, loss of blood. The doctor was concerned about Gary's low blood pressure, so the nurse said something about a blood transfusion.

"Mrs. Dixon, do you know Gary's Blood type?"

"No, I don't think I do."

All of a sudden Gary was bright and perky.

"I know what type of blood I have—it's red."

Everyone buckled over with loud laughter.

Mom, Ginny, and Frank stayed several hours with Gary at the hospital. He regained his strength quickly and a transfusion wasn't necessary. After receiving a tetanus shot he was allowed to go home.

Considering the number of children she was responsible for, Mom did an outstanding job of making sure we all received the required shots and vaccinations and that our immunization records were accurate and up to date.

Curious as to what had punctured Gary's hand, we carefully inspected the ground by the fence and saw several rusty barbs half buried among the rocks and dirt. We eventually concluded that a barb had punctured an artery in his palm. I was lucky; it could just as easily have happened to me.

The creek and falls at the bottom of Kevin Lane was a frequent hangout. Sometimes we went fishing, but more often we went wading in the creek looking for crawdads. That summer we were surprised when we had encountered two or three black snakes there in less than a week. Normally we would see only one or two the entire summer. Nonpoisonous black snakes were very common. Poisonous copperheads were spotted too but—thankfully—not so often.

Sometime in August, Paul, Gary, and I heard the sound of fire engine sirens. From our front yard, we believed the sound was coming from the bottom of Kevin Lane near the falls. Some of us ran down to the bottom of the lane to see what was happening. When we arrived, we found a fire engine blocking traffic at the curve, and several firemen were cordoning off the area near a large wedge-shaped rock on the falls side of the road. We could see dozens of dead snakes in the middle of the road, and firemen wielding long poles were smashing many more. Most of the snakes were trying to escape into the cliffs on the opposite side of the road.

We also noticed smoke coming from the falls side of the rock. I asked Paul what he thought the smoke was about. He said that it looked like they were burning something to smoke out the snakes from their den under the rock. It seemed to be working very well. After an hour of watching, I don't think a single snake got away.

The county must have received several complaints about the snakes. Hospitals could have received a few bite victims too. Why else would they have invested the time and energy on exterminating the snakes? Now we could enjoy the falls, creek, and surrounding area a little more.

Paul said, "Tommy, the chinkapins are ready for picking over by the abandoned old house. Do you want to go with me to pick some?"

Chinkapins (or chinquapins) are similar to chestnuts, except they are smaller and grow on smaller trees known as the Allegheny Chinquapin. They're hardy and attractive trees, and when their spiny and prickly shells dry and crack open in early fall, they reveal a delicious, sweet brown nut.

"You bet! Can I do some of the picking too?"

"Okay, but I'll have to make another tool for ya. Right now, we only have one."

I joined Paul at his tackle/tool box where he had the implements we needed for picking the chinkapins. Using a hack saw, Paul cut a sharp angle on one end of a six-inch long pipe nipple. After removing the metal burrs with a file, he tied a sock as a reservoir around the other open end. When collecting the nuts, we wore an old leather glove on one hand to hold the prickly burr. Then we scooped out the nuts with the sharpened pipe end, and they rolled down the pipe into the sock.

With both of us using one of these tools, it took about an hour to fill each sock with nuts from the low-hanging branches of our neighbor's tree. Most of the tree limbs were too small to support our weight, so not having a ladder was the only thing that kept us from picking more.

Chinkapins were very popular at school that time of year. The trees were scarce and collecting the nuts was so labor intensive that only a few kids brought them to school. Those who did usually only brought a handful.

During recess, Paul and I shared our nuts. We'd pop one in our mouths, bite the shell in half, scoop out the nut using our tongues and teeth, and spit out the empty half shell. Heck, with a pocket-full of chinkapins, even the bullies were extra nice to me. Normally, if a bully chased me, I'd run to Paul. The frustrated bully would often say, "Your big brother ain't gonna be around forever, Dixon." Then he'd walk away maintaining a healthy distance from Paul.

Paul and I were very popular the next two weeks. Then we ran out of nuts.

Wesley (18) serving proudly c. 1960.

Ronnie (17) serving proudly c. 1961.

Tricks and Treats

Halloween was a favorite time in our family. In addition to the usual tricks and treats, I have a faint remembrance of our 1959 celebration back on Newhill Road, when Wesley and Ronnie somehow convinced our mother to dress up for the event. The jovial mood that had gripped the entire household for most of the day reached its pinnacle as we watched my mother and brothers walk out the front door. Ronnie and Wesley were dressed in high heels, skirts, nylon stockings, and headscarves that only partially obscured their lipstick and make-up. Their transformation was surpassed only by Mom's. She wore military boots, a pair of blue and white stripped bibbed overalls over a light blue, collared, long-sleeved shirt, and a blue and white locomotive engineer's hat that concealed her long, dark brown hair.

"Hey Wesley," Ronnie said jokingly, "your mother wears army boots!"

"Oh yeah! Well then ... the same to you—brother!"

That was our best and most enthusiastic Halloween—ever.

Mom didn't have to buy much candy for the trick-or-treaters in those days. We rarely saw more than a hand full of visitors willing to challenge the steep grade of Kevin Lane. On the other hand, Paul, Gary, and I sometimes walked for two hours to collect goodies. Due to two significant and personal events, this Halloween would be especially memorable.

It was Monday night, the night before Halloween, and some of us were working on our costumes. Mom was sewing garments for Gary and me while Paul was working on a secret costume that he was only going to reveal when finished.

Paul was the family artist. Throughout the 1960's, magazines and comic books displayed advertisements that offered young people a chance to earn careers in the visual arts field. The famous "Draw Me" advertisement presented sample pictures (a Pirate and a Cowboy were the most famous) for the budding artist to draw and submit for prizes. We all thought his drawing abilities were good enough, so Paul entered himself into a couple of these mail-away contests. Nothing came of it, although Paul was once rewarded with an honorable mention and encouraged to keep up the good work.

Just before dark, most of the family was gathered in the living room to keep warm by the pot belly stove. An open foldout bed was stationed between the stove and front porch window. Paul was working on his costume in the kitchen while the rest of us were listening to the popular "Snoop & Scoop" show airing weekdays on WHIS-TV (channel 6) in Bluefield, WV. The fully attired cowboys discussed local news items in between showings of old movie serials. Listening was about all we could do, since a good television picture tube was a rarity for us in those days. We were also chatting and consuming a rare bountiful supply of popcorn and cheese curls. The bags of snacks had been passed around several times, and everyone except Yours Truly seemed to have had their fill.

I was ecstatic when Donna said, "Here Tommy, you can have the rest." The bag she handed me was over half full of delicious cheese curls.

Other than a good case of worms, it was rare for anyone of us to get our belly full of anything. So, for more than fifteen minutes, I sat on the fold out bed next to the window making a pig of myself.

Just when I had eaten all the cheese curls my stomach could possibly hold, there came a tap, tap, tapping noise from the window less than two feet behind me. A little startled, I turned to see who or what was at the window. What I saw was petrifying—a huge, hideous green face with black bangs of hair cut straight across its forehead. The man—no, the creature—had bloody red scars and stitches across its forehead, jaw, and chin. Strange looking metal rods protruded from its neck.

Frankenstein!

I would have screamed instantaneously had the sight not taken my breath away. Once I regained my breath, I let out the loudest, longest scream of my life. I was shaking all over.

Paul walked through the front door holding his homemade, cardboard Frankenstein mask. It was a masterpiece. He was laughing along with everyone in the room—until I vomited the cheese curls onto the bed and floor.

Many Halloweens would pass before I would taste another cheese curl.

I skipped school the next day because of a mild fever, but I was not about to miss Halloween night with my brothers and sister. As soon as the sun began to set, Paul, Donna, Gary, and I were dressed and ready to make our rounds. Gary was a ghost, Donna was a witch, and I was Frankenstein. Paul felt so terrible about scaring me that he let me wear his mask. Also, at 14, Paul was under the impression that he was too old to be collecting treats and would be our chaperon, instead.

Our first stop was the Wells' house next door. We said the usual hellos and they complimented us on our costumes. Next we walked down the road and around the mountain along Mud Fork Road. Collecting candy in our pillow cases, we covered about 15 houses, working our way from Falls Mills Road to the Falls Mills Dam. After we returned to Falls Mills Road, we headed east on Post Office Road.

That's when Donna said, "I'm tired. I want to go home."

Not surprisingly, she wasn't used to walking as much as us boys. We escorted her to the foot of Kevin Lane and watched as she disappeared into the abrupt darkness.

Paul's flashlight, a few front porch lights, and the dim glow of a rising moon were all we had to see our way through the valley. The three of us continued collecting treats on Post Office Road, where flashlights and trick-or-treaters were more concentrated than usual. The going was tough here; we were constantly bumping and brushing against other kids.

It happened so quickly. Some kid grabbed my loaded pillowcase and took off running.

Paul's pursuit was so quick that he slipped on loose gravel and fell to his hands and knees. Back on his feet in a flash, Paul went racing down the road and up Sue Lane, a side street, in hot pursuit of the thief.

Flustered and almost in tears, I stood with Gary on the side of the road guarding our remaining goodies. A few minutes later, Paul returned empty handed. He said he had lost the thief in the darkness. If my brother had caught him, that young man would have suffered serious and painful regrets.

Meanwhile, I choked back my tears. Paul said, "Tommy, do you want to do it all over again?"

Since I was determined and in great shape for a nine year old, I said, "Sure Paul."

We hustled the one fifth mile back to the house and told Mom what had happened. She said, "Damn those hooligans."

"It's still early enough, Mom," Paul said, "I'd like to take Tommy back out there."

With Mom's permission, Paul and I both picked up a pillow case and headed down the lane retracing our earlier path, minus the cumbersome costumes. By the time we were back at the Post Office, we were on guard (Paul especially) for suspicious looking thieves. It was a little past eight, and we had collected the same amount of goodies as before.

"Tommy, if you aren't too tired, there are a few more houses we can hit. Do you want to keep going?"

Aside from a sweet tooth, anger and adrenaline were my motivation.

"Let's do it, Paul!"

This time we hit about 10 of the clustered houses along Post Road and 15 or more along Brushfork Road. We even detoured back to Falls Mills Road at Hales Bottom for another 15 houses. Although many were still giving away goodies, a few people thought it was a "little late" to be trick-or-treating. When we told them my candy had been stolen, some people gave us extra treats.

A few minutes after nine, Paul and I headed for home, carefully guarding our stash. We had more than made up for the stolen candy. We slept well that night. Paul and I shared our treats with our siblings the next day, and I had a good story to tell the bullies and others in school.

Dad hated cats. To prove his distaste, he had often used them for target practice with his .22 revolver. He especially hated black cats for the usual superstitious reasons—they were evil and brought bad luck. Or, maybe that was just an excuse to shoot at something he deemed insignificant, or something live and posing the rare challenge of a moving target.

I still harbor the image of a stray black cat running through the high grass of our front yard in Elgood. Indeed, running for its life. Although it took him three shots, Dad was dead-on. The cat died rather quickly, but not before coughing up some blood. I can still see the dead cat lying in the grass, bloody tongue hanging from its yawning mouth, and Ronnie or Wesley dragging it away by its tail.

When Dad was around, our family had few opportunities to enjoy a litter of puppies or kittens unless they were someone else's.

But that was the past; things were different now. Sometime during the summer our family adopted a six-week-old female kitten. Since she was gray and black with a single white paw, we named her Whitefoot. We considered her a lucky kitten since many stray cats and dogs died an early and horrible death in the mountains. A strong bond developed between Whitefoot and me.

It was almost Thanksgiving when Whitefoot was expecting her first litter. Her abdomen grew larger while Mom and the rest of us got more and more anxious.

One night shortly before bedtime, Donna, Gary, and I were sitting on the foldout bed. Whitefoot was on the floor, struggling to join us. I thought she was too pregnant to jump, so I reached down, lifted her onto the bed, and cuddled her in my arms. When she started to growl, I ignored her complaints. Instead, I placed my face next to hers and rubbed noses. She hissed at me and someone in the room said, "Tommy, you're making her mad. She's going to smack you."

In a fraction of a second, Whitefoot sank her teeth into the delicate bridge between my nostrils. Her aim was perfect. I screamed as we let go of each other. Tears blinded me. My nose stung like hell, and began to bleed.

"She bit me!"

"That'll teach you," Mom said. "Someday you'll learn, Tommy Mack."

Why would my cat want to be with me one second, and then bite me the next? In a flash, I realized I had ignored her signals at the wrong time.

That night, Mom and Ginny sensed that Whitefoot was about to go into labor. We lined a small cardboard box with old rags and cut out most of one side for easy access. We placed Whitefoot and her bed, along with a bowl of water, by the fireplace in the corner of my bedroom.

While we were all sleeping, I felt something touch my face. Somehow Whitefoot had managed to jump or climb onto my bed. I placed her between my legs hoping we both would be comfortable. Soon, in the darkness, she began to emit weird choking sounds.

"Is that cat in bed with you Tommy?" Paul asked.

"Yeah, Paul, and I think she's sick."

"Then you better put her on the floor," he warned.

With a gentle touch, I lowered her onto the floor. Before I could close my eyes, she was back.

"Paul, she's on the bed again."

Now considerably agitated, Paul said, "Okay, that does it."

He jumped from his bed, turned on the light, lifted Whitefoot from my bed, and placed her back into her own. When he reached for the pull-chain to turn out the ceiling light, I saw something.

"Paul, what's that stuff on the floor?"

Upon closer examination, Paul and I realized that Whitefoot had started giving birth in my bed. She had smeared blood onto my bed and the floor.

Paul pulled on his pants and called downstairs for Mom. By now everyone in the house was awake. Mom stopped at the head of the stairs and looked into Whitefoot's bed.

"Well, would you look at that," she said.

Everyone rushed to the corner of the room to take a look. Whitefoot was licking and cleaning up after her first newborn kitten. We stood there for several minutes, some of us in underwear only, admiring the miracle of birth.

"Okay," Mom said. "She needs peace and quiet, so everybody go back to bed. We'll see what the litter looks like in the morning."

Someone did a quick cleanup of the mess, and the lights were turned off. Minutes later, we all were asleep.

The next morning everyone was presented with a litter of three beautiful kittens. One looked like the mother, one was mostly white, and the other was all black. Unfortunately, two didn't survive the week, but the black kitten did and was appropriately named Midnight.

Making Ends Meet

To some, my mother's life would seem like drudgery. I could understand that. Were it not for her love and dedication to her children, she may have felt that way. I'd like to think that my mother found her life stimulating and worthwhile. Overall, her life and situation were somewhat typical of many mothers of that era and geographical location. Later in life, all of her children would truly come to understand her and her daily struggles.

With eight mouths to feed, our modest monthly welfare check, along with the government surplus food commodities, rarely lasted the month. Through years of experience, Mom had learned to make the most of the commodities, what we grew at home, and what we bought from the store. But sometimes, no matter how hard she tried, the pantry went bare.

She usually prepared our meals from scratch. Fresh homemade biscuits, dumplings, and cornbread were prepared several times each week. Cornmeal, flour, sugar, baking powder, salt and pepper, lard, and fatback (chunk bacon) were staples for survival. When all the cash was spent, our mother had to step out of her comfort zone to care for us.

We grew up on a steady diet of gravy-n-biscuits and beans-n-cornbread. A healthy chunk of fatback was a necessary ingredient for a tasty batch of pinto-beans. The fatback was for flavoring and wasn't supposed to be consumed. But when the family sat down to dinner, it wasn't unusual to see Mom slurp down several one inch cubes of the stuff. The sight sickened some of us. We eventually realized that this was one of several ways she sacrificed so the rest of us could have more. We never saw her eat that way during better times.

Mr. Ranger was a retired elderly man who lived in a sturdy, red brick colonial directly across the street from the Falls Mills Post Office. A friend of my mother's sister's family, he would sometimes lend us a few dollars to get through the last week of the month. Mom would usually assign Paul the embarrassing task of delivering a note to Mr. Ranger asking for the loan.

Ronnie and Wesley had recently started sending Mom a few dollars every month or two. With our brothers helping out and Mr. Ranger contributing when called upon, the family was eating better and Mom was less stressed.

Nevertheless, I can still remember many nights of going to bed hungry. Our diet pretty much consisted of the same foods consumed by our cousins, the Millers, upon Jenkinjones Mountain, but we had more mouths to feed.

We purchased a package of 40 cookies at the start of every month. Mom tried to make it last two weeks. How successful could that have been, considering she had seven hungry kids, each with a powerful sweet tooth, staring at her? Heck, a pack of forty cookies couldn't last a week. Mom usually made a monthly batch of sweetbread biscuits too. We loved the homemade treats just as much as the store-bought cookies, and they went just as fast.

Milk didn't last long either. At the time, a gallon of milk cost about three pennies over a dollar. Yet, with a working refrigerator, Mom tried to make the gallon last a week. Doing the math, that's only two cups of milk per person per week. We could stretch store-bought milk by mixing it with a solution of water and powdered milk from our commodities. Half the time the refrigerator wasn't working and we had to drink our milk within a few hours before it soured. During the cold of winter we frequently stored milk and other perishables outside, sometimes stuffing them into a bank of snow.

Speaking of snow, I remember wishing for heavy snowfalls every winter so we could make homemade ice cream (the poor folk's way). We spooned clean snow into a serving bowl, added a little sugar, food coloring, and a few drops of vanilla flavoring, and wolfed it down in a flash before it melted. Our snowy ice cream was especially delicious when we added some of Mom's canned blackberries or raspberries to the mix. Mom told us we couldn't eat snow from the first snowfall. She said a good snowfall or two was necessary to flush dirt and pollutants from the air.

Mom was really good at baking cakes and pies. As long as the staples were available, she would bake one or two desserts each month—usually on birthdays, and we had plenty of those. I fondly recall the arguments my siblings and I had when it came to who would have the honor of licking cake batter from the spoon, or scraping fudge from a bowl.

"Mommy, it's my turn! Donna got the spoon last time!"

Our neighbor, Harv Edmonds, was a World War II and, possibly, a World War I Army veteran. A mild-mannered alcoholic, he was in his late fifties or early sixties and lived in a two room ranch house just a stone's throw down the hill.

During our stay on Kevin Lane, Mom and Harv developed a casual friendship. You could say it was a give and take relationship, but the focus was more on what Harv could do for us than what we could do for him. We noted that he was a nice, well dressed old man, especially when he remembered to pull up his zipper. He often smelled strongly of nicotine and alcohol, and sometimes urine. He almost always wore dark colored suits with a dress shirt and a dark brown hat, but rarely, if ever, a necktie.

At least once each week, Mom would visit Harv with several of us kids in tow. Sometimes he'd serve us two or three cookies with milk or soda pop. Mom always joined him for a drink—a good drink with name-brand alcohol, none of that homemade rot-gut stuff when Mom was around. They'd also share some smokes and conversation while we kids were consumed by the television.

Without a television, we were always on the look-out for a good source like Harv to satisfy our cravings. In addition to Bonanza and The Three Stooges, cartoons like The Huckleberry Hound Show and The Flintstones were some of our favorites.

Mom had become addicted to Bonanza. Since Donna was in love with Little Joe and Ginny was in love with Adam, I naturally thought that my mother had her eyes set on Ben Cartwright. Considering what Mom had for a husband, Ginny and Donna figured Mom deserved at least this one little fancy. But she never let on about it.

Once Mom was comfortable leaving us alone with Harv, we were allowed to stop by his place on Saturday mornings to watch cartoons and occasionally on a week-night to watch The Three Stooges. We never had a problem with Harv, and he never seemed to have an issue with us kids. Sometimes he drank too much and passed out in his sofa chair. We always snickered about having to snuff out his cigarette or pipe on the way out the door. If the place caught fire and burned down, I thought, it would be difficult to find a TV-viewing host as nice, as friendly, and as convenient as Harv.

A year or so later, Harv's financial picture improved when he started collecting Social Security, so he moved to a nicer place about a mile away. This reduced but did not stop our regular visits and TV watching. However, Harv's move did have a negative impact on Paul.

On a few occasions Harv would walk or get a ride to our house to socialize and drink with Mom. When it came time for him to go home, he could barely walk. It was always Paul's job to see him home safely. Since the old man was about 5'8" tall and close to 200 pounds, Paul warned Mom that he might not be strong enough to prevent Harv from hurting himself.

On one occasion, I helped Paul with his escort duties. It was well after dark, very cold, and Paul and I were trying to keep Harv moving so we all could stay warm. When he fell down, we'd struggle to get him back to his feet. When he fell into a ditch and hit his head, we thought he was dead. But Harv was a remarkable and tough old guy. It took us a long time, but we finally got him back on his feet and walking again. After that scary incident, Mom put a stop to Harv's visits unless he had someone to drive him home.

Harv's sister, Maggie Sadder, lived next to him in a small house just below ours. On the rare occasion she encountered one of us kids outside, she seemed pleasant enough. Maggie always kept her head covered with a colorful scarf or bonnet. Rumor was she had some form of cancer and was bald underneath her bonnet. In our childish ignorance we shied away from her, thinking the sight of her hideous scalp might scare us to death. Yes, we had never seen a baldheaded woman before, and none of us wanted to be the first—at least not alone or after sundown.

Maggie raised a few chickens and guinea hens on a tiny piece of property, and they often wandered into our yard. Knowing how poor we were, Maggie always offered us one of her hens for Thanksgiving and Christmas. Guinea hens are wary and fast creatures, and a shotgun blast was about the only thing we had that could catch one. So we elected to snatch one of her unsuspecting chickens instead.

To kill a chicken, wringing or chopping off the head is the preferred method. At 14, Paul wasn't quite skilled or strong enough to wring a chicken's neck. Although our mother was capable of doing this, Paul usually took the initiative and chopped off the chicken's neck and head. I can still see the headless chicken in its death throes, flopping about and spewing blood all over our yard. It was a sight even the little ones had become familiar with, and we learned early to stand back and let the blood flow.

Ingenuity wasn't a foreign concept to Paul though. Tired of having to tiptoe around a blood-spattered yard, he pinned the neck of the next dinner chicken under the rim of a galvanized wash tub before severing its head. Then little Debbie stood on top of the tub to pin it down, while the chicken flopping and blood spouting was contained inside. It was noisier, but a much less messy and more efficient way of bleeding the chicken before cooking.

Only seconds after immersing the headless and bloodless hen into boiling water, Mom would begin plucking the loosened feathers from its skin. It was a process best done outdoors. A distinct and pungent odor plagued the nostrils of anyone in the house, forcing the weak to vacate the premises until the house was purged. Just like hog butchering, it was not a process for the squeamish or faint of heart.

A few weeks before Christmas, Mom received letters from Ronnie and Wesley. Both would be home on leave from the Army and in time for Christmas.

The reunion included everyone except Dad and Daisy. We eagerly awaited our big brothers' arrival. When the time was at hand, everyone rushed to the door to greet them in turn. It must have been a bad day for hitch-hiking; poor Ronnie had to lug his heavy duffle bag all the way from the bus terminal in Bluefield, West Virginia. It was no small feat, considering it was almost 6 miles, and he had barely recovered from a broken right arm suffered during horseplay with his military buddies in Germany. It was especially exciting for us to see our brothers dressed in Army uniforms. I remember Wesley and Ronnie giving us a demonstration on how to fold a duffle bag and how to spit shine boots—the military way.

It was crowded at night with everyone under the same roof, but nobody seemed to care. The Christmas spirit abounded with better than usual food and plenty of jokes about good times.

The holiday wouldn't be complete without some of Wesley's singing and guitar playing. His rendition of current and past hits reminded me of favorites I had heard on the radio, and would often catch myself singing as I went about my chores and explorations— Johnny Preston's "Running Bear," The Marathons' "Peanut Butter," Brook Benton's "Frankie and Johnny" and "The Boll Weevil Song," The Dovells' "Bristol Stomp," and especially Jimmy Dean's "Big Bad John," about a heroic miner who sacrificed his own life to save many. The song gripped me emotionally then and, to some extent, for years later.

Wesley, Ronnie, and Ginny celebrated the holiday by joining the Wells children next door. They attended a dance and one or two other events.

The day before Christmas, Wesley and Ginny went on a rare double date, while Mom and Ronnie visited one of our good neighbors. During the visit, they all had a few drinks of holiday cheer. Thanks to the unknown neighbor, Mom and Ronnie were able to bring enough of the "cheer" home to commence their own private celebration.

Paul, Donna, Gary, Debbie and I were kept awake by their festivities until about midnight. Gary, 8, and Debbie, almost 6, were especially concerned about the noise.

From the other bedroom, young Debbie shouted, "If we don't be quiet, Santa won't come down the chimney!"

Paul said, "You're right Debbie."

"Hey Paul," I said, "don't you think we should move the potty away from the fireplace? We don't want Santa to get any of that stuff on his suit, do we?"

"That's a good idea," Paul chuckled. "Tommy, since you thought of it, you can move it to the corner where it'll be out of the way."

I got out of bed and, with caution, moved the potty. As I climbed back into bed, Donna said, "Thank you Tommy."

Debbie added, "Yeah, thanks Tommy."

"You're all welcome."

Sternly Paul said, "Say good night everybody."

With understanding, we all said, "Good night."

Come Christmas morning, Ronnie and Wesley were dead asleep. With so much alcohol consumption, Mom probably wished she were dead. However, this was no time for dying; she had to fix our breakfast. Wanting to prolong the suspense, most of us ate our breakfast before opening our single present.

I received the board game Clue that Christmas. Although a small and simple gift, its impact was extraordinary. The game provided stimulating conversation and challenged anyone seriously interested in winning to think and reason beyond the norm: Was the professor killed in the library? Was he killed using a candlestick? We played the game that day until we were exhausted.

Later in the afternoon, we all enjoyed a big dinner—thanks be given to Mom, Wesley, Ronnie, Maggie, and our Father above.

X

FALLS MILLS
c. 1962

Debbie (6) at Falls Mills, Virginia.

The Summer of 62'

While my mother rarely attended church, she didn't discourage us from attending. "If you go to church," she'd say, "watch yourself and don't be a hypocrite like so many other churchgoing people."

On a few occasions, my siblings and I attended church and Sunday school at the Falls Mills Christian Church. Uncle Pig and Aunt Gertie were constantly urging us to attend. They insinuated that God's word would lead us away from the sins of our father, and instill in us family values and morality.

I enjoyed the bible study projects and classroom participation of Sunday school. But as time passed, our attendance dwindled until only I attended. Soon, even I slid from the grip of the church and its potential offerings. My aunt and uncle were disappointed, but I'm sure it was tempered by the hope of reviving our interest down the road. To them, a seed had been planted.

It was a sunny weekend morning in mid-April. Mom was washing clothes and other family members were attending to their chores and hobbies. The properties in the hills around Kevin Lane displayed the wonders of nature. Redbud, dogwood, and magnolias were blossoming or already in full bloom. An abundance of honeysuckle, tiger lilies, and trumpet creepers smothered our roadside fences, as yet another waterfall of forsythia cascaded the steep banks between the house and the lower garden.

While hummingbirds hovered and darted above us, Gary and I played armies-at-war with miniature soldiers, tanks, and trucks. Being careful not to damage Mom's prized daffodils, we molded the dirt bank along the base of the fence into a mountainous battlefield of hills, valleys, roads, tunnels, boulders, and bridges. Gary and I began to argue as we obliterated each other's plastic pawns.

"No Tommy, it's my turn. You already killed ten of my men, and you just blew up two of my tanks."

Was I exerting too much control over the battle?

From behind us a strange voice called out, "Thou shalt not kill, sayeth the Lord." Startled, we turned to see two young men dressed in white shirts, black ties, black slacks, and black shoes.

Looking down at us, one of them smiled and said, "We didn't mean to scare you boys."

"That's okay," I mumbled, "we're just playing."

"Well, hello then. I'm Elder Hansen and my sidekick here is Elder Tribett. And by what name shall we call you boys."

"I'm Gary Lee."

"I'm Tommy Mack."

The Elders asked if they could speak to our mother. I sat on the porch steps with the two men as Gary ran into the house to fetch Mom.

"Well, Tommy, how old are you and Gary?" asked one of the men.

"I turned ten in January. Gary will be nine in November."

"How many brothers and sisters do you have?"

After counting my fingers, I said, "Five brothers and four sisters."

"Wow! "That's a pretty big family. Are all of them living here?"

"No," I said, glancing back to see what was taking Gary and Mom so long, "I have two brothers in the Army and a sister that's married."

Mom and Gary walked onto the porch, with Donna and Debbie sneaking along behind them. After more introductions, they explained the reason for their visit:

They were Elders from the local branch of The Church of Jesus Christ of Latter-Day Saints, better known as the Mormon Church.

They told us the church offered many activities and services for all the families and individuals in the surrounding counties. In addition to the usual church services and Sunday school, there were family picnics, barbecues, pony rides and games. My eyes widened even further when they said they had baseball teams in the summer for children nine to 14 years old. They told Mom they would be glad to provide transportation for us if our family was interested in attending their church services in Bluefield, Virginia.

Mom glanced at each of her children. "I'm not interested, but if any of the kids want to go, they have my permission." Debbie and Donna declined with a shy smile and shake of their heads. Gary was more enthusiastic.

"I'll go!"

"I'll go too!" I piped in.

With that, we made a date to be picked up the following Sunday morning.

As sure as their word, the elders arrived on time at Kevin Lane driving a fairly new station wagon. Gary and I had agreed to meet them at the bottom of the hill since there was no way the wagon was going to traverse such a steep grade without damaging the undercarriage in the process. Two other young men our age were there to greet us.

We continued driving south in the direction of Bluefield, stopping at a few houses. Some parents apologized to the Elders, saying their children had changed their mind about attending.

We had almost reached Bluefield when we pulled in front of a house I recognized from previous trips to the city. It was, like so many houses in the area, a poor looking, one-story house situated close to the road. A huge boulder the size of a dump truck crowded a tiny front yard. The front door was scarred by scrapes and dings, as if it had been used for target practice. The back of the house overhung a 20-foot cliff that ended at the railroad tracks below; it was supported by wooden bracings that appeared to be anchored haphazardly to the rock. When passing by, I had always wondered who lived there. Images of odd looking and strange sounding humanoids danced through my silly mind.

Now I sat waiting nervously for someone—or something—to join us in the station wagon. After a couple of minutes, the elder blew the horn. Still, no one appeared to join us and we continued on. I can't say I was disappointed.

Gary and I felt a little shy and awkward during our first appearance at the Mormon Church. Over time those feelings gave way to confidence and security as we made friends and got to know more members. On May 5, 1962, we were baptized as proud members of The Church of Jesus Christ of Latter Day Saints. We continued to attend the church and its activities as long as we had transportation, usually once or twice each month.

There were several opportunities to choose up sides and play baseball that year. The theme for one of our excursions was: work before play. We soon found out what they meant.

The elders had accumulated two station wagons full of us young and eager boys. Somewhere between Falls Mills and Pocahontas, we turned onto a dirt side road that wandered around the mountain for about two miles. We stopped at an empty lot surrounded by shade trees. Our drivers walked to the rear of the cars, opened the tail gates, and removed several duffle bags. The vehicles contained not only baseball equipment, but grass cutting equipment too.

Soon we were cutting grass and weeds from the lot so we could play baseball. Gary and I were no strangers to the hand sickles we used. It took less than an hour for the ten kids and three adults to clear the field.

As we got ready to play, I noticed three other young men who had made their way to the edge of the field. They were pushing bicycles, and two of the boys were Negroes. I hadn't seen many houses on the way, so I assumed they had biked some distance. Our adult chaperones seemed to have expected them and introduced the newcomers.

Were it not for his familiar first name, I may not have recognized him. Henry, the friendly Negro boy from Jenkinjones who had shared his bicycle with me, was about to join us for a game of baseball. This was the same kid who I had called a "nigger" and shoved to the ground three years previously, an incident that had shamed me. Henry was a long way from Jenkinjones Mountain. I quickly surmised that he and his family, just like my family, had moved.

Our awareness of each other was heightened during the introductions. He knew I was that Tommy, and I knew he was that Henry. My eyes locked with his. We had no expectations, but we did have three choices: 1) avoid, 2) attack, or 3) acknowledge.

The time was the early 1960s; the place was the not-so-deep south, so there would be no avoidance. The race riots, with all their hatred and violence, were at least four years away; there would be no attacking. Instead, we worked our way through the crowd until we stood facing each other. We locked eyes again, smiled, and shook hands.

Since Gary followed me like a shadow most of the time, I introduced him to Henry and reminded my brother about where we had first met. Henry was about nine, somewhere between Gary and me.

Gary and I had played very little baseball and knew few of the rules. Other than poverty, these were the best reasons for not owning a baseball mitt. Even though our hands took a beating that day, our knowledge and abilities increased fivefold. I was very impressed with Henry's baseball skills; he was probably two years ahead of most kids his age. We all had a good time, and Gary and I enjoyed having him on our team. Henry and I reluctantly departed that day. We promised to keep in touch through the church and its activities, but, unfortunately, that was the last time we saw each other.

Later that summer, I received Paul's old mitt and we played many games of catch in the front yard, further improving our skills. Batting practice consisted of hitting rocks, and sometimes chunks of coal into the hollow using an old wooden bat. The rocks chewed up the bat so fast it didn't last the summer. Gary almost got the switch when Mom caught him smashing chunks of coal into dust. In her mind, it was much more valuable as fuel. I think Donna squealed on him.

Around this time we watched our neighbors pack up and move away. From what I'd heard and remembered, the Wells were good neighborly people. Just like the Bright family on Newhill Road, they had shared some good and bad times with us, but mostly good. Mom, Ginny,

Ronnie, and Wesley were the most disappointed to see them go. It was strange and sad to see the big house that loomed over us sitting so empty.

In a matter of days a new family moved into the vacated Wells house, and we wasted little time getting acquainted. Mr. and Mrs. Snowdecker's son, Clarence, was about my age. Their daughter, Susie, was a couple years younger than me. Oddly enough, I found myself paying more than the usual attention to Susie. There was something special about her pretty blond hair, fair complexion, and intriguing smile. Like mine, Clarence's head was sporting a crew cut that his mother clipped regularly. Also, like me, he was very thin.

A few days after the Snowdeckers moved in, I began to spend a lot of time playing and exploring with Clarence. Gary and I, and sometimes Paul, introduced him to many of our favorite hangouts around the mountains and cliffs. During our get-acquainted phase, I discovered that Clarence would be starting fourth grade with me at Falls Mills Grade School. I also learned he was physically out of shape. He became winded and tired much more quickly than Gary and me. Within a week or two he stopped playing cowboys and Indians with us in the woods.

"Nooo, Tommy!" he'd say. "Let's do something closer to home."

I began to consider him a sissy, but Ginny didn't like me calling Clarence that.

"Tommy, you should take it easy on Clarence. You never know— he might have a problem with his heart or lungs."

Maybe Ginny was right. Or maybe his parents sheltered their kids more. Whatever the reason, I was never privy to it. Nevertheless, hanging out with Clarence was fun most of the time.

Paul and I even included him in our secret escape project. Yep, we finally got around to installing a trap door in the floor of the closet under the stairway. Having to skimp on materials, we used pieces of leather belts as hinges and a rusty old latch we found in one of the local trash piles. The project was much more difficult than we imagined.

At our age, we always looked for opportunities to play pranks on each other— pulling chairs from underneath one another, pouring vinegar into someone's Kool-Aid, offering someone a wormy apple. Little things.

One evening I was struck by an advertisement in the back pages of my latest Superman comic book—you know, right there among the advertisements for dog whistles, X-ray specs, and plastic toy soldiers. The ad proclaimed, "Learn how to throw you voice!"

Wow! Wouldn't that be a great trick to play—not only on Clarence, but on classmates and family too? The ad promised that it "fools everyone."

There were a few other tricks I was contemplating—booklets on performing magic tricks, and hypnosis, offers to "paralyze a 200-pound attacker with just one finger" or to "wipe out" two attackers at once. Since it was going to cost a whopping 25 cents to learn how to throw my voice, I went begging, borrowing, and stealing pop bottles for the next few days.

Two days later I had more than enough money. I mailed the name and address form with a quarter wrapped in a sheet of paper, and continued my bottle collection efforts in order to buy more tricks. The "candy coated cockroaches" or the "fake blood" would be next. With these, I could be king of the pranksters.

Soon it was late June or early July. Gary and I crisscrossed our front and back yards several times catching some of the few remaining June Bugs and storing them in one of Mom's mason jars.

Paul used his pocketknife to poke holes in the lid. "You don't want to smother 'em to death, do ya?"

A little later, when Clarence and Susie stopped by, Paul suggested that I show them how to fly June bugs.

"Clarence," I said, "have you ever flown June bugs?"

"What's a June bug?"

Gary saw the question as an opportunity.

"These are June bugs!" he shouted, poking the jar into Clarence's face.

Susie screamed and Clarence jumped back.

I grabbed the jar from Gary. "Come on, I'll show you."

We walked to our back porch where I retrieved some sewing thread from Paul's tackle box. I opened the jar and Gary removed a bug. With a gentle touch Gary held it, while I attempted to tie the thread to one of the bug's rear legs. Unfortunately I wasn't careful enough and off came the leg.

"Ooh, that's gross," Clarence said.

Susie covered her mouth with her hand, quietly staring.

"Well, there are more where that one came from!" I exclaimed.

Gary presented me with another leg, and I looped the thread around it and pulled it snug—although more gentle this time. We walked into the middle of the yard to give ourselves plenty of room.

"Okay, Gary!" I hollered. "Let it go!"

Gary tossed the bug in the air. The June bug sensed freedom. It lifted itself into the air and began to fly in circles around us as I held the thread. I circled my arm above my head so I wouldn't get dizzy.

"Hey, that looks like fun," Clarence said.

"Here, you try it," I said, handing the thread to Clarence.

I watched Clarence, sharing his joy. I also noticed how cute Susie looked, with her blond hair and pretty smile. A few seconds later the leg broke off and the bug flew away.

We all took turns flying bugs and breaking off legs until Paul told me to quit. Mom said I had chores and the garden to attend to. Gary played with Clarence and Susie for a while until they had to go home.

A year or so later, our tradition of June bug flying gave way to a new sport when we purchased a kite at discount from Ward's Store.

Late May through June was the best time to gather wild strawberries, and the far northeastern slopes of the Snowdecker property had some of the best pickings. Mr. and Mrs. Snowdecker weren't even aware that this delicious fruit proliferated on their property, and we did a good job of keeping it a secret. Paul, Donna, and I, containers in hand, snuck around the Snowdecker property in a counterclockwise direction. Without making a sound, we climbed around boulders, rocks, vines, and poison ivy in an effort to evade detection. From mid-morning until the early afternoon, we worked the steep slopes in the hot sun and picked over five quarts of strawberries. We were very tired by the time we got home. That day I got my first really bad sunburn. Mom treated it with a mixture of vinegar and water that, despite its unpleasant odor, always soothed and cooled my burning skin.

I had just cleaned up from working in the garden when Mom handed me a letter.

"What's that?" I asked, looking a little surprised.

"It's for you. Didn't you order something from that funny-book a few weeks ago?"

"Oh yeah," I said, "I guess I did."

I walked away and hustled upstairs to my bedroom for some privacy. I started to open the envelope when I heard the stairway squeaking. Someone was sneaking up.

"Gary, what are you doing up here?"

"I just wanted to see what you got in the mail."

"I'll show you later," I said. "Just go away and leave me alone for a while."

"You promise?"

"Yeah, I promise. Now go away!"

I opened the envelope as I watched my brother disappear and close the stairway door behind him.

This was the first piece of mail I ever received that was addressed to me personally, and I felt important. But I was expecting my throw-your-voice kit to arrive in a more substantial package. Was this really the kit?

The envelope contained a cheap device made of plastic and metal, about the size of my thumb, along with instructions.

For the rest of the day when no one was around, I placed the device in my mouth as instructed and tried repeatedly to make it work. All I managed was a squeaking noise. That night I cleaned the device and hid it so that Gary wouldn't find it. The following day I kept trying whenever I found a moment or two of privacy, but to no avail.

Finally, on the third day, I was so frustrated that I asked Paul to try it.

"Tommy, I'm not gonna put that thing in my mouth. I don't know where it's been."

"It's clean, Paul. I just washed it. You can wash it again yourself if you don't believe me."

Paul took the device, washed it, read the directions, and made several attempts at making it work.

"This is a piece of crap," he said, handing it back to me. "You'll never throw your voice with that. Face it, Tommy, you've been gypped."

Paul's comment put the whole situation into perspective for me, but I wasn't ready to give up yet. I kept practicing for another day or two until the device broke. I was truly disappointed. That's when I finally showed it to Gary and told him how I had been cheated out of 25 cents.

"Gary, let this be a lesson to you. Never order anything from the back of those funny-books. They're all just a bunch of junk!"

Several years would elapse before I again ordered anything from magazines. I spent what little money I had on comic books and sweets.

<u>Truth and Consequences</u>

Ginny was 16 now and, with Mom's permission, was allowed an occasional date. Mom held very strict rules for her children—daughters especially—and she promised painful repercussions if they weren't followed.

One of Ginny's first dates was a double date with Billy Donnerton and another couple. At first they drove to Bluefield and enjoyed some hotdogs and Coca-Colas while joking around in the car. Then, after driving to the top of a mountain, they parked and started making out. A few minutes later, the other couple took a blanket and a flashlight and disappeared into the woods.

Billy now thought it was okay to take extra liberties with his date. Ginny enjoyed the kissing and some of the caressing, but when Billy started fondling her and demanding special privileges, she became nervous and uncomfortable. She felt like her intestines were being tied into knots.

"No, Billy, don't do that!"

But Billy didn't seem to understand the word *no*.

Ginny struggled to keep him at bay. She finally managed to break free and fell from the car onto the ground. In a state of panic, she ran down the road toward home until she was out of breath. More than a little angry, she left Billy and the others far behind.

As she walked, she wondered why boys were so rude and disrespectful. She also wondered if she would ever find a boy who didn't tie her stomach into knots. Ginny gasped when she realized how late it was. She started to cry as she increased her pace.

Ginny had walked about four miles when a car pulled up beside her. It was Donnerton and the other couple. He apologized and offered her a ride the rest of the way home. Ginny accepted the apology and was dropped off at the bottom of Kevin Lane.

Some of us were still awake, concerned about our sister's well-being. She was way past her curfew, and Paul, Donna, and I knew that Mom was waiting on the porch, a cigarette in one hand and a switch in the other. Worry and anger had worked Mom into a frenzy, and she was in no mood to listen to Ginny's excuses, no matter how sincere.

I can still picture Mom chasing my sister in circles as she delivered a nasty thrashing. I can still hear Ginny's screams too as the beating started on the porch and continued on into the house.

"Please don't do it, mommy!"

Whack! Whack!

"No, Mommy"

Whack! Whack! Whack!

"It wasn't my fault!"

Whack!

"Nooo, mommy!"

Whack, whack, whack!

"Noooo!"

Sticking my fingers in my ears and pulling the covers over my head just wasn't working.

The next morning Ginny didn't join us at the breakfast table. Her wounds were too fresh for advertising. The welts would heal quickly, but the other scars would take much longer.

I couldn't make any sense of Mom's fury. What could my sister have done to deserve such a beating? Ginny may have done some growing that night and perhaps Mom also. She probably realized her anger had overcome her reasoning, because I don't think she ever disciplined Ginny again.

A few days later Mom received some money from Daisy in the mail. She used it to buy Ginny a bus ticket to Lancaster, Ohio. Alone, Ginny began her first bus ride all the way to Ohio to spend the rest of the summer with her big sister.

Before Ginny left, I overheard Mom and her having what they thought was a private conversation. Ginny was providing some of the details of her nightmare-of-a-date with Billy Donnerton.

I thought I heard Ginny say, "Mom, you don't understand. Billy tried to *rake* me."

I didn't hear much more of their conversation, but I remember walking away deep in thought: Billy used a rake on her? How horrible it must have been for Ginny! If someone attacked me with a garden tool, I'd be just as upset. Ginny was lucky she didn't come home all bloody and bruised. No wonder she was late getting home!

When Ginny arrived in Ohio, living with her big sister wasn't easy. She couldn't relax with Daisy like she could with Mom at home. Daisy and Chester returned her just in time for school. She had been glad to get away from the Bluefield area, but now she was just as glad to be home.

Daisy brought our little nephew (now almost two) with her. Little Chester Junior didn't seem to like visiting our house on the hill. He kept repeating, "This place stinks. This place stinks." Other than *Mommy* and *Daddy*, I think they were the only words he knew.

Apparently, little Chester wasn't acclimated to real country living.

More Adventures

In a flash, the summer was over. Looking back, I faced the new school year with a surprising degree of determination and grit.

One thing was different this time. My neighbor Clarence was my buddy. I knew it the instant I saw booger stains on his front pockets. A few weeks after classes started, we began working on homework together. Whenever I didn't quite understand something, he was there with an answer, although not always the correct one.

One Saturday morning I dropped over Clarence's house. Susie opened the door, her mother standing behind her.

"Hi Tommy."

"Hi Susie. Mrs. Snowdecker, can Clarence come out and play?"

"Clarence is upstairs getting dressed, Tommy. He isn't feeling well."

"I'll tell him you're here," Susie said, running up the steps.

"You can wait here, Tommy," her mother said, pointing to the freshly waxed stairway landing. "Feel free to watch the cartoons on television."

As she walked away, I got the impression she had noticed how dirty my pants looked. Her suggestion that I sit on the stairs and not on her upholstery was a good idea. My pants were pretty dirty.

Mrs. Snowdecker didn't have to ask me twice to watch cartoons. I hadn't seen more than a couple hours of them in the last month.

Susie returned, informing me her brother was in the process of washing and dressing and would be down in a few minutes. For a while Susie and I sat on the stairway watching Mighty Mouse, one of our favorites. I enjoyed that little bit of quality time with her. During commercials I would glance around, admiring how well constructed and clean their house was. I even stood up and walked around a little so I could get a view of the new kitchen I heard they had put in.

It sure wasn't like ours. I found myself wishing that someday my family could have a house like this.

Before I knew it, half an hour elapsed and Clarence was finally walking down the stairs.

"Oh, you're still here," he said.

"Of course I'm still here. What took you …? Wow! What did you do to your hand?"

With his right elbow tucked into his ribs, Clarence held his bandaged right hand motionless in front of his chest.

"I cut it yesterday on a piece of glass in the backyard," he replied. It sounded like bragging when he added: "I have two stitches."

Clarence was fresh and clean and in no mood to play. So we watched some more cartoons and around noon I called it a day.

For several days Clarence favored that hand as if his whole arm was broken. Again, I couldn't help thinking I had the biggest sissy for a friend.

The day after he had the stitches removed he still wore a bandage. In a casual manner I grabbed his wrist, asking, "Hey, can I see your scar?"

He jerked his elbow into his rib cage, screaming, "Noooo!" You'd think I had committed bloody murder against him.

He wouldn't let anyone see his wound for several more days, saying it was still sore. After two weeks I finally got a peek. The wound was nothing more than a scratch. It took about a month for Clarence to stop favoring that injury.

The Falls Mills Grade School c. 1987.

Fourth grade was my year of awakening as a student. I don't recall being on the blackboard line, getting paddled, or being sent home with a note from the teacher at Falls Mills Grade School. Either I was a good student or she was an easy teacher.

I do, however, remember our school talent contest that fall. Entire classes from grades one through seven competed for prizes by doing the Hokey Pokey, while individual students competed by doing the Limbo, the Hula Hoop, and the Twist. (Chubby Checker recorded the Twist in 1959, and the dance became popular on the Dick Clark Show in 1960.)

The fact that I volunteered for a twisting contest was proof that I was losing some of my shyness. The rhythm and beat of a good song also helped. I can still recall the aching pain in my side as the dance progressed. Just when I felt like it was going to split, the song ended. My classmate Shirley Stevenson and I had taken first place. There was hope that I had at least a little rhythm in my hips and feet.

By winning the contest, I think Shirley finally forgave me for pulling that chair from underneath her as she was about to sit down. It was the usual thing to do when you had a crush on a girl. Shirley and Regina Sarver were two of the cutest girls in the whole school. But if I had known Shirley would hit her head on the cinderblock wall, I wouldn't have tried such a stupid stunt.

All the rhythm in the world won't help you when you get caught doing stupid things in stupid places.

It was a cool, damp fall morning. One of the season's first frosts hadn't quite evaporated with the rising sun. I had been looking for discarded pop bottles along Falls Mills Road and Kevin Lane when I saw them—a dozen or more unbroken whiskey bottles recently dumped onto a ledge off the side of the lane.

Wow, I thought, Harv or somebody must have had a busy week. The bottles beckoned me.

I picked up a stone and threw it at the bottles. *Thock*! I threw another. *Thrack*! The bottles shattered. Looking down, I saw a three-foot piece of rope that gave me a brilliant idea. I tied one end to a rock about the size and shape of my foot.

Tool in hand, I jumped down to the rocky ledge. Swinging the rock like a savage, I smashed the bottles with reckless abandon. As I stepped forward to smash the few remaining bottles, I slipped on a wet rock and tumbled forward, hands first to break my fall.

Alarmed, I sprang to my feet. I can't believe I did that, I thought, I'm not usually that clumsy.

Brushing glass shards from my hands, I surveyed the damage. A few small cuts or scrapes on my right hand, but nothing serious. Then, I saw it.

My right wrist had been slashed. Like Clark Kent opening his shirt to reveal Superman's mighty chest, my skin had parted to reveal red meat and tendons. I began to drool. The incision stared back at me, its bloody tears dripping to the ground. I started to cry and at the same moment threw up my breakfast. I made a frantic dash for home.

Someone heard me crying as I approached. Mom and Paul were beside me in an instant.

"Oh no, not again," Mom said. "Tommy, how did you do this?"

Scared and sobbing, all I could say was, "I was … playing in … Harv's trash pile."

The wound was ugly, but for some odd reason not bleeding much. Mom gave Paul the responsibility of escorting me to Dr. Porter's office in Pocahontas.

"He'll need more than a few stitches for this," she declared, wrapping a clean t-shirt around my wrist. Upon hearing that, I started sobbing louder.

"Come on Tommy—let's go," Paul said, and ushered me out the front door.

In emergencies like these, it was sometimes quicker to hitchhike to the doctor's office than to find a neighbor with transportation. Mom avoided hitchhiking, probably due to some bad experiences in her younger days, so I can remember walking five miles with her from Falls Mills to Bluefield, Virginia, for dental appointments. Sometimes we walked six miles to Pocahontas for doctor appointments. But this was no time for walking.

We hurried to Falls Mills Road. I held the bloody t-shirt tight against the wound while Paul stuck out his thumb. We got a ride from the first driver headed our way.

But our relief was short-lived. The middle-aged man, thinking I had attempted suicide and my life was at stake, drove recklessly. Paul tried to tell him there was no emergency, but he didn't believe us. Preoccupied with my injury, I wasn't aware that our rescuer sped and swerved and passed on curves and bridges. Paul was pretty sure he smelled alcohol in the car. I thought I was going to bleed to death. Paul thought we were going to die in a car wreck.

But by the grace of God, we made it there alive. Later that day I returned home—in slower fashion—with six or seven stitches in my wrist.

On the following Monday, my teacher and classmates wanted to know what happened.

To avoid the embarrassing details, I simply said, "I fell on a piece of broken glass."

The skin, drawn tight by the stitches, worried me. I was hesitant to bend my hand at the wrist, afraid I might tear open the wound. I favored the wound even after the stitches were removed.

So much so, Ginny said, "Tommy, you're beginning to look like Clarence holding your hand that way. Do you want us to call *you* a sissy too?"

Ain't gonna happen, I thought, I'll never be as wimpy as Clarence.

To compensate, I attempted to write left-handed. Even though the word ambidextrous was not yet part of my vocabulary, I had always wanted to be versatile with both hands. Well, that wasn't to be. My right side was so dominant that I couldn't even pick my nose left-handed.

Today I carry a well-defined reminder of my glass-breaking adventure. Over the years, people have made more than a few teasing insinuations about how I acquired a scar across my wrist.

Tag Along

Ginny turned 17 in late October. As part of her birthday celebration, she asked Mom if she could go to the drive-in movie with her friend Alvin, who had recently joined the Army and was on leave from basic training. Ginny and Alvin had known each other for a few months and had already been on a couple of short dates. But Mom wasn't ready to cast off the last bindings to her daughter, especially since the incident with Billy was still fresh.

"Ginny, you can go if you take Donna or one of your brothers with you."

"Oh, Mom!"

"No, I mean it," Mom said. "You should have someone else with you at the drive-in."

At first Mom suggested Paul, but he wasn't going to tag along with his big sister to just any old movie.

"What's playing?"

Ginny said, "It's *Kid Galahad* starring Elvis Presley."

If it had been a war, western, or monster movie playing, Paul would have jumped at the chance. "No thanks," he said, "I don't think I'll like that one."

Ginny ruled out Donna, the blabbermouth, as her chaperone. So I was left as the least objectionable choice.

"Tommy, do you want to go with Alvin and me to watch Kid Galahad at the drive-in?"

I looked at her with my mouth agape. "For real?"

"Sure. It's an Elvis Presley movie, and it's supposed to be a good one."

"Okay, I'll go. Thanks Ginny!"

"Good," she said, "Alvin will be here to pick us up in an hour. So, go wash up. You look dirty, and I don't want you stinking up the car!"

I wasn't exactly thrilled about protecting my sister's virtue. But I was excited about seeing a movie on the big screen—for the first time.

The ticket agent at the drive-in charged Alvin for two adults. If he'd looked a little closer, he would have seen me lying on the floor in back, covered with a blanket. Those two were so happy about sneaking me into the movie.

Alvin parked the car and it was time to hit the snack bar.

"Guess what, Tommy?" Alvin asked.

"What?"

"Congratulations, you win the grand prize!"

"What's that?" I said, with a puzzled look.

"Tonight you get a hotdog, a soda, and the honor of sitting in the front seat."

"That's okay with me."

They told me to wait in the car, and I watched the two lovebirds stroll away, hand-in-hand, to the snack bar. I was beginning to like Alvin.

The hotdog was a rare treat for me. It was fun eating and chatting with Ginny and Alvin. Soon the movie started, and the three of us settled into our viewing positions. I sat proudly behind the steering wheel, a rare Coca-Cola in hand.

Thirty minutes later I was enjoying the action, but having trouble understanding most of the plot and dialogue. Perhaps this wasn't the best movie for a 10-year-old. Also, the windshield was clouding-up, and the smacking sounds emanating from the back seat were becoming a distraction.

"Hey, you guys," I said, "I think fog is setting in. It's hard to see the movie screen."

Ginny and Alvin straightened up.

"Oh, that's not fog, Tommy," Alvin said, "that's condensation." He handed me a dollar bill. "Here, take this to the snack bar and buy yourself another hotdog. And take your time coming back."

I hesitated for a moment before taking the money. I didn't think Mom would mind me leaving them for a few minutes. They were only kissing. What kind of trouble could that lead to?

As I walked away from the snack bar with my hotdog, the air was pleasant and cool, much better than the hot, stuffy car. I sat on a swing in the kiddy section, watching a movie I didn't understand. Then I headed back to the snack bar to buy another Coca-Cola with what was left of Alvin's dollar. I didn't think he would mind; after all, he was paying me to stay away.

I had been gone almost 45 minutes when I decided to head back to the car. In the process, I got lost. Every row of parked cars looked the same. The reflected light from endless chrome bumpers and grills—freshly waxed—made the task even more difficult. Frantically, I tried to retrace my steps and recall what Alvin's car looked like.

I'd been wandering around the darkened drive-in for about ten minutes when someone honked. I walked in that direction and spotted the car. Alvin and Ginny were laughing.

"We saw you walk past two times," Alvin said, "and thought you might be lost."

"Oh," I said, "I knew we were parked here somewheres."

Alvin had moved to the driver's seat and Ginny sat next to him. I climbed into the back seat. Twenty minutes later, the movie was over.

I said, "I have to go pee."

"Can it wait 'til we get home?" Ginny asked. "We're leaving now."

"I think so," I said, ignoring the pressure in my bladder from drinking two large Colas.

Alvin started the car, Ginny unhooked the drive-in speaker, and we joined the line of exiting cars.

I had no idea it would take so long just to leave the drive-in. By the time we reached the highway, I felt my bladder would explode. Sensing my discomfort, Ginny said, "Do you want us to stop somewhere and let you go?"

"It's … it's okay, I … I can make it."

Just when I thought I was going to pee all over myself, the car stopped at the foot of Kevin Lane.

"Tommy, you go on home. Tell Mom I'll be there in a few minutes."

As they drove away I walked briskly up the lane, fumbling with my zipper as I went. At the trash pile, I let it go. It was the greatest physical relief I had ever experienced. I would have to wait four more years to match such a pleasure.

I made it back to the drive-in several more times after that. Sometimes Paul and I hitchhiked, and sometimes we walked the four miles. We usually tiptoed across the rocks in the creek, snuck through a hole in the fence, and watched the movie from under the trees by the bank. I don't think we ever paid. Occasionally, when the mosquitoes were biting, we would be brave and enjoy the movie from the swings in the kiddy section. Afterwards, if we couldn't thumb a ride, the walk seemed to take forever, and by the time we arrived home our hair and clothes would be damp from the late night fog. We always slept well after a night at the drive-in.

My sister Donna would be 13 in a couple of months. Her girlfriend Patty told her that a young man named Walter wanted to meet her. Since Walter was a member of a new church that had just formed in Bluefield, a date was set for them to meet at an evening service. Mom gave Donna permission to attend as long as I went with her.

When the evening arrived, Patty and her parents drove us to the church. It was cold outside, and we rushed through the introductions to enter the warm building.

Before the services had even begun, I was feeling uncomfortable with so many strangers and so many introductions. However, I was much more relaxed when the minister began speaking. His voice seemed to have a calming effect. He asked some in the audience to come forward to confess their sins, speak to the Lord, and receive His hand. Many people, including Donna, Patti, and Walter, marched to the front of the church. I insisted on staying behind, not knowing what was to come.

The people around me were behaving in odd ways. Some were standing and waving their arms in the air while others were rolling in the isles. At the same time, they were saying strange things in strange ways, especially up front where my sister was. It sounded like a foreign language; I couldn't make any sense of it. Thinking that dozens of eyes were upon me, I began to sweat from stress and nervousness. The whole scene began to feel like a nightmare that I could barely wait to escape. Was God forcing me to acknowledge my sins? But I was only 10 years old—what sins could I have committed?

I can't recall how much time Donna spent with Walter that night. She met with him only a couple of times after that. But it was often enough for Walter to present her with a Christmas present, a bottle of Evening in Paris perfume. Yes, the same fragrance in the same little cobalt blue bottle that had tickled Daisy's fancy nine years earlier. Donna was quite pleased.

I told my family they couldn't drag me back to that church again.

"It scares me, Mom."

"I don't blame you, Tommy." Mom said. "No one is going to make you go back there if you don't want to."

"Good!"

The Christmas Tree

In late November, Ginny and Alvin were sending letters back and forth to each other. Probably in love for the first time, my sister had no desire to continue her education. In fact, she later admitted, "I never even opened my books that year." Just like her brothers and sister before her, Ginny quit school. She was in the eleventh grade.

Ginny told Mom that she and Alvin were planning to marry when he was home on leave in January. She spent the remainder of the year helping Mom and getting to know her future in-laws.

Wesley and Ronnie were making the most of their military careers. They were also continuing to help Mom with finances as much as they could.

Wesley was steadily progressing in rank. His guitar playing was improving from playing in a couple of upstart rock-n-roll bands. While stationed in Germany, his love life took a positive turn. He wrote home, enclosing a picture of his new sweetheart—an attractive, dark-haired German girl. Mom and the rest of us were impressed.

Except for some in-law squabbling, Daisy was doing well. Chester was a good husband and provider.

A few days before Christmas, the county had a whopper of a snowfall. Seeing all that beautiful snow, I found myself filled with holiday energy and spirit. So much so, I boldly took it upon myself to provide the family with a Christmas tree. In past years, Dad or my older brothers and sisters provided them. This year I decided to beat them to the task.

In preparation for the hunt, I wore my warmest winter clothes. I pulled on a pair of well-worn black galoshes with metal clip fasteners. My regular winter jacket covered a wool sweater, a long sleeved cotton shirt, and a t-shirt. I donned a woolen scarf and a winter cap with earflaps (thinking Paul wouldn't mind). I chose a small bow saw because it would be easier to carry and use than an axe.

I snuck out the back door, telling no one about my mission. I headed north and skirted the Snowdecker property, crawling under several fences. When I reached the old deserted house, there were about four inches of snow on the ground with more on the way.

I came to the base of a small yet fairly steep hill sprinkled with magnolia and rhododendron. I saw these as minor obstacles. Continuing on, I encountered many decomposing tree stumps and sometimes found myself crawling on hands and knees through the snow-covered leaves. When I finally crested the steep hill I was out of breath and forced to take a rest.

I gazed at the beauty of the small valley below, now wrapped in snow. There was a stark and wonderful difference between this view and my first back in the summer of 1960. I saw the ruins of what once had been an impressive brick house, the only man-made structure in view. I scanned the valley and the hills in the distance for signs of fir, pine, and spruce. The steady snowfall made this task more difficult. I saw few choices.

I made my way down the slope and entered the valley. A large spruce tree stood near the foundation of the ruined house. Too big. The chimney and fireplace were still intact. I imagined the house in its prime, with Christmas stockings stuffed full of goodies and the family sitting by the fire. Charred roof rafters peeked from under the snow near my feet, giving me a hint of what might have happened.

I felt the first tingle in one of my big toes. I knew my hands and feet would soon feel the same bite. I hurried on through the valley, scouting one evergreen tree after another. I couldn't find one worth taking home. I felt frustrated and indecisive. Would I have to return empty handed? I wanted so much to bring my family a tree.

I looked back at the spruce near the ruins. From where I stood, the upper part looked perfect.

I dashed back to it. God, it was tall—at least sixteen feet! Time was ticking away, so I decided to cut down the whole tree and trim off the top.

I remember being afraid and extra careful it didn't fall on me. If it didn't kill me, I was sure Mom would. Still, I felled the tree in less than ten minutes.

I cut away some of the lower limbs and began sawing through the seven-inch diameter trunk. Exhausted and sweating, I opened my jacket and stuffed my wet cotton gloves in my pockets. Finally, I succeeded.

I rubbed my fingers and stomped my feet in an effort to warm them. "Please God," I cried, "give me enough strength to drag it home."

I grabbed a sturdy limb at its base and began hauling. At first the tree glided over the snow, but the further I dragged it, the heavier it became. There were about five inches of snow on the ground and it just kept coming. When I reached the base of the hill, the thought of giving up nagged at me.

But I was too stubborn to admit defeat. I exhausted myself again by sawing another three feet from the tree. Even this wasn't enough. I could pull it only halfway up the hill. I was wet, cold, and way too tired. I gave up and headed home.

It was around noon when I arrived and the snow had stopped. I took off my wet clothes and huddled close to the potbelly stove. Nobody had any idea of what I had done that morning.

After lunch I developed a plan. I approached my sister as she read a book.

"Donna," I whispered, "will you promise to keep a secret?"

She looked surprised at my offer.

"Sure," she replied in a curious tone.

In a hushed voice I said, "I cut down a Christmas tree this morning, and I need your help dragging it home."

"Why me?" she whispered.

"Well, Paul's not here. You're stronger than me, and it's going to take the both of us to drag it home."

Perhaps Donna saw this as an opportunity to show me she could be trusted. Or perhaps I caught my sister in an adventurous mood. At any rate, she agreed to help.

We dressed and left in a hurry, telling Mom we were going out to play. We didn't expect to take long. To save time we cut through the Snowdecker's property, hoping Clarence and Susie wouldn't see us and want to follow.

When we reached the base of the steep, snow-covered hill, Donna stopped.

"You didn't tell me it was going to be this far."

"You didn't ask," I replied. "Besides, it's just over the top of this hill. Come on!"

Huffing and puffing, slipping and sliding, we reached the top and coasted down the other side.

"Well, there it is. What do you think?" I asked proudly.

"It's too big! Tommy, why did you pick such a big one?"

"It was the only good one I could find," I said, sounding defensive. "Besides, I had to cut it two times to get it this far."

"Oh well," she said, "let's try dragging it."

We took hold of the tree and started pulling it up the hill.

"Wow, this sure is a lot easier with you helping."

But about thirty feet from the top of the hill we started slipping and sliding, and our enthusiasm began to crash.

"Let's cut some more off," she suggested.

"Okay."

Donna looked at me and I looked at her.

"Oh no! Donna, we didn't bring the saw!"

"Tommy!"

"I didn't think we needed it!"

It was snowing again. In fact, it was snowing so hard I could barely see the ruins of the old house about two hundred yards away.

"It's snowing too much now," she said. "It's just too slippery on this slope, Tommy. We'll have Paul come and help us tomorrow."

I watched Donna turn and walk away.

"Wait!" I shouted. "I know what—let's sweep a path through the snow with our feet."

"Oh, come on Tommy!" she screamed. "Stop being so stubborn. I'm cold and wet. Aren't you cold yet?"

"No! Donna, please. Let's give it one last try, and if we can't do it, then we'll come back with Paul tomorrow. Okay?"

"Okay," she said. "Let's hurry, then. My toes are getting awful cold."

We shuffled up and down the slope, clearing a path through the snow. We scattered a few dead branches along it for added traction.

Then, both of us grabbed hold of the tree and charged up the hill, grunting, groaning, and lunging until we finally crested the top.

"We made it!" I shouted. We smiled proudly at each other.

"Come on, Tommy, let's get this thing home before we freeze to death!"

The rest of the trip was mostly downhill. To avoid two fences, we dragged the tree across part of the Snowdecker's property. We hoped they wouldn't notice or mind the transgression.

With our hands and Donna's toes nearly frozen, we dragged the tree into our yard and left it near the front porch where it could be seen. Excited, we burst into the house.

"Hey everybody!" I shouted. "Look out the window and see what we brought home!"

Mom, Gary, and Debbie scrambled to the window for the surprise viewing.

"Look Mom," Gary shouted, "it's a Christmas tree!"

"I declare. Tommy, is that what you've been up to all day?"

"Yeah, Mom. Donna helped me. What do you think?"

"We'll have Paul check it out tomorrow. But if I find out you took that tree from someone's property, I'll have your hide, Tommy Mack."

"It's okay Mom, I promise. No one will miss it."

"You'd better be right young man."

The next day, Paul and I prepared the tree to fit on its base.

"Why did you pick such a big one?" he asked.

"Oh no, not you too," I moaned. "Paul, it was the best I could find."

"Well, we'll have to cut off some more."

The section I brought home was about eight feet tall and Paul cut off an additional foot. We proudly decorated it with multicolored paper chains and other homemade decorations, topped off by a cardboard star covered with aluminum foil.

We received the usual presents that Christmas. But perhaps the tree was the best present of all.

XI

FALLS MILLS
c. 1963

<u>Gary (9) Falls Mills</u>

Birds and Bees

Mom signed the marriage certificate, and Ginny and Alvin were wed early in January. In fact, the county office informed them they were the first couple to tie the knot that year in Tazewell County, Virginia. As a reward, they were given a case of laundry detergent and a case of soap.

Alvin's leave ended shortly after the wedding, and he returned to military duty in another state. For the next few months Ginny continued to divide her time between her mother-in-law and our family on Kevin Lane.

Spring planting was upon us again. One day Paul and I were working in the main garden below the house when I heard a strange sound coming from the woods. Using it as an excuse to take a break, I followed the sound into the woods and stopped at the fence bordering Harv's and Maggie's property. I waited under a buckeye tree, hoping to hear the sound again. I keenly remember that tree. It was the only one of its kind for miles around, and I always thought God had put it there just for the buckeye necklaces Donna and I made.

I heard the sound again and knew right away that it was puppies. I couldn't see them in the heavy underbrush, but could tell they were only a few feet beyond the fence. I dashed back to the garden.

"Paul! Paul! There's puppies in the brush!"

Paul dropped his garden tool and followed me. When he heard the whimpering, he said, "Tommy, you stay here. I'm going to get a closer look." He crawled through the fence and almost disappeared into the fresh spring overgrowth. From a distance of about 20 feet he called back to me.

"I see two puppies. Their mother isn't here, and I don't think we should be here when she gets back."

Paul and I returned to our work, but thoughts of the puppies kept clouding my mind. "Hey Paul, do you think Mom will let us keep them?"

"I don't know. Hey, look at what you're doing. You're missing a lot of the weeds on your side of the rows! Now pay attention—there'll be time to talk about the puppies come dinner time."

"I'm sorry."

While eating dinner that night, Mom cautioned us to stay clear of the puppies. "If the mother gets too nervous, she might carry them to a quieter place." Later that night, Paul said we could sneak a peek at them every two or three days.

As soon as Gary and I arrived home from school the next day, we tossed our books into a corner, and dashed outside to see Paul already working the garden. When he saw us, he put his fingers into his mouth, whistled, and motioned for us to join him.

"Tommy, I looked in on the puppies a few minutes ago and saw them nursing with their mother. I know you guys want to see them, but the mother growled at me. I don't think she's ready for anyone to get close to her and the pups."

"Oh, can't I just take a peek?"

To satisfy our curiosity, we walked into the woods and crawled through the fence, stopping just a few feet from the new family. The pups looked so cute. They appeared to be about three weeks old and were lying on a dirty rug nestled beneath a rusty piece of tin roofing.

The mother stared at us with a clear message: DON'T COME ANY CLOSER! Again, we returned to our chores.

"Hey Paul, how do you do that whistling thing with your fingers?"

"Oh, you mean this?"

He placed his dirty fingers in his mouth and whistled so loud it hurt my ears.

"Wow! Yeah, like that. Can you teach me to do it?"

Gary and I walked closer to study his method. After forming the letter V with his fingers, he rested the point of the V on his tongue just inside his lower front teeth. He took a deep breath, closed his puckered lips, and blew hard. This produced another shrieking whistle.

"Now, you try it," he said, as I wiped away his spit.

Paul coached as I tried whistling several times. With each try I produced nothing but air and spit. Gary too.

"Keep practicing," he said, "you'll get it someday."

For the next two weeks I watched the puppies grow and tried to teach myself to whistle.

It was only a few weeks before summer vacation. In the fall I would be moving on to the fifth grade, Debbie would enter the first grade, Gary the third, and Donna the seventh. Paul would be leaving Falls Mills School and entering eighth grade at Graham High in Bluefield. A few school bullies would be glad to see him go, but I had little concern because I was beginning to hold my own in the schoolyard.

Paul had failed the second grade at Abs Valley, while Donna and Paul had failed the sixth grade at Falls Mills. Looking back, I think Paul flunked sixth grade because he had girls on his mind. One could have been his very attractive sixth grade teacher, Miss French. A year after flunking Paul, Miss French would refuse to send Donna on to the next grade. This kept her two grades ahead of me. Donna thought her teacher was mean, but Paul, despite being held back, enjoyed Miss French.

For nearly two years Paul had been suffering from repeated bouts of sore throat and fever. Now, every two weeks he'd get sick, recover, and then get sick again. My brother's illness placed such a huge emotional and physical burden on Mom that she demanded an answer. The doctor found that Paul suffered from severe bouts of tonsillitis and needed his tonsils removed.

It was a big day when Paul came home from the hospital. We all gathered around as he tried sitting up in bed to down a glass of apple juice and eat a small helping of ice cream. He was still so out of it that he was lucky to nod or shake his head. But the next afternoon, Miss French came to the house to see how her star pupil was progressing.

During the visit, Paul was as lively as a 19-year-old on his honeymoon. As a get-well present, Miss French gave him a watercolor set and some coloring books, and she told him to hurry up and get well. That was all Paul needed to hear. The next day he was running around much quicker than expected.

There was one drawback from having his tonsils removed; he was no longer able to run far without getting a sore throat. From that point on, Paul's ability to participate in competitive sports was seriously diminished.

Paul was approaching 16, and I noticed he was beginning to talk more and more about girls, a subject we had rarely, if ever, discussed.

"Hey Tommy," he said, "let's go down to the cliffs and swing on the vines."

"Okay, but we better hurry before Gary sees us. He'll want to come too, and I don't want him tagging along."

"Yeah, good idea," Paul said, "he might get hurt down there."

Halfway down the lane we turned left and trampled across the forsythia and honeysuckle growth that carpeted a trash pile of countless rusty cans, buckets, tubs, and bottles. About 30 feet beyond, we came to a 15-foot cliff. We easily navigated our way to the bottom, using familiar hand and footholds, then scurried down a steep bank to a large rock outcropping.

Thirty feet below that, we grabbed the tree vine we had severed from the ground at waist level. Taking turns, we ran down a steep slope, jumped as hard and as far as we could, and sailed in a wide arch 15 feet above the edge of Falls Mills Road before landing on the other side of the tree. No matter how many times I did it, I could never shake the cold and hollow feeling in my gut as I looked down at the highway from high in the air.

Paul and I were careful not to swing when traffic was in sight. Someone might report us to the sheriff. Finished with our swinging, we tied the vine to the tree trunk and sat together catching our breath on the gnarled and massive roots. We enjoyed the shade, the silence, and the view of the road and creek.

"Tommy, if I tell you a secret, will you promise not to tell anyone?"

Wow, my big brother wanted to confide in me.

"Sure Paul," I promised, "I won't tell a soul."

"You know I'll kick your butt if you do, don't you?"

"Yeah, I know. Don't worry. I'll keep my mouth shut. What's your secret?"

"I come here after school sometimes," he said, "to watch the traffic zoom by."

I grew perplexed. Was that my big brother's revelation? He watches traffic? I'd have no problem keeping that a secret.

"Really?" I said.

"Yep. Usually I come here right after school. That's when most people are starting to leave work and a lot more cars are on the road."

We fell silent. A few more cars passed through.

"So Paul, you don't want me to tell anyone that you like to watch cars?"

"No silly," he said, raising his voice, "what I don't want you to tell is that I like to look at girls' legs when they drive by."

"Oh!" Suddenly my brother was making sense—well, just a little.

"Yeah, this time of the year the girls wear short skirts and from here you get a great view."

I shifted my position and focused on a stream of cars rolling by.

"Watch Tommy," Paul said with excitement, "here come some now."

Due to the dangerous curve at Kevin Lane, many of the cars slowed to a crawl, giving us a clear view through the open passenger side windows. That's when I caught a glimpse of what my brother was enjoying.

"Yeah, I think I see what you mean."

"Sometimes I get to see some real nice ones," he added.

"What kind of legs do you like, Paul?"

"I like the ones that aren't too fat or too skinny."

"I think they're my favorite, too," I agreed.

We watched cars and legs pass for a few more minutes, and I got to thinking.

"Paul, have you ever kissed a girl?"

He thought a moment. "No. Oh, wait a minute—there was a group of girls back in Elgood that kissed me while we were hiding behind the stage."

"Wow!" Now I was beginning to get excited.

"Oh yeah, I almost forgot. I did kiss a girl one time when I played a game of Post Office at our neighbor's house in Jenkinjones."

When I heard Paul say the words Post Office and kiss in the same sentence, I was shocked. I had forgotten about the game. Now I wanted to know more.

"Paul, what's kissing have to do with the Post Office?"

"It's just a silly game, Tommy. But it can be fun if a lot of people are playing."

"Like how much fun, Paul?"

"Well, the boys and girls separate into different rooms called the Post Office. Each boy takes a turn visiting the girls and gets a kiss from each of them. Then each girl takes a turn visiting the boys and getting a kiss. It's something like that."

"Oh, I see."

Paul and I watched the cars roll by.

"Paul, why do boys like kissing girls and looking at their legs?"

He stood up.

"You shouldn't worry about those things just yet," he said, brushing leaves and dirt from his pants. "You'll find out when you're a little older. Come on, we better be get'n home now." He scrambled up the steep hill on all fours and I was right behind.

As I went about my chores and games the next few days, my mind kept wandering back to the kissing game. Just when I had almost forgotten the subject again, Clarence and I saw Debbie and Susie on the back porch playing tea. The sight prompted me to form a plan.

"Clarence, have you ever kissed a girl?"

"No. Have you?"

"No, I haven't, but I'd like to. Would you like to kiss a girl, Clarence?"

"Maybe, but it would depend on who she was."

"Yeah, I wouldn't kiss an ugly girl," I said. "Have you heard of the kissing game called Post Office?"

"I don't think so. What is it?"

I explained the game. Once I had sparked his curiosity, I said, "Would you like to kiss my sister Debbie?"

"Oh, I don't think so, Tommy. She's too young."

"Would you rather kiss Donna?" I countered. "She's three years older than you."

Clarence quickly stood tall. "You bet!" And then he shriveled back down just as fast. "But I would be more scared to kiss her. I don't think she would want to kiss me."

"Look, Clarence," I said, "if I can stomach kissing your little sister, you should be willing to kiss one of mine." Clarence had no idea how eager I was to kiss Susie. "You're ten years old and I'm eleven," I persisted. "Don't you think it's about time we kissed our first girl?"

"Well, okay, I guess I could start with Debbie. But it don't mean I like her."

We approached our sisters on the porch, who pretended to sip tea. I told them about a new game called Post Office that none of us had ever played before.

"Yeah, it's supposed to be a lot of fun," Clarence added.

The girls were curious and eager to find out more. For our plan to work, Clarence and I found a secluded location—the smokehouse beside Clarence's driveway. On the way there I explained the game and promised the girls they wouldn't be kissing their brothers. I added that it's more fun with more people, but we had enough for our first time.

When we arrived at the smokehouse, Clarence insisted that Susie and I enter first.

"Okay, but you better take your turn when we're finished."

"I will," Clarence promised.

Except for a few shattered mason jars on the floor and shelves, the smokehouse was empty. Holding the door open, I warned Susie to be careful of the broken glass. Looking directly at Clarence, I said, "Count to one hundred, then you can knock on the door."

"Okay," he promised.

I stepped in behind Susie and closed the door. With a crooked smile, she returned my look with a curious intensity. For a brief moment I wondered if she had done this before.

I heard Clarence counting, "One ... two ...."

I approached Susie and placed my hands on her shoulders. As I pulled her closer, I felt her nervous resistance. She began to retreat and I followed. I pressed her against a shelf where she could no longer retreat and moved my lips close to hers.

"Six ... seven ... eight ...."

With our eyes wide open and our lips puckered, we anticipated the kiss with a slight shift of our feet.

"Nine ... ten ...."

"Aiyeee!" Susie screamed.

I jumped backward. Clarence stopped counting and opened the door.

Looking down, I realized Susie's sandals had provided zero protection from the broken glass. The side of her foot was slashed.

"She cut herself!" I shouted. "Help me get her to your house!"

While Susie screamed and cried, Clarence and I shepherded her across the driveway to the kitchen door where Mrs. Snowdecker already waited. The nasty wound bled heavily.

"Mom! She cut her foot on a piece of glass in the smokehouse!"

Oh no, I thought. Boy, are we going to get it.

Sure enough, Mrs. Snowdecker asked, "What were you doing in the smokehouse?"

"Just playing," Clarence replied in a sweet and innocent tone.

"Good Lord, what are you kids going to get into next?" She wrapped a dish towel around her daughter's foot. "Tommy, you and Debbie go home."

A few minutes later, Debbie and I watched from our front porch as Clarence, Susie, and their mother drove past, headed for the doctor's office.

Susie wasn't going to like getting stitches. And from the looks of her foot, she would need a few. In fact, I wouldn't be surprised if Clarence got jealous.

As they drove out of sight, other thoughts ran through my mind, none of them pleasant. The quest for my first kiss had turned into a nightmare.

The following day, Debbie approached me at our garden.

"Tommy, Susie's mom was just at our house talking to Mommy about something. I think it was about us playing in their smokehouse."

Uh oh, now I was in real trouble.

A few minutes later, Donna yelled from the kitchen doorway.

"Tommy Mack! Mommy wants to see you in the house! Now!"

When I walked into the kitchen, Mom was staring at me with an angry look in her eyes. Goose bumps collided along the hairline at the back of my neck, as I sensed what was coming.

"Tommy, was it your fault Susie cut her foot yesterday?"

"Uh, I guess so."

My eyes bugged out when I spotted the freshly cut switch lying on the table. Gripping me with one hand, Mom whacked me hard across my shoulders and back.

"Ouch!"

"Ow!"

"Ow!"

She kept beating me, but never below my waist, where thick pants protected me.

Finally the switch broke and she thought I had learned my lesson. I fought back tears and dashed to the privacy of my bedroom.

For some time afterwards, I cursed Clarence's parents for not clearing out the broken glass. Besides school, I saw little of Clarence and Susie after that.

One day, about a week before the end of the school year, I was sitting alone on my front porch. I heard a noise and saw Susie sneaking through a hole in the fence between our properties. She was walking fine and wore no bandages

"I've been trying to catch you alone, Tommy. We're moving away tomorrow, and I just wanted to say goodbye."

Before I could say anything, she leaned over and placed a fleeting but firm kiss on my lips.

"Bye, Tommy."

"Bye, Susie." She flashed me her patented Susie smile, said nothing more, and was gone. I never saw her or Clarence again.

Donna, Gary, and I had just walked home from our school bus stop near Ward's store. As we climbed the front porch, we heard loud male voices coming from the driveway of the vacated house next door. We poked our heads through an opening in the fence to see what was going on.

To our surprise, we saw two pickup trucks and some men and women moving furniture into the house. Wow! We're getting new neighbors already?

The three of us rushed into the kitchen to tell Mom the good news. Of course, she already knew.

As the week wore on, we learned that our new neighbors were the Stetterman family. Mr. and Mrs. Stetterman had three sons. John was almost 18, Ronnie was 16, and Ricky was about my age. Ricky was one grade ahead of me in school because he hadn't flunked a year. Two weeks into the summer vacation I had shown Ricky Stetterman all the cliffs, swings, and swimming holes I could think of.

There were no Stetterman girls to consider kissing, and for the longest time I thought it was God's way of punishing me for my sins.

We continued checking in on the puppies and their mother, and after a while she began to trust us. By July the dogs were running around our property and having a good old time. They were Labradors. The black one we named Prince, the brown one we called Scruffy. (We couldn't call him Brownie, as there would never be another dog like that in the Dixon family.) We treated the dogs like family, feeding them scraps from the table, but Mom insisted they weren't allowed in the house.

Scruffy had mange, and as the days wore on his condition worsened. Paul and I tried baths; flea powder; and even motor oil, a desperate, old-fashioned remedy, all to no avail. There was no way we could afford a veterinarian, so Scruffy started to lose weight. He walked away one day and never came back. A few days later, a foul odor near the cliffs led us to his decomposing body. Paul and I buried the carcass with a small wooden cross as a marker.

Prince, on the other hand, seemed very healthy. He hardly had an itch to scratch, let alone a skin disease. From then on, Prince was a constant companion for my siblings and me.

Years later I would learn that it was not unusual for one puppy to succumb to mange and a sibling to thrive without a trace of the disease. Some were born with resistance and some were not.

Not long after, Prince's mother disappeared. I figured she was either taken in by someone or more likely killed. Many dogs and cats don't live long in the mountains, even with a good home.

Mom received two letters in late June. One was from Daisy, telling us that Chester had been assigned to Lackland Air Force Base in Texas. By the Fourth of July, her family was living in San Antonio.

The other letter was from Wesley. He was coming home for a three-week leave in September. Afterward he would be assigned to duty at Fort Hood, Texas. That wasn't too far from Daisy in San Antonio.

It had been well over a year since I had seen Wesley and I was excited. In preparation for his arrival, I tripled my efforts to learn how to whistle and, with encouragement from Paul, I started lifting weights.

Paul and I had made dumbbells by filling two Hi-C juice cans with cement. Before the cement hardened, we imbedded into it a one-foot long wooden handle. Several times each week we'd practice our lifting exercises on whichever porch was shadier. I had high hopes of being as strong as Paul, so I could work the well pump with just one hand. Until that happened, I'd have to continue placing my entire body across the pump handle and ride it down, a process I repeated until I collected all the water I needed. Heck, collecting water had become a good workout all by itself.

The Feud

Paul and I met at the vine swing below the Stetterman property. It was around three-thirty in the afternoon—quit-n-time—and our plan was to swing and watch the rush-hour traffic (and legs) go by. I had swung only a couple times when it was Paul's turn. He had made a good, wide swing over the edge of the highway, when he let out an alarming scream. I watched as the vine slowly lowered him to the side of the road below, unhurt.

The smaller supporting vines attached near the tree-tops had rotted to the point that it could no longer support his weight. The good thing about vine swings is they seldom break all at once.

After a good belly laugh, Paul climbed the steep bank to rejoin me. We sat back to watch the traffic and girls whisking by, acknowledging that there were no more good vine swings so close to home. Paul and I were about to leave when we heard footsteps rustling the leaves on the rocky outcrops above us.

"Oh no," I said, "it's Gary." He had finally found our hiding place.

"Mommy's looking for you two. She wants you to come home now."

Paul and I got up from our tree roots and began climbing.

"Gary, stay there," Paul said, "we're coming."

Upon reaching the top, we noticed that Ricky and Ronnie Stetterman had just walked past Gary and were standing in the pathway directly in front of us.

"What are you doing on our property?" Ronnie asked.

I said, "Just playing and swinging."

"Well, this is our property and my dad wants you Dixons to keep off."

"No way," Paul said, "this ain't your property."

"My dad says it is."

"This is state property," Paul said. "We've been playing here for three years and we're not stopping now."

Paul and I were standing downhill from the Stetterman brothers with our backs to the cliffs. Not the best defensive position.

"That's what you think," Ronnie boasted.

Gary sensed trouble.

"I'm going to tell Mom!" he shouted, turning and running for home.

I was surprised and confused by the sudden confrontation. I took my eyes off Ricky and Ronnie to glance at Paul and didn't see it coming.

Ronnie pushed me backwards and took a running charge at Paul. I struggled to keep my balance, overcome by a sense of helpless freefalling. Instinctively, I reached out and grabbed Ricky's shirt. I guess I didn't want to make the trip alone.

Ricky and I landed in the trash pile below. We rolled several times, stopping less than three feet from the edge of the 12-foot drop-off. We were lucky—the vegetation had cushioned and slowed our fall. Ricky and I rose to our feet, trying hard to maintain our balance on the spongy vegetation.

Ricky scrambled his way back up the steep bank with me in full pursuit. I had taken three or four steps when Ricky turned and pushed me backwards again. Upon landing, I felt a sharp pain in my hand. I ignored the pain and continued the chase. Once I reached the top, Ricky was already out of reach. Ha! He was scared of me! Then I saw Paul on top of Ronnie, serving him the last of several knuckle sandwiches. Maybe Ricky was afraid of Paul, not me.

I noticed I was bleeding from a gash on the back of my hand. Seeing all that blood, I started pouting.

Paul left Ronnie on the ground, battered and dazed.

"What's the matter, Tommy?"

"Ronnie pushed me into the trash pile," I cried. Then, I pointed at Ricky: "And ... and *he* made me cut my hand!"

Seeing the blood running down my fingers, Paul became infuriated. He lit out for Ricky, who cowered in the distance. Ricky didn't stop running until he was safe inside his house. On the way back to attend to me, Paul passed a bruised and limping Ronnie who shied away, giving my brother a wide berth.

Paul took a closer look at my cut hand.

"Oh, it's not that bad. You won't even need stitches."

He wrapped my hand with my clean handkerchief and examined me for more cuts.

"Are you okay? Are you hurt anywhere else?"

"I don't think so. Paul, I think Ronnie was trying to push me over the cliff!"

"Yeah, they're some crazy neighbors. I guess we'll have to keep a close eye on them."

Paul and I were halfway home when Mom and Gary met us at the lane. She was disturbed by our story. We had always gotten along with our neighbors. She wondered what could have turned the Stetterman boys so ugly all of a sudden.

Mom said we weren't allowed on their property anymore. So, we promised her we'd stay off the Stetterman property from now on, but we occasionally sneaked to the lower cliffs, where no one bothered us.

A day or two later, Paul, Gary, and I were playing over in the cow pastures adjacent to the Stettermans' pigpen. For the last two weeks, Paul had been making a bow and arrows. He spent hours searching for the right sized hickory sprout. Then he'd whittle it down to the perfect size and weight. Arrows were fashioned from young and straight sprigs of hardwood. Small tree suckers usually worked well. He used heavy duty fishing line for a bowstring and bird or duck feathers for the arrows. Arrowheads weren't necessary since we rarely shot into anything other than the air, ground, or cardboard. Occasionally, a wasp's or hornet's nest would be the target. Then the tip of the arrow would be wrapped in rags, dipped in kerosene, and set afire.

The cow pastures provided plenty of room for testing our new weapon. Facing uphill with our backs to the Stettermans' fence, Gary and I watched as Paul fired arrows high into the sky. We'd study the arrow's flight, and when it reversed course and headed for earth, we'd listen for the distinctive *sssuumph* sound when it penetrated the ground. What a satisfying sound that was! Sometimes Paul would misjudge and shoot a little too high above us, or the wind would carry it back to us. We'd have to skedaddle out of there to avoid an arrow in the head. If anything like that happened, we knew we'd also get the switch.

THOMAS DIXON

We were smack-dab into the middle of our shooting when we heard a deep and manly voice behind us.

"Go on, get your ass over there!"

We turned to see Ricky, Ronnie, and their big brother John walking briskly toward us, with Mr. Stetterman right behind. As they approached the fence, Paul, Gary, and I backed away.

I thought it was nice that they were going to apologize for their earlier behavior.

Once again, Mr. Stetterman shouted, "John, either you get over there and kick that boy's ass, or I'm going to kick your ass right here and now! Ya hear!"

I was petrified. John was almost two years older and considerably bigger than Paul. But then again, Paul had easily gotten the best of Ronnie. He probably could handle John too—I hoped.

John climbed the fence, jumped to the ground, and charged headfirst into Paul. My brother sidestepped him, pushed him to the ground, and jumped on top of him. That's when the cheering started.

Ricky and Ronnie shouted, "Get up, John! Get up!"

Mr. Stetterman screamed, "John, get your ass off that ground!"

Gary and I were shouting, "Go, Paul! Go!"

As Paul and John wrestled, I noticed they were about a foot away from a fairly ripe cow pie. John was on his stomach soaking up punches to his head and making futile attempts at dislodging Paul from his back.

"You'd better do something real soon, boy!" Mr. Stetterman shouted. "You're pissing me off!"

"Watch out for that cow pie, Paul!" I shouted.

Apparently Paul had a plan of his own. Gary and I watched as he slowly worked John's squirming body toward the cow pie. Once they were close enough, Paul pressed the side of John's head into the manure, breaking through the hardened crust to the fresh, juicy, and smelly mush inside.

"Oooh!" Gary and I groaned.

That's when Mr. Stetterman lost control. "I'm gonna come over there and kick your ass right now!" The big man charged the fence and I shouted a warning.

"Get up Paul! He's coming! Hurry up, Mr. Stetterman is coming!" Paul gave John's face one last christening before he jumped to his feet.

My brothers and I were vaulting the lower pasture fence to gain the safety of our garden when we heard Mom.

"You leave those boys alone! You're a grown man! You should be ashamed of yourself!" She was pissing angry.

We looked back to see Mr. Stetterman cursing and dragging John across their pigpen. It looked like he may have been pulling John by the ear. No doubt it was the clean one. Ricky and Ronnie stumbled along behind them.

As we walked across the backyard, Mom rapped her knuckles real hard atop Paul's noggin.

"Ouch!"

"You boys just can't seem to stay out of trouble, can you?"

When we told her the whole story, she tried to hide her crooked smile. She was letting us know she was proud of us. No one in the Stetterman family bothered us after that, and we didn't bother them either.

We heard the shouts throughout the house. "Wesley's here! Wesley's here!"

We ran to the front porch to greet him. He was standing next to a bright red, sparkling new 1963 Volvo. It had to be the most beautiful thing I had ever seen upon the hill at Kevin Lane. Wesley was sure proud of it.

"Whacha think, Mom?"

"It looks real nice, Wesley. I especially like the color."

Along with sparklers and cherry bombs to celebrate the occasion, Wesley brought along small surprises for each of his siblings. Mine was a handsome Barlow pocketknife with a three-inch blade and a brown-speckled ivory handle. It was my first knife and the best gift I had ever received from one of my brothers. Gary was disappointed he didn't get one, too.

"Gary, you're too young to have a knife just yet," Wesley warned. "You might cut yourself."

Gary dropped his head, curled up his lip, and gave a sigh of hurt and disappointment.

During his leave, Wesley was a busy young man. Besides celebrating the Labor Day week with fireworks left over from the Fourth of July, he had several dates with an attractive redhead named Kay. Apparently, his relationship with the pretty German girl hadn't worked out.

A couple of days later Wesley piled several of us into his Volvo and drove to the west side of the dam. When we got there, he offered Paul, Donna, and me 50 cents each to wash his car. At the time, it may have been the most money I had earned in a day. While the three of us were at work, Wesley, Kay, and Ginny went swimming in the muddy water. It was real hot and sunny that day. I wanted to join them, but the water looked too deep and muddy for me. Ginny and the two lovebirds were having so much fun they forgot to keep an eye on young Gary. Tired of watching the fun, he grew bored, striped to his underwear, and decided to go swimming. By the time Wesley rescued him, Gary had swallowed more than a mouthful of that muddy water. Gary had no fear.

Shortly after his arrival in Texas, Wesley wrote home to say that he and Kay were engaged. It turned out that Wesley and Kay knew each other through Ginny and had exchanged a few letters during the preceding months. I would soon have my first sister-in-law.

I wasn't able to work the pump with one hand before my big brother left. And it was just a few days after Wesley departed that I squeaked out a little-bitty whistle. Or at least I thought I did.

"Paul, I think I've got it!" I shouted. I tried it again as he watched, but produced nothing more than spit. "Darn, I thought I had it, Paul."

"Keep working at it, Tommy."

I had to quit trying when my lips started to cramp.

Early the next morning I got dressed, enjoyed a refreshing pause in the reading room, washed up, and ate breakfast. When I walked onto the back porch, I stood next to the well pump and looked out over the cow pastures in the distance, wondering what chores I had to do. Then the strangest thing happened. I placed my fingers in my mouth and what came out was a sound that Paul would be proud of—a near-perfect whistle. After succeeding in three out of five attempts, I ran to find Paul.

I found him in the house and managed several ear-piercing whistles.

"Alright, Tommy," Paul said, "I think you've got it."

My success was also apparent to Mom.

"Okay, okay, you've made your point. Now take it outdoors!"

Learning to whistle was one of my proudest moments.

Sometime during early summer Mom received word from Dad. He was due home in late September. Mom also received a letter from Ronnie in July. He wanted to save money to buy a car and would no longer send her military allotment checks. He said Dad should be able to get a job.

Now I had two weeks to get used to the idea of my father being around. Would he be barking out orders? Would he go back to getting drunk? Would he buy another gun and start beating on my mother? To be honest, that was the essence of how I remembered him.

Meanwhile, Paul began to intensify his weight-training regimen. I didn't know it at the time, but he was more worried about his father's return than anyone and was serious about being able to defend the family. After all, he had been the man in the family ever since Ronnie had left home.

The Homecoming

When the Dixon kids charged into the woods for recreation, all critters (large and small) would head for cover. In addition to playing Cowboys and Indians, we pretty much acted like Indians on the warpath. That's probably why my siblings and I rarely encountered snakes and other varmints in the woods.

It was the second weekend after the start of school. Gary, Paul, Prince, and I had spent an hour or two playing Cowboys and Indians among the cliffs and rocks above the Stetterman property. With Paul and Prince in the lead, we were slowly working our way homeward.

"Don't move," Paul shouted, waving his arms above his head.

Gary and I froze; we thought Paul had spotted some type of varmint. He pointed toward the side of the pathway about 20 feet away. He crouched low and moved in slow motion as he picked up a sturdy stick lying nearby. Gary and I were clueless, but we knew our brother. He wouldn't behave in such an odd way without a good reason. Before Paul could approach the mystery critter, Prince charged onto the scene. That's when Gary and I saw what Paul was stalking.

What looked like dead wood on the forest floor was actually a snake, and clumsy Prince had forced it to give away its position. Paul was quick. Before the dog spotted it, he clubbed the snake just below the head, breaking its neck. Paul had to use both hands to lift the dead snake with the stick. Close to five feet in length, it was one of the biggest blacksnakes he had ever seen, let alone killed.

We resumed our trek homeward, pausing for a drink of water in a stream at the base of the final hill. We had tasted the water before and, as usual, it was refreshing. While Paul and Prince poked around the rocks, Gary and I searched for a tree.

Of all our childhood activities, climbing trees had to be one of our favorites. On the other hand, climbing young saplings and bending them over wasn't the most environmentally friendly twist to add to the game. Nevertheless, the Dixon boys had perfected the sport.

Gary and I raced to see who could climb and bend over the biggest tree. He bent a skinny sapling 30 feet downhill from the stream. I climbed a bigger one less than three feet from Gary's. Then, in triumph, I leaned my sapling over and parallel with Gary's. As I dangled in the air above my little brother, I worked my way hand over hand further out the sapling, until it lowered me close enough to step on Gary's hands as he held on to his sapling. Gary yelled in pain and let go. I had won.

Gary accepted defeat by climbing back onto his bent tree with me. Now four to five feet off the ground, Gary and I stood side-by-side as I bounced up and down on his sapling.

Gary shouted, "Stop shaking the tree, Tommy!"

I bounced harder and harder as my brother screamed louder and louder.

"Stop bouncing, Tommy! Stop bouncing! You're gonna make me fall!"

Paul shouted a warning: "Tommy, stop picking on him!"

It was too late. Gary's feet slipped and he fell off the tree. I could tell he wasn't hurt, but his pride was. Hurt enough for him to pick up a rock and throw it at me. Fortunately, it missed its mark.

"Paul, Gary's throwing rocks!"

I watched Gary as he scrambled about. I wondered if he was looking for another rock. Now Paul was concerned about Gary's behavior.

"Gary, you better behave yourself!"

I knew Gary wasn't paying attention. He stooped over and picked up something. I wasn't going to wait to find out what it was. I dismounted the sapling and ran splashing across the stream with Gary chasing me. I stopped about 30 feet up the hill, turned around to face my attacker, and saw my brother cradling a large rock in his palm.

"Paul, Gary's trying to hit me with a rock!"

Gary stared up at me with an ugly frown. His face was flushed with anger and his chest was heaving.

Paul stopped what he was doing to pull the fuse from the argument.

"Gary, put down that rock!"

I moved another 10 feet up the hill, then turned to face my brother again. I was dripping sweat and every heartbeat pounded at my ear drums. Before Paul could stop him, Gary heaved the fist-sized rock high into the treetops above me. I heard it brush leaves and snap twigs, but couldn't see it. I strained to pick up its flight path. Should I move or stand still? Do I move left or do I move right?

I took one step to the left, and the rock struck the left side of my forehead. I fell back on my behind as my scalp split open. A metallic taste slid across my tongue and I almost lost consciousness. Paul heard the cracking sound too, followed by my screams.

When Paul and Gary reached me, I was griping my head with bloody hands.

"Ah shit, Gary," Paul muttered, "what have you done now?"

Prince was curious, poking his nose into my face and sniffing my bloody head and hands.

Panting like a dog himself, Gary just stared at me. He seemed surprised that his rock had done such damage. Indeed, he may have been proud of his accomplishment.

Paul wrapped my head with Gary's t-shirt. With Prince close behind, we rushed for home.

"Gary," I gasped between tears, "you're really gonna get it when Mom sees what you did."

With a forlorn look, Gary said, "Well, you asked for it."

When we got home, Mom was livid.

"For crying out loud, Paul, how did this happen?"

"Gary hit me with a rock!" I cried.

Paul said, "Mom, I told Gary several times to put the rock down, but he wouldn't listen."

We turned to hear Gary's sorry defense, but he was nowhere to be found. Just before we entered the house, he had apparently taken a detour.

The weather was supposed to be quite cool that night. Gary had to come home and face the music sometime, and without a shirt it wouldn't be long.

It was six o'clock that afternoon. Gary had spent the last two hours in the familiar embrace of Harv Edmonds' sofa, watching television.

"Gary, I think you better be getting home now. Your mother is probably starting to worry about you."

"If I go home, she's gonna whip me. Can't I stay the night here?"

"I'm sorry Gary, but you have to go home sometime, and I think it's time for you to get on home and take you punishment like a big boy."

Harv ushered Gary out the front door, saying, "Now you be careful; stay off the road, and don't stop til you get home."

It was almost dark when Gary arrived back at Kevin Lane. Instead of going directly home, as Harv had ordered, Gary took another detour and spent more than an hour milling about the cliffs below the Stetterman property, still trying to summon up enough courage to crawl back home and take his punishment. Around nine o'clock he was sitting on our back porch, shivering from the cold, and thinking about the warm bed waiting for him upstairs. Gary was finally realizing the predicament he was in. That's when he decided that Mom's quick and fiery punishment would be less painful than shivering in the cold for all eternity. I was awake and watching him when he sneaked into his bed that night. Others could have been awake too, yet no one said a word.

The following morning, Gary timidly joined us in the kitchen. Mom was waiting for him with the switch. My rock-throwing brother received a big dose of her wrath and didn't even get to eat breakfast.

Once again, I had another haunting scar to wear.

Dad arrived home around the middle of September. He had just missed Wesley. Released early due to good behavior, he was fortunate to have served only five years of his eight-year sentence. I recall that he stood on our front porch, joking and kidding with each of us. He called Donna "Little Miss Mooneyes" and asked her for a hug. Then it was my turn.

"Tommy, what happened to your head there?"

"Gary hit me with a rock."

"I'll bet it hurt. Didja get'm back?"

"No, but Mom gave him a good whippin'."

Dad just chuckled and winked at Gary.

289

"See that? Bad deeds don't go without just punishment."

I figured he must have learned that one in prison.

Later on, he handed each of his boys a new belt as a present. "Keep your britches up," he said with a nasty grin, "and don't give me an excuse to use it on ya." I sensed he was trying to make a favorable first impression.

Less than a week later, he would impress the entire family by using some of his hard earned prison money to purchase a used wood/coal stove for the living room and a used but working refrigerator. The cracked potbelly stove was put to rest. Less than a week after that, he shocked us by installing a padlock on the refrigerator door to eliminate the snacking that depleted our food supply. He and Mom were the only ones with a key.

Around that same time, some of us were curious when we came across Mom and Dad, in the middle of the afternoon, propped up in bed with their bedroom door open. They were laughing, joking, and enjoying what must have been the afterglow of an after-sex cigarette. It was the first and last time I remember them looking so happy together.

It was the last weekend in September and Paul was turning 16.

"It's my birthday," he said. "I don't want to spend it hanging around the house listening to Dad's nasty mouth. C'mon boys, let's go fishing."

Gary and I helped gather the equipment and we headed for the dam.

At the time, anyone 16 or older was required to have a fishing license. Paul didn't have one, but with the three of us sharing one pole he was willing to take a chance.

We walked out the back door and headed for the cow pastures, our shortcut route to the dam. Halfway across the yard, Paul stopped us dead in our tracks, again.

"Look at that," he said, pointing toward the pastures.

Clouds of smoke billowed from the hills beyond.

"Maybe we should take the main road to the dam," Paul cautioned. "I don't like the looks of that smoke. Someone is over there burning something."

Gary and I followed Paul down Kevin Lane. We walked a few hundred feet south on Falls Mills Road, turned west on Mud Fork Road, and traveled the final half mile or so to the dam. We threw in our line at the usual spot below the spillover steps. The location offered shade and privacy. We took turns holding the pole and watching for the float to bobble. Paul was the only one having any luck. He caught two that were barely big enough to cook.

An hour later we climbed the steep bank to the paved road carrying four fish in our bucket. As soon as we stepped onto the blacktop, a game warden driving by stopped us.

"What do you boys have in the bucket?" he asked.

"Four fish," Paul said. "My brothers caught them."

"Young man, how old are you?"

Afraid to lie again, Paul said, "I just turned sixteen."

The Warden got out of his truck and walked around to confront us.

"Well, young man, since you're the one carrying the pole, I have to assume that you were the one fishing. Do you have a license?"

"No sir."

The Game Warden proceeded to take our names and address.

"Oh," he said. "You must be Sleepy Dixon's boys?"

Paul said, "Yes sir."

"I heard that he's ... uh ... home now. Has he been behaving himself?"

"I guess so," Paul answered.

"Well, I tell you what I'm going to do. If you boys are willing to help me, I'm willing to drop all charges against you for fishing without a permit."

"What do we have to do?" Paul asked.

The warden pointed toward the dam. "Do you see the smoke coming from the tops of those mountains up yonder?"

We all said, "Yeah," having also smelled it from the moment we left the house.

"We've been battling some small scattered brush fires up in the hills between the dam and the Stetterman property. I want you boys to go home, get a shovel, and hike up there and find those fires. And when you find them, shovel some dirt on them to put them out. Okay?"

"Yes sir!" we shouted.

As we hurried off, he said, "Now remember to use dirt only—not leaves—to put out the fires!"

Paul hollered back, "Yes sir!"

"Mom! Mom!" Gary yelled, as he ran ahead of us into the house. "The warden told us to put out the forest fires or else Paul will get locked up."

"What?"

Paul jumped in to explain. "No Mom, that's not true. Gary, I'm gonna kick your butt. Mom, the warden caught us with these fish here and told me I could work off my fine by helping them put out some fires up in the woods yonder."

Paul and Mom began discussing the merits of young kids fighting a forest fire. Paul explained that there was no forest fire and the Warden just wanted us to fight isolated hot spots. After a little more discussion, Mom said, "Well, okay. You boys be careful up there." We headed for the garden tools stored under the house.

"Gary, you get your butt back here!" Mom shouted. "You're a bit too young to be fighting fires!"

"Oh Mom! You never let me do anything."

Paul and I headed for the fence, each carrying a shovel.

"I want you boys home before dark and before your father gets home."

"Okay, Mom," Paul said. "Don't worry—we'll be fine."

We had just climbed over our neighbor's fence and were walking across the pasture when we heard a noise behind us. Gary jumped from the fence to the ground.

"Gary, didn't Mom tell you that you can't go?"

"Yeah, Paul, but she changed her mind."

"Well, you get your butt on home and tell her that I sent you back. I don't want you along on this trip."

Gary started to argue with Paul until Mom's voice broke through.

"Gary, I'm gonna cut a juicy switch for your behind if you don't move it back over here!"

We heard Gary grumbling as he headed back. He was beginning to fib, giving Mom reason for concern.

We followed the billowing smoke to a scattering of small fires around the ruins of the brick house where I had cut down our Christmas tree almost a year earlier. Paul and I began shoveling dirt onto the smoldering embers.

Fishing hadn't tired either of us, so I began singing a chorus of the song "Smokey the Bear."

Smokey the Bear, Smokey the Bear.
Prowlin' and a growlin' and a sniffin' the air.
He can find a fire before it starts to flame.
That's why they call him Smokey,
That was how he got his name.

Paul wasn't much for singing, but it was such a catchy little tune, I caught him humming along with me.

Most young boys growing up in the 1950s and 60s can remember the story of how Smokey Bear became a "living legend" in 1950, when as a young bear he was caught in a wildfire in New Mexico. A year or so after his burns were treated and he was nursed back to health, he was delivered to the National Zoo in Washington D.C. In 1952, Steve Nelson and Jack Rollins wrote the "Smokey the Bear" song. Smokey lived a good life at the zoo until his death in 1976. All young kids remember his famous words: "Remember—only YOU can prevent forest fires."

After working for a while we heard voices from the other side of the hill and went over to investigate. We saw dozens of tiny fires with about half a dozen men working at a frantic pace to put them out. Paul and I added our shovels to the task.

While dashing here and there to put out fires, we became separated. Then I caught sight of Paul talking to one of the young men, who turned out to be young John Stetterman. They seemed to be having a friendly chat. It was good to see them talking and not fighting. Minutes later we met Ricky and Ronnie, also battling the fires.

The Stettermans and the Dixons headed home late that afternoon, dirty, sweaty, and exhausted. Nevertheless, we were talking and laughing. I think I learned a good lesson that day. Working hard as a team can mend broken friendships. After some awkward moments, the feud was over.

When Paul and I walked into the house, Mom said, "Lord-all-mighty! You boys get them clothes off and clean yourselves up! You smell to high heaven!"

Yep, that's the way she talked sometimes.

Oddly enough, a few weeks after our firefighting mission, a real forest ranger stopped by the Falls Mills School. He talked about forest fires and Smokey Bear. Everyone was given a coloring book, a comic book, or a poster depicting parks, rangers, and Smokey. That was the first day I gave serious thought as to what I wanted to be when I grew up—a forest ranger.

Even more than spring, October seemed to provoke boundless energy in my siblings and me. One of our favorite places to channel this energy was in our neighbor's cow pastures. This neighbor (whose name I cannot remember) never complained about the Dixon boys running about his property and acting like a bunch of wild Indians. Maybe that's why I can't remember his name.

In addition to shooting bows and arrows, we sometimes chased and were chased by Blackie, his big black bull. When we teased him, we did it near the fence to ensure a quick getaway.

One October day we got careless. Donna, Gary, and I were busy collecting walnuts from one of the few trees inside the pasture and about a hundred yards from the safety of the fence. Once we had collected as many nuts as we could carry in burlap bags, we'd take them home and spread them under the house to dry.

We had just started collecting the few good walnuts scattered about the ground when we heard Gary hollering.

"Look out! He's coming! He's coming!"

Gary was sprinting toward us with Blackie right behind. My eyeballs were big enough to pop. Reacting on instinct, Donna and I scampered up the walnut tree. Gary joined us just in time. The bull snorted and stomped in frustration at the tree's base, then pawed at the bag of walnuts lying on the ground.

"Gary, what the heck did you do?" Donna asked.

"I just shouted and waved my hanky at him."

We noticed that Gary's hanky was one of those cowboy type bandanas. It was also red. Blackie circled the tree, glancing up with big black eyes as we held on tight.

Donna said, "Gary, don't you know that red colored things make bulls mad?"

"I know, but I just wanted to see for myself."

We were so frightened when we climbed the tree we didn't notice how high and scattered its limbs were. The lowest limb was about six feet off the ground. Fortunately, we all were experienced tree climbers.

We watched the bull methodically scratch his stubby horn against the tree, as if to send us a message. But after about ten minutes Blackie lost interest and slowly trotted off without looking back.

Of course, Donna told Mom about the stupid thing Gary had done.

"I don't want any of you kids over there messin' with that bull. That animal could have killed any of you! Do you hear me, Gary?"

"Sure Mom."

He was lucky he didn't get the switch.

A week or two later, Paul, Gary, and I were back at the pastures again. This time we brought along a couple of large pieces of cardboard that had been discarded by Ward's store. A favorite pastime was sledding the pastures.

At that time of year the grass was usually thick and anywhere from eight to 18 inches tall—the best conditions for a smooth ride down the long hill. A long dry spell made the sport even more enjoyable. Occasionally we'd collide on the way down. Sometimes we'd gather so much speed we'd have to spill out of the cardboard to avoid hitting the barbed wire fence. And we always had to watch out for the cow pies.

Another game we played in and about the pastures, as well as on the school yard, was Mumble Peg. There are several versions. Paul taught me the one I know, as Ronnie or Wesley had taught him:

There are two players, each with a knife. (Or the players can share one.) Thanks to Wesley, I had my own pocketknife to defend myself.

To start the game, the two opponents stand at attention facing each other, feet together, about three feet apart. The player who goes first throws his knife into the ground beside the other player's right or left foot. If the knife sticks, the player must place his closest foot against the knife. If it doesn't stick he does nothing, and now it's his opponent's turn.

The knife throwing is repeated until one player's feet are so far apart that he either loses balance or cannot separate his feet any further.

At that point the loser has to pull out the mumble peg—a wooden twig about three inches long and about a quarter inch in diameter. The winner drives the peg into the ground using his knife as a hammer, giving the peg three taps with his eyes open and three taps with his eyes closed.

The loser has to pull the mumble peg from the ground with his teeth by the count of 100. If not, the winner takes the loser's knife, or whatever prize was agreed to before the start of the game.

Most of the time we played the game just for fun. Paul almost always defeated me, but I usually won against Gary.

After Mumble Peg, we finished up by sliding down the pasture until we wore out all the cardboard.

Sometimes, after returning from the pastures, Dad would grumble and complain that we were wasting time and not doing our chores. That time of the year I had very few chores. Paul had more than a few and, contrary to our father's opinion, always completed them with enthusiasm.

I believe Dad was trying to keep a low profile during the first months of his return. He spent just as much time away from home as he did at home, usually drinking. At home he was often loud, obnoxious and hung-over, but not too pushy. That would change soon enough.

When nights began to get cool, Paul was up extra early to stoke the stove fires while Mom prepared breakfast, school lunches, and warm water for washing up. She placed the pan of wash water on a rickety old chair that rested against the wall between the new heater stove and the kitchen doorway. Every morning and evening, before school and bedtime, Mom draped a clean towel across the back of the chair. A mirror, hanging on the wall above the chair, was used for combing our hair and other hygienic inspections. We took turns at the wash-pan, sometimes arguing about whose turn it was. The sooner you washed up, the cleaner the water. If it wasn't too cold outside, we'd line up on the back porch with a glass of water in one hand and a loaded toothbrush in the other. Being careful not to soil our school clothes, we brushed and rinsed our teeth, spitting into the drainage ditch below. Many mornings I watched my younger siblings leave the house with toothpaste stains on their shirts or blouses.

One night, following a quick sponge bath, I transferred everything from the pockets of my dirty pants to my cleaner school pants for the next day. That's when I realized my knife was missing and began to panic.

"I can't find my knife! Paul, I lost my knife! Gary, did you take my knife?"

"Now take it easy, Tommy," Paul said. "You probably lost it in the pastures while you were sliding down the hill."

"Yeah," I said, "that's where it is. I'll go look for it tomorrow after school."

The next morning it rained. On Tuesday it rained again. On Wednesday I searched in the damp cow pasture but couldn't find it. The following weekend, Paul, Gary, and I looked again without success. The idea of Gary taking my knife kept clouding my mind. But no, he wouldn't dare do that!

I knew what rain and the elements could do to things left outdoors. All I could think about in school was my knife collecting rust. If I ever did find it, it would be so rusty I wouldn't be able to open it.

About two weeks after losing the knife I was playing in the pasture again. I'd all but given up on finding it. Nevertheless, I paused near an area where I thought I might have dropped it. I checked the ground here and there without luck and then headed home. About halfway down the hill, I saw it. Although snuggled between clumps of tall grass, it was still in plain sight. I don't know how any of us could have missed it.

The knife was indeed rusty. However, with Paul's help, I was able to open the blades, perform some light sanding and sharpening, and give it a good coating of oil. It was like finding a lost friend and nursing him back to health. I felt so relieved. I also felt a little guilt and shame for thinking Gary had taken it.

It was early afternoon, Friday, November 22, 1963. The principal stuck his head into our classroom and motioned for Mrs. Tabor to meet him at the door. The two huddled for a moment and I heard her gasp out loud. Then the principal made an announcement.

A hush fell over the class as we struggled to grasp the meaning of such a momentous event.

At about 2:15, President Kennedy was declared dead and all grades were dismissed early. I walked home with David Smith, a fellow classmate and budding friend. I told Donna that David had invited me to his house to ride his bicycle.

The Smiths lived in a nice ranch house about a 25-minute walk from school. I met his mother, and within 15 minutes learned to ride David's bike. Yes, at age 11, I had finally made this rite of passage.

Just before I went home I met his father, who was watching the assassination news on TV. David and I listened for just a minute or two, content not to dwell too much on the sad event. I declined an invitation to stay for dinner, and was elated when David offered to let me ride his bike home.

"Oh, boy! Thanks David! Now I can be home in a flash!"

And, since it was Friday, David's father said I could enjoy the bike for a couple of days. He said they'd drive over on Sunday afternoon to collect it.

At 4:30 I headed home. For the first time I made the three mile trip completely alone. I felt mature and responsible. Yet, I was still afraid Mom might be angry with me for not coming straight home. I rationalized that she might be less inclined to give me the switch if I came home riding my friend's bike.

I hurried on my way, staying well to the side of the road to avoid traffic. I passed a pony, a few sheep, and some goats in a field. I greeted the pony, saying, "Hey boy, how ya doin'?" The pony rewarded me with a shake of his head and strolled over to the fence to greet me. I dropped the bicycle in the grass near the shoulder of the road, eager to pet him. I petted the pony with my right hand, while running my left index finger along one of the fence's thick silver wires. Immediately I began to experience a strange tingling sensation in my left wrist. Curious, I squeezed the wire more tightly.

"Damn!" I shouted, jumping back from the fence. In an instant, it was clear—the fence was electrified.

Feeling lucky to be alive, I walked back to the bicycle and hurried on home, refusing to stop for anything.

Mounting Pressures

During the weeks leading up to Christmas, Ginny was depressed. Her mother-in-law had been writing Alvin, accusing Ginny of infidelity and "wasting" some of her husband's allotment money on food and clothing for our family.

Ginny was an attractive young woman. She had succumbed to the natural desire to socialize with young men and women her own age. She also didn't think Alvin would mind her spending a little money on her siblings, especially when it was for food. She was wrong. Circumstances, rumors, and gossip had all but destroyed her hope of a happy marriage. He cut her off emotionally and financially, and divorce was impending.

Floundering in her discontent, Ginny spent a lot of time visiting friends and family. One day she stopped in to see our Aunt Tini. When she looked into her aunt's bedroom, she was stunned to see our father sitting on the bed, naked and hung over. Aunt Tini, wearing a bathrobe, was hung over as well.

"Ginny," Dad said, "please don't tell your mother you saw me like this." Infuriated and disgusted, Ginny stormed out of her aunt's house and never returned.

For the next several weeks she was haunted by what she had seen. She wanted to do or say something about it, but she didn't want to hurt Mom, having felt the sting of what rumors and gossip can do.

Near the middle of December, Wesley informed us by letter that he and Kay had been married earlier that month. He had been given a six-day pass, but it had taken him seven and a half days to drive to Bluefield, Virginia, get married, and drive all the way back to Fort Hood. When he reported for duty he expected to be reprimanded, but his commander, knowing Wesley was in love, may have feigned ignorance. Taking the hint, Wesley kept quiet about it.

Mike Edmonds, rumored to be a nephew of Harv Edmonds, was one of Paul's best buddies. Mike lived on the other side of the creek and railroad tracks where we could easily see his house from our front porch.

Dad was home the day Mike stopped over to see Paul. Mom was heating up the entire house as she used the cook-stove to prepare dinner. Gary, Prince, and I were playing outside and had attracted the attention of two stray dogs. One kept chasing and trying to mount the other, who looked like she could be Prince's mother. I held Prince and asked Gary to go inside and tell Paul and the others.

Paul and Mike walked onto the back porch with Dad right behind them. They broke into loud laughter when they saw the two dogs mating. Dad walked over to the pair, laughed again and placed a hard kick into the ribcage of the male. The dog yelped in pain. Mike added another kick into the female's stomach. The poor dogs couldn't run away because they were stuck together.

I kept a tight grip on Prince and watched in shame as Dad and Mike repeatedly kicked the dogs. Paul was just as uncomfortable with their brutality as I was. Having seen enough, he dashed to the water pump and filled a bucket with cold water.

"Maybe this will cool them off, Dad."

The three kept splashing the dogs with water until they separated and ran off.

Paul was struggling with eighth grade at Graham High. His grades were falling off the charts and nothing made sense to him. He dreaded being left behind for the third time. Paul loved Donna, but attending classes with his little sister and other much younger kids would be way too embarrassing. A few days before Christmas, he walked into the principal's office and dropped his books onto the desk.

"I've tried and tried," he said, "and it just ain't sinking in."

The principal tried to talk him into reconsidering, but Paul's mind was made up. He walked out and headed for home.

On the way he thought about all the chores he could get done now that he didn't have to go to school. He also thought about getting a job to help with family finances. He'd also be home now to protect his mother from abuse, a responsibility that had been handed down, like worn-out clothes, from one sibling to the next.

After walking a mile or two, Paul stuck out his thumb. Within minutes two cars pulled over. The man in the first car offered to take him to the pulp plant three miles up the road. Paul said that was fine.

When the man let Paul off, the second car was eager to offer him another ride. As soon as he got in, my brother felt suspicious. They had traveled less than a mile when the man said, "Have you been having any luck with the girls?"

With a nervous chuckle, Paul replied, "No, not really."

The man placed his hand on Paul's knee.

Caressing Paul's thigh, he said, "If you want, I can turn off onto one of these side roads."

Paul was doing some quick thinking. He was getting angry too, but wanted to avoid a fight.

Actually, this wasn't the first time Paul found himself in such a pickle.

It was a few months past my second birthday when we were living under the hill on Boissevain Mountain. Dad had been plowing a small piece of Mama's property that was located directly across from her house on Tank Hill Road. Paul, age 6, was helping his father by making water runs to our fresh water spring over the hill. Using the dipper, he filled a mason jar and carried it back to Dad, being careful not to drop it. Halfway to his father, he decided to take a shortcut through a neighbor's property and was instantly stopped by a young Negro girl who lived in the house.

"Let me see what you got in them britches," she said, as she proceeded to pull down his pants.

Paul struggled while the young girl held his pants down and began examining his anatomy. Paul was wondering what she was up to when he heard the back porch screen door slam shut. Looking up, he saw the girl's mother stepping from the porch and walking toward them.

"Girl, you better leave that little white boy alone!"

Startled, the girl turned around and ran to her mother while Paul struggled to pull up his pants. As he hurried on with his jar of water, he could hear the woman's anger along with the young girl's cries.

Not long after, Paul and Ginny were hiking the well-worn trail down Boissevain Mountain to the small company store in Tipple Hollow, the same route the sheriff had taken that morning in 1958 to arrest Dad for the shotgun shooting. They had been sent to fetch groceries and were told not to dally. When they passed a young man lurking in the woods off the trail they didn't think much of it, until he accosted them on the way back.

"Give me a dime," he demanded.

Ginny said, "We don't have a dime."

"Then, give me all your pennies!"

"We don't have any money."

The boy grabbed Ginny's arm and shouted, "Then give me some pussy!"

Upon hearing such a vulgar and unusual request, Ginny broke free, and she and Paul started running for home. The young man began chasing and throwing rocks at them. My brother and sister stopped running and sat down the bag of groceries. Unbeknownst to their young assailant, these two siblings had taken several country courses in rock throwing, and they were elated that he was interested in playing their game. Ginny and Paul didn't hesitate in making an impression. Soon, they were peppering the young man with an overwhelming flood of rocks. It was just too much; the bully fled downhill toward the hollow—out of sight and out of range. Paul and Ginny returned home scared but unscathed.

Now, in his current pickle, Lady Luck was still with Paul. He saw the small country store up ahead and asked the stranger to stop so he could get something. Paul dashed into the store.

My brother grew nervous as he waited for the man to leave. Ten minutes later the man took the hint and drove away.

Paul will always remember his unveiled thoughts and emotions as he walked home that day. A high school dropout for less than an hour, he had already learned a good lesson not taught in public schools. It was a "dog-eat-dog world" out there, and you had better be prepared.

XII

COMING
AND
GOING
c. 1964

Ginny (17) Graham High School

The fourth weekend in January fell between my birthday and Donna's. Mom often adhered to the principle of killing two birds with a single stone, so she used the weekend interval to bake a three-layer cake for the two of us. Everyone present received a piece, but she made sure that the birthday child, or children in this case, received two pieces. Mom wasn't about to spoil any of her children by promising them more than two pieces of cake on their birthday.

According to the 1960 census, 78 percent of American households had an operating telephone. By 1970 that figure had increased to 87 percent. That's an increase of almost 1 percent per year. So, in 1964 the Dixons were still among the 18 percent that did not have a phone—or, in our case, could not afford one.

Three years earlier Paul had installed the family's first facsimile of a telephone, composed of two Del Monte fruit cocktail cans attached to a 30-foot length of wire. This allowed us to practice make-believe conversations with other family members. Yes, Paul's contraption was the closest thing we ever had to the real thing.

Letters were therefore our most convenient way to communicate with distant family members. The method was cheap at five cents a stamp, but it didn't work very well when it came to last-minute changes in plans. On February 13th Ronnie was officially discharged from the army. His letter said he would be home in late February. Come March, when there was still no sign of him, the family started to worry.

"When's Ronnie coming home, Mom?"

"Lord willing, Tommy, he'll be here anytime now."

After spending a few weeks with some friends near Baltimore, Ronnie arrived home the first week in March driving his first car, a green and white 1956 Oldsmobile. Dressed in civvies, he looked older and healthier.

We all had a lot of catching up to do. Dad hadn't seen Ronnie since he was sent to prison and, from the way our mother and father were fussin' over him, you knew they were proud and thrilled to be with him.

(A few months earlier, Ronnie had been shipped stateside from Germany to have a bullet removed from his foot—the one fired from Dad's .22 caliber pistol more than six years earlier.)

Dad was always eager to celebrate a good cause and asked Ronnie to join him in a toast of homebrew. Yep, once out of prison Dad had wasted little time in convincing Mom to help him whip up a small batch or two, just for "medicinal purposes."

A couple of hours later Ronnie changed clothes and drove Dad to Pocahontas. My brother had a few buddies there, and I'm sure they had a lot of stories to catch up on. Dad wanted to tag along, but Ronnie and his friends wouldn't have it. I'm sure Dad felt rejected. A few hours later, Sleepy Dixon was slouched on his favorite stool at the Cricket Saloon in Pocahontas, well on his way to a full-blown inebriation. I wouldn't see Dad until the next day, and Ronnie for several days after that.

Early morning ice patches could be seen about the edges of the creek in Falls Mills, yet many buds were beginning to sprout new life. Warmer weather was just around the corner.

I was doing my best to keep a stray two-month-old puppy out of my father's way. Probably an offspring from the mating dogs Dad and Mike Edmonds had abused back in December, the pup kept hanging around the house and wouldn't go away. Worse than that, it had the mange.

All that jail time must have mellowed Dad. Why else would he allow us to keep Prince, Whitefoot, and Midnight? He knew the dog was no good at hunting. Dad wasn't waving loaded guns at anyone either, and it was also encouraging that he hadn't laid a finger on Mom since his return. Some of us were feeling—or at least hoping—he was a changed man.

Paul had been helping Mike Edmonds with his newspaper deliveries. One day, with the chore finished, Paul and Mike were in the house talking with Dad. I left the puppy on the front porch and went inside to see what they were talking about. I noticed Dad drinking some of his rotgut homebrew, and now he was offering Mike and Paul some.

"Come on, Mike! Have a sip. It'll grow some hair on your chest."

Just like me, Paul couldn't stand the smell of the stuff, let alone drink it. Mike, on the other hand, wasn't shy about taking as big of a swig as Dad would allow.

Minutes later, Mike said, "Well, I guess I better be gettin' home." When he opened the door to the porch, Dad saw the puppy scratching near the doorway.

"Hey Mike!" Dad shouted. "I'll give you fifty cents if you get rid of that mangy pup for me!"

Mike's eyeballs lit up as he glanced over at Paul, then at the puppy, then back to Dad. I was in shock.

"Make it a dollar," Mike replied, "and I'll drown it in the creek."

"No!" I screamed. "You can't do that!" I rushed for the door but Mike blocked my way.

Crossing the room, Dad said, "Wanna bet? Here's a dollar for ya, Mike. Get rid of the mutt!"

Mike snatched the money from Dad's hand and barged onto the front porch with me right behind. He chuckled while pushing me out of the way and scooping up the puppy. He headed quickly down the lane.

I ran after him, shouting, "No! Don't do it, Mike! Please!"

I chased him all the way down the lane, the hundred yards to the bridge, and the sixty feet to the middle of the bridge. I kept jumping and reaching for the puppy, yet Mike just kept giggling as he held it high above his head.

From behind me I heard Paul's voice. "Let it go, Tommy."

"Nooo!" I cried. "Paul, stop him! Don't let him do it!"

When Mike turned to face me, the puppy was already headed for the icy water 12 feet below. I heard the splash, but the puppy instinctively surfaced and began to swim toward the concrete support platform underneath the bridge. His nails clawed at the hard concrete in an effort to not be swept downstream. The current was fairly swift and I sensed he wouldn't be able to hold on for long.

"Dammit!" Mike cried. "Now I gotta climb down there and finish the job!"

"No Mike!"

As Mike began his climb, Paul said, "Tommy, the dog's going to die anyway. This will be quicker."

I was beside myself as I watched Mike toss the puppy into the water again. The dog once again swam back and, shivering, clung to the slippery concrete. Now Mike was pissed. Screaming a string of curses, he grabbed a big stick of driftwood that had been wedged against the bridge support.

"This'll fix him," he muttered.

Mike smashed the puppy's head, sending him back under the water. Seconds later he resurfaced, paddling furiously and gasping for air. Mike hit him again, hard. The dog went under and a few seconds later his limp body surfaced. Before the current could sweep the puppy away, Mike smashed him hard across the skull one last time and he disappeared.

Mike rejoined us on the bridge. The three of us stood watching for the dog to resurface somewhere downstream.

"Hey Paul," Mike chuckled, "if I had known it was going to be this hard, I would have asked your dad for more money."

Paul smiled but said nothing.

"Well, see ya later Paul. I should have been home an hour ago."

As Mike turned his back and walked away, I thought about the stick he left lying in front of me. Fortunately Paul was there.

"Come on, Tommy, let's go home. You'll get over it."

I wiped the tears from my cheek.

"No, I won't," I promised.

For the last three weeks I had seen very little of Ronnie. By the time I got home from school, he was already hanging out with friends in Pocahontas, Boissevain, Jenkinjones, or somewhere else; and, more than likely, spending the night with one of them. I'm sure he was having a better time with his friends than he was with Dad or the rest of us.

The next Saturday afternoon Ronnie returned home. Some of us had just finished eating lunch and were sitting around the kitchen table when he walked in.

Mom said, "What have you been doing, Ronnie? Did you find a job yet?"

"Not yet, but Ricky says he knows somebody who might want to hire me to install fences. I'll be checking into that this week sometime."

"Good," Mom said, "a job is what you need. It'll keep you out of trouble, too. I don't ever want to see the sheriff up here, knocking on my door again."

"Mom, you don't have to worry about that. What you have to worry about is that old man of yours."

"Oh?"

"Yeah. I saw Dad at the Cricket in Poky this morning. He'd been drinking a lot, and I don't expect he'll be home tonight."

"I'm not surprised," she said. "I guess he'll never change."

We heard Paul mutter something from the living room. I couldn't quite make out what he said, but he seemed to be affirming my mother's opinion of Dad.

Ronnie said, "Did you say something, Paul?"

"Never mind, it's not worth repeating."

Sensing a bit of tension in the house, Ronnie decided to change the subject.

"Hey, I saw some geese swimming along the banks of the creek the other day. Has anyone seen their nests?"

"Yeah, there's a bunch of 'em," I said. "And some of the nests have eggs."

"Hmmm. Mom, would you like to scramble us a few goose eggs for breakfast tomorrow?" Ronnie asked.

Oh boy! My brother was gonna spend the night.

"I don't see why not," she said, "as long as you promise to leave at least two eggs in each nest. That way the mothers will have a better chance at hatching a little one."

I thought this was sounding pretty interesting. "Mom, can I go with them?"

With her permission, I was allowed to traipse along the creek banks with my big brothers. Looking back, I think Ronnie wanted to spend some quality time with his little brothers. Gathering goose eggs would fit the bill.

We had already spent a good bit of the afternoon scrambling about the creek banks in our search when Ronnie called for silence.

"Did you hear that?" he asked.

Seconds passed as we froze in place, turning our heads this way and that.

"What?" I asked.

"It's a woodpecker," Ronnie said. "Yeah, there he is in the tree over there." For a few seconds we watched the bird do what he does best.

Paul said, "Yeah, he's sure peckin' a lot of holes in that tree."

"That reminds me of a poem," Ronnie said. "It's about the only one I can remember. It's called "The Woodpecker." Let me see, it goes something like this." And he began to recite.

> The woodpecker pecked out a little round hole
> And made him a house in the telephone pole.
>
> One day I watched as he poked out his head,
> And he had on a hood and a collar of red.
>
> When the streams of rain pour out of the sky,
> And the sparkles of lightning go flashing by,
>
> And the big, big wheels of thunder roll,
> He can snuggle back into his telephone pole.
>
> Elizabeth Roberts (1881-1941)

"Wow! That's a good one, Ronnie. I like that. Will you write it down when we get home, so I can memorize it?"

"Sure will, just you remind me later."

It was close to dark when we decided to quit. Paul carried four big goose eggs tucked away in towels inside a burlap sack. We walked a hundred feet or so away from the creek, climbed an eight-foot embankment, and stepped over the guardrail onto Brushfork Road not far from the Falls Mills School. We joked and clowned around as we headed home along the narrow shoulder of the highway.

Hoooonnk!

"Get out of the road!" the man yelled as he drove by.

Ronnie lifted his middle finger at the truck as it chugged down the highway.

Errrrrrrkk!

The truck slammed on its brakes and was backing up.

"Oh no, let's run!" I shouted.

"No, I'll take care of this." Ronnie said.

Two men, both about Ronnie's size and age, jumped out of the truck, and the driver walked right up to Ronnie.

"You got a problem?" Ronnie asked, standing guard.

The man gave no warning. His left jab connected with Ronnie's forehead. He followed with a right that barely caught my brother's jaw. Trying to duck, Ronnie slipped to the pavement but was back on his feet in a flash.

By now they were jabbing as they danced around each other. Had Ronnie learned to box in the army? Paul and I kept an eye on the other man standing by the truck. Assured that he only wanted to watch, we refocused on the fight as Ronnie connected with a couple of jabs and a good right. The sound of bone against bone was a first for me. It was a little scary and something I would never forget. After another minute of dancing and jabs, the fighters were so tired they just gave up.

Ronnie and his opponent shook hands. Out of breath, they joked around apologetically and made light of the event. Five minutes after the truck had stopped, the two young men were gone.

On the way home we joked and laughed about the confrontation.

"I think you won, Ronnie," I said. "Don't you, Paul?"

"Yeah, you did good Ronnie. I think that guy bit off a little more tobacco than he could chew."

Ronnie smiled as he wiped the blood from his nose and lips.

As promised, Ronnie dictated the poem to me that night. I memorized it and a few weeks later recited it to my teacher and fifth grade class. Mrs. Tabor had given the class a book of poems to study, and I couldn't resist telling her about the "The Woodpecker." One poem from her book stuck with me:

The Little Turtle

There was a little turtle.
He lived in a box.
He swam in a puddle.
He climbed on the rocks.

He snapped at a mosquito.
He snapped at a flea.
He snapped at a minnow.
And he snapped at me.

He caught the mosquito.
He caught the flea.
He caught the minnow.
But he didn't catch me.

Vachel Lindsay (1879-1931)

It was late April or early May. Ginny had decided her life was going nowhere, both at home and in Tazewell County as well. Things were headed downhill with Dad at home. Almost every dollar that he'd earned in the last six months had been wasted on alcohol. Ginny had had enough.

She spoke with Wesley by phone, and he promised her that life in Texas would be better. She accepted his offer to stay with him and his new wife. She had very little money, but more than enough for a one-way bus ticket to Texas. It was as good a place as any to make a new start, look for a job, and file for her divorce from Alvin.

For some strange reason, I have vivid memories of my sister's last days on the hill at Kevin Lane. Ginny wondered if she would ever reunite with us, and I too felt strangely sad about her living so far away from the family.

Someone had a camera that day. While we waited for Ronnie to drive Ginny to the bus station in Bluefield, she asked me to take her picture. I was being silly, not a bit serious, when I asked her to pose while standing on the fence post that divided our front yard from Kevin Lane. I giggled as the tomboy we had come to love climbed the fence barefooted and stood atop the post more than five feet above the ground.

"How does this look, Tommy?" she asked proudly.

She wore a beautiful sleeveless dress with a multi-colored floral print. Facing away from the camera, she clasped her hands behind her neck, and with her eyes gazing up the lane I snapped her picture.

"You look great, Ginny. It's gonna be a good one."

During the days that followed, a haunting emptiness seemed to cloud my normally cheerful disposition. Ginny had been more than a sister to us. Like our mother, she was a fantastic and loving caregiver. Her absence, along with the puppy incident and my discomfort with my father's presence, contributed to a nagging feeling of dread. It would soon be overcome by more urgent demands.

Ginny (18), striking a pose at Kevin Lane.

In early May we had finished preparing the upper and lower gardens for planting. It was easier and quicker this year since we had some help from Ronnie. The two gardens were more than enough acreage to meet our needs. But Dad, in typical fashion, didn't think so. He called a meeting in our yard to explain his gardening ambitions to Paul, Donna, Gary, and me.

"Our trash pile is spread out too far," he observed. "We can increase the size of the garden by moving all that trash yonder to a small spot just below the outhouse."

We were shocked. Was he joking? We looked at him and each other, but apparently he wasn't. We raised a chorus of complaints—it was too much work, it was dangerous, it was just a stupid idea.

"I don't want to hear any of your griping!" he shouted. "You have all week to get it done, because I want to plant seed this weekend!"

After Dad walked away, we looked at the trash pile and thought of how much time and work it was going to take to complete the task. I was sick and disgusted and my siblings probably felt the same. There were hundreds of rusted cans, broken bottles and jars, and numerous discarded household items dating back years before our arrival on the property. I saw myself slipping and cutting myself once again.

When I came home from school the next day, Paul had started moving the trash pile. I reluctantly joined his effort. A few minutes later, after Mom had reminded them, Gary and Donna were helping with some of the small stuff. No one complained more than Donna. Little Miss Mooneyes wasn't used to performing manual labor.

Neglecting our schoolwork, we were back at it again the next day. While several of us were raking the trash, we heard a car coming up the lane. By now we had become familiar with the sound of the Oldsmobile, and we guessed it was Ronnie returning with Dad. He had picked up his father at the Cricket Saloon before he had time to get staggering drunk.

As the Oldsmobile climbed and maneuvered its way up the steep, rocky, and cratered terrain, Ronnie couldn't help bragging about the car's performance.

"This baby can go anywhere!" he said. "Dad, have you ever seen an Olds handle like this?"

"I don't reckon I have," Dad said. He leaned over to get a closer look at the strange position of Ronnie's feet.

"Where's the clutch?" Dad asked.

"Dad," Ronnie chuckled, "this car has an automatic transmission. It don't need a clutch."

"Well, I'll be damned!" Dad said. "I heard about them automatic transmissions, but I didn't know they got rid of the clutch."

Ronnie parked the car, and as he and Dad walked into the house, we could hear Ronnie laughing so hard we thought he was going to crack a rib. At the time, we didn't know it was all about Dad's lost clutch.

Dad came out of the house a couple of times to grin at us, give instructions, and admire the work in progress. Ronnie stopped by too and asked us what we were doing.

I said, "Our stupid father is making us move the stupid trash pile."

"Why?" Ronnie asked.

"Dad wants to make the garden bigger," Paul replied.

Ronnie laughed. "That sounds like something he would make somebody else do."

The following Saturday morning we ate breakfast and returned to the task. In addition to his regular chores, Paul still did the bulk of the trash work while the rest of us were in school. I was amazed at how much work we had accomplished. But the job needed another day. Paul thought we had extra time, because Dad had stayed out all night and probably wouldn't be home until later that morning or early afternoon. Most likely he would be drunk too.

A little past noon, Mom called us into the house for a well-deserved lunch break— commodity cheese or peanut butter and jelly sandwiches, most likely. After eating, Paul, Gary, and I played fetch and tug-of-war with Prince. With so much work going on, we thought we had neglected him. He was such a handsome devil.

XIII

THE ESCAPE
c. 1964

The Cricket, Dad's favorite watering hole.

Dad was drunk again. Ronnie dropped him off at the house and, not wanting to be around him any longer than necessary, skedaddled out of there. As soon as Dad got us in the house, off came his belt.

After he gave me the beating of my life, I cried myself to sleep. But just before I drifted off, I made a promise to God: "If you can make my dad go away forever, I'll never ask you for anything again."

It would be many years before I learned all the details of what took place while I slept.

Dad was complaining about Ronnie and his friend Ricky Bright. Paul said it was because they were going out on the town, having fun, and not including Dad in their drinking.

"If those kids come over here drinking again, I'm gonna kick both their asses."

Paul gave a low chuckle.

Dad said, "Oh, you don't think I can do it, do you?"

"No."

Using a phrase he probably learned in prison, Dad said, "If you stub-up on me boy, I'll kick your ass too."

Paul just smiled.

"Oh, you don't think I can kick your ass either, do you?"

"No."

"Then step outside, boy!" Dad commanded.

"Okay, but you better take out your teeth," Paul suggested, as they walked to the door.

Mom shouted at her son, "Paul, don't you dare go out there and fight with your father!"

Paul had been counting on the day when he could have a chance like this. His father had challenged him, and he wasn't about to miss the opportunity. But Mom knew her husband better than her son knew his father. Sleepy Dixon wasn't about to fight fair.

"Don't worry Mom, this won't take long."

"Paul, you better come back here! Don't do it, Paul!"

Dad had removed his false teeth and joined Paul in the side yard just above the garden. Dad tried to kick Paul in the groin but missed, striking him in the hip instead. Paul returned the kick, catching Dad on his ass. With a growl, Dad charged Paul putting him in a face to face bear hug. The two squeezed tighter and tighter until Dad gave out a loud and painful moan. He collapsed backward with all of Paul's weight driving into his chest. The impact nearly knocked the breath out of Dad. They wrestled around on the ground with my brother in control.

"Let me up," Dad demanded.

"I'll let you up if you promise not to do anything."

"I won't."

Paul released his grip and stepped back. Dad recovered in a flash and seized a grapefruit-sized rock, then dropped it when Paul ran to the front yard. Dad dashed across the back porch and into the kitchen. He grabbed an iron poker from the stove and confronted Mom, who was coming through the front door. Those five miserable years in prison must have flashed through his mind as he raised the poker above his head. But then he dropped it and began pushing Mom through the door, screaming obscenities at the top of his lungs.

I was awakened by noises from downstairs. I could hear my mother and father shouting and screaming at each other. Stomping and shuffling feet, resonating through loose floorboards, hinted that there was also a struggle going on. It sounded like someone was being murdered in our living room. I realized that I had cried myself to sleep after the beating Dad had given me.

The screams and shouting continued as I walked to the stairway railing and looked down. I could see nothing, so I slowly tiptoed down the stairway, turned left at the landing, and descended to the bottom. As I peeked through the stairway door, I saw Dad give Mom a final push through the front door onto the porch.

"I'll let you back in when you can show your old-man some respect!" he shouted. Then he closed the door and secured all three locks.

A light bulb flickered inside my head—I might be the only other person in the house. Trembling with fear, I watched him walk back toward the kitchen. An urgent voice told me to get out of there before he notices me. I opened the door just enough to peer around the corner toward the kitchen. No sign of him. I noticed the sofa was pushed up against the door to the emergency trap door exit under the stairway. There was only one way out.

I jumped from the stairway and scrambled to the front door where I unfastened all three door locks. I flung open the door, ran across the front porch and, while jumping to the ground, cleared all four porch steps in one leap.

I huddled in the front yard with Donna, Gary, Debbie, and Mom, who held young David. Mom, with tears in her eyes, pulled me close to her side.

I looked toward the house and saw Paul hiding beside the chimney with a stick in his hand. What was he doing? I thought. A moment later we saw Dad sneaking through the alleyway on the back side of the chimney, gripping a butcher's knife. Dad started to throw the knife but stopped when Paul ducked back behind the chimney. Dad continued forward, holding the knife in front of his body. Paul stepped forward and, with the stick, knocked the knife from Dad's hand. It landed on the ground between them. Looking Dad straight in the eye, Paul slowly reached down to pick it up. Dad swung, but my brother was quicker. In one fluid motion, Paul tossed away the knife, dodged the punch, and punched Dad in the chin knocking him backward. But the knife was now at Dad's feet again, and he quickly rearmed himself. Paul backed away, joining us in the front yard.

Contemplating his next move, Dad slowly walked across the porch and down the steps toward us. He reminded me of a Wild West gunslinger lining up for a fast draw, his jaw and lips pressed firm with determination. No, the threat was too great. Everyone but Paul began to retreat further across the yard until we were standing on Kevin Lane.

"Paul, that's enough!" Mom cried. "Let's go to Ward's and call the sheriff."

But Paul wasn't moving.

"No Mom, I'm not running anymore."

My mother, near hysterics, pleaded with Paul in vain. Now he and my father were face to face, just a few feet apart.

"I've been away too long, and you kids need to learn who's the boss in this family!"

"Drop the knife Dad!"

Taking several steps toward Paul, Dad waved the weapon. "Let's see if you're man enough to take it."

Paul grabbed Dad's wrist and the two wrestled for control of the knife. Paul was cut on the hand, and Dad was stabbed in the knee, but within seconds, my 16-year-old brother had pinned our father to the ground.

"Donna!" Paul shouted. "Take the knife from his hand!" Donna wouldn't budge. We were all frozen with fear.

"Mom, take David with you to Ward's, and call the sheriff. Hurry!"

Dad grunted and gasped for breath as he struggled to maintain his hold on the knife and throw off Paul. "The law … ain't gonna help ya … when they hear … what you've done, boy."

"All you kids," Paul shouted, "run to the cliffs!"

"You heard him! Let's go!" Mom cried, as she ushered us down the lane.

Donna, Gary, Debbie, and I ran to the lower cliffs and scrambled down the familiar rock faces to our usual spot. Mom and David continued on to Ward's Market to call the sheriff.

Through sheer grit, Paul wrestled the knife from his Dad's grip. He had subdued his father and was now in control of the situation. But the sight of his father at his feet, so defeated and diminished, only fueled his disgust and anger.

"Get up Dad … Get up!"

Dad rose timidly to his feet, only to groan and collapse from the sharp and stabbing pain in his knee. The prolonged struggle had sobered him a bit too. Now favoring a cut and an injured leg, he managed to regain his feet and limp toward the house.

"No you don't!" Paul shouted, stepping in front of him. "You're not going back into our house. Not now! Not ever!"

Dad gave Paul a hateful stare.

"I mean it Dad."

Dad turned and retreated down the hill. Now aware of how treacherous he could be, Paul followed him at a distance holding onto the knife. When Dad reached the lane, he turned and looked back.

"You've cut your father with a knife boy. That's no way to treat your father. I guess I'm gonna hafta swear out a warrant on ya."

"Go ahead," Paul said, "see if I care."

Dad's pride must have been shattered. It was the second time one of his sons had stood up to him without a weapon and won. Years of drinking, years of inhaling coal dust and tobacco smoke, and too many years in prison had taken his strength and dominance. On the other hand, Paul's diligence to his chores and weight-lifting had instilled confidence and seen him through. Yet, Dad surprised us one last time when he made a quick detour to appear at the top of the overlook, about 70 feet above us.

"I know you kids are down there!" he shouted. "I'll be deal-n with you later!"

Paul shouted, "Keep movin', Dad! And don't stop until you get to Poky!" We peeked around a huge boulder and watched him walk away.

We cheered when Paul—remarkably unharmed—joined us. Two minutes later we looked down through the trees by the old vine swing and saw Dad limping north on Falls Mills Road. He was hitch-hiking. Son-of-a-gun, someone was already offering him a ride.

Paul told us to stay there and be quiet while he went to Ward's to see how Mom was doing.

Mom told Mr. Ward about Dad's drunken assault with a deadly weapon. He called the Game Warden first, who then contacted the sheriff in Pocahontas.

When Dad saw the sheriff approaching, he said, "I want to press charges against one of my boys!"

"Sleepy, it's too late," was the reply. "You're under arrest."

Many years later, in quiet solitude, I reflected back on that day. While I was sleeping upstairs, Mom was trying to get back into the house, knowing I was the only one left inside. My father, forgetting that I was upstairs, kept pushing her out the front door. But Mom couldn't tell her drunken husband that she was trying to rescue me.

Dad was charged with violating his parole; the offenses being public drunkenness and assault with a deadly weapon. The judge told Mom that he would be held for up to 30 days, pending the results of a hearing in two weeks. In preparation for Dad's eventual release, the judge suggested that the family make plans to move as far away from the area as possible.

Two weeks later, Ronnie loaded Mom, Paul, Donna, Gary, and me into his Oldsmobile and drove us to Tazewell, Virginia, for the hearing. David and Debbie were left in the care of a family member.

Ronnie parked the car on a busy street about a block from the County Courthouse. He left Gary and me inside while everyone else went to the hearing. About 30 minutes later Donna came back and said Ronnie and Paul were the only children the judge needed to hear.

As the afternoon wore on and the sun began to bake us, we decided to evacuate the car for the shade of a tree. We sat, played a little, and tried to behave ourselves as much as possible during what seemed like an endless wait.

I studied the expressions on my family's faces when they returned. Or should I say lack of expression.

"Well, Mom, how did it go?" Donna ventured.

"We'll talk about it later."

We piled back in the car and headed home.

Later on, Mom said, "Judge Perry knows your Dad like a book."

"Dad had a lot of nerve," Paul said. "He looked Judge Perry straight in the eye and said, 'Paul doesn't do anything around the house.'"

Turning his attention to Paul, the Judge had asked, "Young man, don't you have any respect for your father?"

Paul replied, "No, because he don't have any for me."

The judge asked Mom if we had a safe place to move to. She said we did. Then he sentenced Dad to 30 days, minus the 15 already served.

Why he received only 30 days for such a gross violation of parole, I'll never understand. We had just two weeks to pack up and disappear.

Mom, Ronnie, and Paul had several discussions about our moving options. One option, strongly recommended by the judge, was to move to Delaware where my aunt was eager to help us make a new start. The other was a three-room house in a dark hollow near Hales Bottom. Since it was one of Dad's earlier suggestions, it was quickly dismissed. Aside from the house being dilapidated, Ronnie and Mom knew Dad had "ulterior motives" for that quiet and isolated spot. Mom and the family made plans for a one-way trip to Delaware.

Because of our domestic situation, our school year was cut short about a week. Near the end of May we received our report cards; not surprisingly, we all had passed to the next grade. I was excited and nervous about starting the sixth grade in a strange school in a stranger state. I had no idea where Delaware was.

It was around the first of June, another pleasant spring day, when we started loading our belongings. Ronnie had rented an 8-foot U-Haul trailer for the few possessions we were taking with us, about as big as the Oldsmobile could pull. Several boxes of pots, pans, dishes, pictures, personal documents, clothing, and knick-knacks were stacked around two end tables, a coffee table, two lamps, a sofa chair, and a set of bed frames. Even if we had enough room, we couldn't bring along our best mattress; we didn't want to risk transferring bed bugs to Aunt Catherine's house.

327

Many of our personal items did not make the move. Our comic book collection—a stack over three feet tall and possibly worth hundreds, if not thousands of dollars today—may have been relegated to the outhouse. But leaving Prince, Whitefoot, and Midnight behind was by far the most difficult part of the move. I worried about them for days and thought about them for months after arriving in Delaware. God forbid Dad should take out his anger on any of them. I could only hope and pray they found peace with the Stettermans, or another kind neighbor. I would never see them again.

By mid-morning we were ready to leave. Ronnie drove the load alone to the bottom of the rocky hill. The rest of us made our final walk down Kevin Lane before climbing inside that poor Oldsmobile. Ronnie shifted the transmission into drive, checked his load, and revved the engine. The car seemed to hesitate, then lurch forward onto Falls Mills Road.

EPILOGUE

We seemed to have made our escape that day. However, Mom and Ronnie were worried about how well we would be able to get by in Delaware. Ronnie thought of the past and how Dad—thanks to Mom's goodness—had always seemed to worm his way back into the family cell. At that time, I guess most of us were harboring our own personal reservations as to whether or not our father's *hollow reign* had really ended?

To be honest, our painful family journey wasn't over yet. We weren't going to reach the *Promised Land* by running to Delaware. Nope, there would be a lot more hard work in front of us.

The years and events you have just read about—not surprisingly— have had an amazing effect on all members of the family. Yes, including me. From the oldest down to the youngest, our family turmoil and good times have imbued each of us with separate and unique outlooks on life. What baggage we brought from Tazewell County, Virginia, in 1964, will be unpacked in Delaware and tried on for size. A few pieces will be discarded, some will be modeled for the public, and other pieces will be hidden away for a rainy day.

On average, our family's life in Delaware will be an improvement over the last twenty five years. Yet, living in the city would not provide everyone the peace and tranquility we sought so desperately. As my family and I adjust to living and growing up in the city, we will encounter and struggle to deal with a plateful of individual and family issues. That's another story.

SOURCES OF REFERENCE

- The <u>Bluefield Daily Telegraph</u>, Newspaper. Bluefield, WV

- Mercer County Circuit Court, Records. Princeton, WV

- Tazewell County Circuit Court, Records. Tazewell, VA

- Family, Friends, Pertinent Others, and A Lifetime of Personal Interviews.

THEN

NOW

ABOUT THE AUTHOR

THOMAS DIXON spent 30 years working in the chemical research field before retiring in 2008. Five weeks later, his mother's death spurred him to collect notes and memories for a long overdue family history. He finally found something he truly enjoyed—writing about his life. *TOMMY MACK: An Appalachian Childhood*, a memoir, is his first book, and he plans two more based primarily on the evolution of his life with bits and pieces of the Dixon family. Tom is the father of two daughters and lives in Newark, Delaware with his wife and best friend, Mildred.

NOTES

CPSIA information can be obtained at www.ICGtesting.com
Printed in the USA
BVOW042130071211

277841BV00001B/6/P